1385

Calf's Head and Union Tale

Calf's Head & Union Tale

Labor Yarns at Work and Play

Archie Green

University of Illinois Press   *Urbana and Chicago*

Publication of this book was supported by grants from the L. J. and Mary C. Skaggs Folklore Fund and Henry P. Anderson.

© 1996 by the Board of Trustees of the University of Illinois
Manufactured in the United States of America
1 2 3 4 5 C P 5 4 3 2 1

This book is printed on acid-free paper.

Library of Congress Cataloging-in-Publication Data

Green, Archie.
    Calf's head and union tale : labor yarns at work and play / Archie
  Green.
      p.   cm.
    ISBN 0-252-02248-3 (cloth : alk. paper).—ISBN 0-252-06553-0
  (pbk. : alk. paper)
    1. Labor and laboring classes—United States—Folklore.
  2. Working-class—United States—Folklore. 3. Trade-unions—United
  States—Folklore. 4. Tales—United States. I. Title
  GR105.3.G74   1996
  398.2'08'623—dc20   95-50190
                                               CIP

Contents

Acknowledgments

Colleagues and companions across the land helped collect and comment upon this book's tales. I have credited storytellers and scholars directly in source citations and contextual background notes for particular yarns. Many other friends helped move this compilation from initial idea to published volume.

As I pulled together folktale study and labor-history research, Lynn Bonfield and Sandra Cate made possible my preliminary-gift chapbook, *Labor Tales* (1993), for the Labor Archives and Research Center, San Francisco State University. Librarians Greg Castillo, Joe Garity, Ivan Hudson, Vicki Rosen, Greg Swalley, and Harriet Talan sought and obtained rare material. Doug Alexander, Mary Quinn, and Arlene Ursini helped me with modern office machine technology. Bucky Halker and Jim Leary read early drafts of my typescript.

Picture searching engaged a diverse crew: Julie Ardery, Debra Bernhardt, Beverly Brannan, Janice Capecci, Judy Clark, Norm Cohen, Carlos Cortez, Joanne Delaplaine, Tom Featherstone, Rachel Frew, Diane Hamilton, Joe Hickerson, Jens Lund, Barbara Natanson, Oscar Paskal, Mary Proenza, Bob Reynolds, Franklin Rosemont, Robert Rush, Susan Sherwood, Lee Stone, David Taylor, Susan Teller, Tom Walker, Bob Walls, and Terry Zug.

As I worked on this book, Louanne Green heard all the included stories many times over. Finally, Judith McCulloh and Patricia Hollahan guided *Calf's Head and Union Tale* through the maze at the University of Illinois Press.

"Mill Village Loungers."

Introduction:
Tales Heard and Told

Language flows constantly, energizing labor as it notes pain, pleasure, or promise within each act of work. Do we tote, tear, burrow, or blast in antiseptic silence? Talk jumps from field row to packing shed, factory aisle to loading dock, office module to clinic lab. Talk surrounds every worn machine in decaying mills and every gleaming computer in science-fiction cells. Whether we're harnessed to old or to new technologies, we seek words to dramatize our experience and mark our identity. With great impartiality, job speech forges both shackles and scalpels.

In rusted shell and marble tower, individual workers banter, blabber, and ballyhoo. Speech at work consists of meandering gossip, barked command, sullen retort, cheerful wit, mournful plea, and self-contained stories. These latter narratives, under varied tags ("tale," "yarn," "legend," "myth," "saga," "parable," "drollery," "joke," "whopper," "windie," "anecdote"), roll from assembly line to shopping mall, hospital corridor to harbor dock, public bureau to runaway plant.

Calf's Head and Union Tale holds a set of representative stories—imaginative, formulaic, familiar, eccentric—drawn from and commenting upon work. In these, raconteurs slip from random talk to structured tales. Such self-contained narratives resemble glistening dewdrops caught in the spider web of ordinary speech. Although different physical elements constitute web and droplet, the latter rests within the former. In time, the sun and wind dissipate both the web and its watery jewels. Yet spiders continue to spin as the morning dew finds its way to fresh webs.

I call up this metaphor of web and dewdrop to underscore the relationship of daily talk to enclaved story, as well as to the latter's autonomy. While most job experience can be milled into speech, only some acts jell into legend or myth. In my book, I am particularly interested in traditional narratives, usually named *folktales*. Some readers will prefer to drop such items into other bins: "personal experience narrative," "oral history," "life story," "social reportage."

Aware of linkages that tie together all forms of verbal art, I favor tales understood by storytellers and their hearers as discrete—set apart by special signs; holding life beyond casual chatter. Over the years, I have been fortunate to hear choice job yarns spun by artisans unfamiliar with fine literary canons, but conscious of their own vernacular power as well as the lines between ever-present "spider web" speech and "dewdrop" story.

On occasion, fellow workers recall and retell tales of Sinbad, crafty sailor; Hiawatha, noble hunter; Davy Crockett, frontier scout; Florence Nightingale, devoted nurse; John Henry, deathless steel-driver; Mother Jones, defiant friend; Paul Bunyan, giant logger; Joe Hill, Wobbly martyr. At times, we deploy the adventures of these exemplars to anonymous workers in everyday settings.

Narratives about legendary artisans—builders or dreamers—told at work, home, saloon, or hall become our beacons for conduct. Even after discounting stories spun as fantasy, we salvage from each account useful elements that amplify our own lives. We persist in chartering personal paths by referring back to magical or martyred helpers.

To bring crews of mythic or human workers to everyday scenes, to place Joe Hill and his companions on our jobs, we borrow and build upon landscape features: mountain, hill, vale, dell, cliff, pool, river. John Henry tunneled through treacherous rock. Joe Hill organized miners seeking mountain ore. Unionists on freedom marches sang "Go Tell It on the Mountain" and "On the Rock Where Moses Stood." Paul Bunyan "drove" logs down river to hungry sawmills, thus housing an entire nation. In tales expanded far beyond forest camps, Paul altered nature itself.

We assert both good and bad fortune by oceanic allusions. Generations of children have thrilled at Sinbad's adventures. His long voyage began at wharfside in a gulf port before he braved the open sea. His chronicles, moving in rakish and measured tones, help return us to our own piers and gulfs, to bedrock realities.

Herman Melville's Captain Ahab stands at the wheel with every present-day mariner. Does dour Ahab guard, threaten, or command? On and off the waterfront, we refer to Davy Jones's locker. Curiosity impels our questions: Who is Davy Jones? Where does he live? Has anyone seen his locker? How long will his name resonate among seafarers?

Memories of particular gods of toil—brother blacksmiths Weland and Vulcan—recede on the steelmill or foundry floor as plants close down or run across borders. Iron puddlers and rollers in Pennsylvania dramatically named their first union the Sons of Vulcan. Where do we now hear of Roman deities in rust-belt mills?

Yet we do not lose all links with past myth, for speech threads us to antiquity. Nautical vignettes make the point as we personalize experience in Poseidon's tongue: Her life ebbed with the tide. The gang lowered the boom on the boss. Deep six the cable. Our mate walked the plank. Let's keel-haul the fink.

Some workers reflect upon the consequences of their verbal skill. They enjoy the plaudits of companions when stories are well received. Alternately, they know that words as well as sticks and stones break bones, and, at times, they deflect blows with the adage "Talk is cheap." Who has not heard barbed retorts to a blowhard ranting about how he'd handle a tough scab? After loudmouths exaggerate amatory prowess, their buddies may sound off, thus reducing the braggarts to size. A temptress in the copy room gloats over last night's conquest. Her sister substitutes a silent putdown. Here, subverbal shorthand, with a wink or a hand gesture, replaces "Talk is cheap."

Traditional one-liners serve as spoken exclamation points to punctuate pomposity or hypocrisy: Get lost, Pipe down, Silence is golden, Don't use your mouth as a flytrap. Such orders signal that talk, far from cheap, is much too precious to be wasted, and that the gift of speech, although abundant, must be treated with care. Hence we relish the image of verbal power as a double-edged sword, a tool to cut down fools and exploiters, a blueprint for personal and group identity.

Laboring in mine and mill, or steno pool and copy room, workers exchange speech in all its dimensions from technical direction to poetic fancy. A shipwright struggles all day to set a bulkhead, summing up the task with "It's straight as a frozen rope." A keyboarder calls up new locutions to fend off unwanted attention: "I'm not programmed that way."

We string lone words into pithy sayings and find pleasure in hearing them repeated. Similarly, we combine single sentences into plotted stories—some of which boomerang as they return to us. Reflecting on such material, we expand our thoughts to penetrate the mystery and reveal the prophecy contained in folktales. Language retains fascination for its users. Accordingly, shop-floor savants speculate on word origins, criticize peers for talking trash, and pontificate on the meaning of their own stories.

Although students of dialect have compiled vocabulary lists for specific trades, and linguists or lexicographers have delved into the vernacular speech favored by working people, no comprehensive tome has gathered English-language job talk in its entirety. Anthologies containing urban legends about alligators in sewers or poodles in microwave ovens do hold a few job-oriented stories, but, again, we lack a popular garland of occupational narratives.

At times, a television newscast features work talk derived from an antique tale, or a soap opera enacts a job yarn in all its lurid dimensions. Also, a political-convention orator may shape the facts of a chicken-plant fire into a moral tract, thus bringing industrial terror into individual hearts removed from the factory site. Essentially, we need published collections of labor language/literature in multiple formats for diverse audiences.

Wobblies, Pile Butts, and Other Heroes holds among a set of case studies one on "Marcus Daly Enters Heaven," a Butte copper-mining tale recorded in 1952 with antecedents in thousand-year-old Norse mythology. In that book, I also explored two story clusters: sneaking-home-from-work sexual misadventures and shortened-shovel-blades-and-handles as defiant acts of on-the-job sabotage.

Other folklorists, from George Korson, Ben Botkin, and Wayland Hand to Bob McCarl, David Taylor, and Jim Leary, have unearthed particular occupational tales. Most recently, Tom Walker has looked at two subjects—sailors' lore and soapboxing. In this latter area, he breaks new ground by treating the rhetorical strategies of anarchist firebrands, socialist dreamers, and trade-union pragmatists. In sum, scholars from Korson to Walker have focused attention on work-rooted narrative. Readers may wish to place our findings next to the contemporary folktale analysis of beanstalk-climbing apprentices and brother toilers offered in *Jack in Two Worlds,* edited by Bill McCarthy.

For those new to laborlore studies, I assert simply that folklorists are not peddlers of rags, bottles, and papers who scavenge on city streets or country lanes. Nor are we vacuum cleaners sucking all the dust and lint in our paths. We arrive at mine or mill with tested tools; we animate our collections and related commentaries with some degree of affection for working people. We struggle to find purpose in our studies; we seek not to elevate our achievements beyond their bounds.

Here, in the compass of *Calf's Head and Union Tale,* I present a set of representative work narratives, ancient and recent, solemn and ribald, didactic and innocent. Carried to the United States from distant shores or born on this continent, a few with known analogs around the globe, our set of tales amplifies the many accents in which American workers caress and curse their tools, troubles, and triumphs.

Wherever possible, I note precise sources for each selection: the storyteller's name, craft, and locale; the tale's initial appearance in a book, journal, or sound recording. I identify other collectors and add references for further reading or listening. The matter of "proper" titles remains troublesome. Over the years, scholars such as Antti Aarne, Stith Thompson, Linda Dégh, and Herbert Halpert have helped standardize names such as "The Smith and the Devil" for stories scattered across the globe and existing in multicolored forms. I have respected the tale titles given by previous collectors, providing my own where none were found.

Scholars offer conflicting standards for "handed down" narratives and disagree with considerable passion over distinctions between the categorizing labels *tale, legend, myth.* In this book I use *tale* broadly as a cover for such interwoven items. Thus, *tale* becomes my shorthand term ranging from barebones vignettes offered as truth to cloudland adventures beyond belief, from pithy anecdotes to perambulating sagas.

Dictionary makers who struggle with the term *folktale* stress anonymity, antiquity, oral circulation, and inattention to fixed norms of time or place. I have tried to qualify such platonic qualities by invoking a three-pronged definition for *tale* when tied to occupation or unionism: (1) a narrative shaped on the job or at the hall that

"Gospel Truth."

jumps fences of time, place, skill, and belief; (2) one found in variant forms; (3) one commenting upon the experiences and aspirations of its tellers and hearers.

I do not imply that academicians alone, whether literary specialists or critics, relish occupational lore. Many scholars share affection for job narratives with blue-/pink-/white-collar yarn spinners, bull slingers, and truth stretchers. In short, emblematic work tales do appeal beyond the construction site's keep-out fence or the office tower's coffee bar.

With a canvas of swapped tales and linked analysis, workers who use pen or hammer contribute to the broad American dialogue. A casual story may outflank an angry polemicist; a bohemian allegory may soften a puritan's heart. Accordingly, I seek to persuade seminar students to meet union-hall raconteurs—above all, to join in word juggling and tale hawking.

How do listeners recognize a folktale or distinguish one from other forms of literature? While observing workers exchange stories, I found only a few who felt at ease with the nomenclature of campus folklorists or literary scholars. Although no revealing signal flashes to indicate traditionality or to certify folk status, I have seen on-the-job listeners grin or gesture to indicate that their bard had kissed the blarney stone, or that his yarn was old when Noah launched the ark. In short, a laugh or wink can signify *folktale* without falling back upon the term itself.

Beyond such subtle clues, we look for other signs that *folktale* is a meaningful label. We note that some individuals respond to a tale's form; others, to its message; still others, to its delivery. In all cases, multiple examples (usually called *variants*) become the key to a defining standard, whether by outside critics or those gathered in a storytelling circle. Does the tale resemble something heard before? Has it traveled? Does it recycle wisdom? Has it tied personal history to community memory?

Many storytellers entertain as they play cat-and-mouse with audiences. They mimic, torment, or dazzle. We respect their talent and expect choice fiction. However, others stumble in their efforts—mangling accounts, neglecting juicy bits, rushing into punch lines. Gifted yarners at work do share platforms with incoherent bumblers, with Joe McGees and Sad Sacks. In short, we anticipate high drama and poetry from a few creative souls as we get garbled tales from their peers.

We may recognize tradition from the bones of a tale rather than from its external performance. We hear a work anecdote built like a childhood gift—trolls guard a bridge, musicians defy the Bremen robbers, a fairy godmother transforms a pumpkin into a splendid coach. A casual yarn tugs at our minds as it "looks" like something we heard years ago. Construction stiffs see beneath a tract house's skin to "feel" structural beams and joists. In this manner, these same hands at a talk fest "see" the fit in a story's columns and girders.

We add to a narrator's charm our affection for language and laughter at sharp wordplay. We frown at "big words" that defy un-

derstanding. We respond to familiar phrases holding rhetorical power: that reminds me of . . . ; in the good (bad) old days; wooden ships
and iron men; long years ago; east of the sun, west of the moon.

Such obvious formulas to open and close storytelling sessions
echo among the blueprints, printed codebooks, and project-sched-
ule sheets that guide job procedures. Occasionally, a choice story—
almost a verbal rendering of a Rube Goldberg drawing—serves to
explain complex technology or, metaphorically, to plant flowers at
the cyclotron's concrete edge.

I am especially interested in a tale's inner contours, its plains and
peaks. When a story moves from speech to print, it often loses character. Crevices fill in; granite erodes. In transferring a tale from a
living circle to the published page, collectors and editors differ in
the degree to which they retain the imperatives of vernacular style:
halts, wheezes, yawns, digressions, repetitions, inflections, contrac-
tions, dialect. Conventions of punctuation and paragraphing vary
among typographers, adding to the confusion about how speech
should "look" in print.

Some published tales sound natural, while others appear stilted,
far removed from the zest of the "liar's bench." Happily, we have a
few sound recordings—LP, cassette, CD—of workers' stories (such
as those by Myron Cohen) that carry vocal subtleties away from
particular jobs. In the absence of such aids, readers will benefit from
an old-fashioned appeal—read a story aloud!

Beyond matters of sound, structure, and style, tales become magnets for diverse and contradictory values, for kaleidoscopic scenes.
Some occupational anecdotes hold pragmatic or empirical guides to
national consensus; others, by contrast, assert formulas of class and
ethnic struggle. I have not attempted any statistical breakdown, of this
percentage reflecting belief in the system or that percentage trum-
peting revolution. Readers will make their own evaluations.

The tales scattered in this book display an alphabet of brag, par-
ody, know-how, respect for authority, fear of danger, sexual charm,
tenderness, provinciality, family cheer, opposition to line, ideological purity, union solidarity. Despite such range, my gathering is se-
verely limited in that it holds only English-language stories. I do
know that our contemporary work force includes a babel of tongues.
Thus, I urge others to delve into the lore of all groups constituting
the American mosaic.

From the earliest popular reworkings by Washington Irving and Nathaniel Hawthorne of European lore in the United States, some occupational material has been available to general readers. Mark Twain's stories of Mississippi River pilots stay vital in our national literature. During Twain's lifetime, socialist and anarchist organizers across the United States used sardonic anecdotes in their soapbox spiels. Some of this pungent humor then appeared in print in contemporaneous radical journals.

Red lore resurfaced through the 1930s and 1940s, coming to life during CIO drives. A bit of this period's clangor spilled over into popular fiction or cinema that held considerable vernacular substance. I cite a novel and a film: John Steinbeck's *In Dubious Battle* and *On the Waterfront*, starring Marlon Brando. We continue to hear defiant soapbox echoes in "modern" movements: civil rights, feminism, gay and lesbian recognition, ecology, reinvigorated populism.

New Deal relief project writers such as Jack Conroy counted union activists as cohorts. In 1939, WPA collectors coined the term *industrial folklore* to include a blend of regional sketches, local-color fiction, living theater, topical poetry, and vernacular expression. In Franklin Delano Roosevelt's era, one might find a work tale in an anthology, enacted on stage, packed in fiction, shown visually in a post-office mural, or used to introduce a blues song or ballad at a folksong concert.

In the 1920s and 1930s, some communist writers, flying banners of "proletarian literature," incorporated traditional anecdotes into sectarian strike novels and plays. Many of their books have turned to dust, doomed by shifts in party lines or by mechanical treatment of the creative spirit. Yet even dreary propaganda sketches and trite Popular Front fiction included job-speech items or work-scene descriptions bedded in gritty experience. Thus our search for occupational narrative leads from present job site to quiet archive, from literary classic to discarded manifesto.

I have not divided my findings into bins of diamonds or pebbles— correct, olympian, austere, holy. Nor do I certify the tales found in my book as gospel truth. Far from it! Audiences search for their own clues to detect error. Even after listeners have subjected stories to reality checks, those they deem false can be enjoyed for their affective role.

Storytellers range in performance style from factual reportage to

lackadaisical exaggeration. On many jobs we observe workers who
joke, brag, mimic, improvise, and complain to make it through the
day. Historically and functionally, a line of continuity runs from Mike
Fink's ring-tailed "roarers" told by Ohio River flatboaters to the
"propwash" pranks related by attendants during flight delays.

Because we hurried to span a continent to link Atlantic to Pacific,
much American work lore vivifies construction gains and glorifies
participants in extractive industry. Who has not heard stories about
brave miners or giant loggers? Such accounts have surfaced not only
in mine patches and woods camps but also from sea to shining sea
along wagon trails, canal ditches, steel rails, telegraph lines, and
interstate highways. We can assume that satellite dishes and fiber-
optic cables will stimulate stories about future Paul Bunyans and
John Henrys.

Reflecting on these continental treks, past and present, I turn
back to personal creeds: I seek to understand the contrast and continuity within tales, whether about grounded flatboats or soaring jet
planes. I wish to serve working people as they treasure the gold
nuggets and reject the iron pyrites in their story bags. I encourage
readers to praise or criticize the narratives that drift into their range.

In this book I comment more fully on some tales than on others.
Curiosity does not operate mechanically to discover equal sums of
background detail for each story. In treating "Furuseth's Credo"
(about a sailors' leader), torrential luck has enabled me to find abundant information leading to a case-study essay. For a few items (such
as "Smoking in the Dynamite Room" and "Kelly Girl"), voids remain
and I have no substantial notes to offer. I trust that others will fill
in the gaps and "dig where they stand," thus joining the ranks of
folktale explorers.

Critics will bring diverse perspectives to this book; I welcome
alternate interpretations. Each selection holds multiple possibilities
for commentary. In days past, wordsmiths peddled their wares from
Boston's wharfs to Seattle's "shark's dens" (employment offices),
from Sault Ste. Marie's locks to Laredo's streets. No corner of this
land, no union-action event, no vision of labor's goal, no calling has
escaped the attention of our raconteurs. These widely scattered stories deserve sophisticated analysis.

Conscious of laborlore's variety, I caution that my tale trove alludes
only tangentially to parallel folk constructs: song, shanty, sermon, rid-

dle, proverb, customary belief, ritual act, material artifact. Perhaps an anthologist will bring together in a single volume work wisdom cast in molds different than mine. Meanwhile, readers may sharpen their particular sense of similarity and difference within verbal lore by asking: What distinguishes a saying or slogan from a tale?

Two decades ago, Ada Louise Huxtable, a *New York Times* critic, reported an adage of great wisdom:

> Our favorite environmental comment comes from a lady correspondent who had a Tuscan father and an English mother and has been married to an American, and watching New York architecture for most of fifty years. She has seen the old buildings go down and the new buildings go up. Observing a typical apartment house rising on York Avenue recently she asked a workman, in Italian, "How do you build them so fast?"
>
> "Senza rispetto," he replied, "without respect." There is nothing more to add.

Neither Huxtable's friend nor the anonymous workman turned the latter's wistful retort into a full-scale narrative. During my own building-trades years, I heard wood-butchers and rod-busters comment bitterly on shoddy methods, corner cutting, and speed. They talked about the danger in ignoring safety measures and their disgust at working for gunnysack contractors on dingbat tracts or scarecrow facades.

I have no memory of anyone summing up his distress with as terse a maxim as "Senza rispetto," nor did I hear any extended tale built around this thoughtful ending. Yet I do not rule out the possibility that a rounded tale, which could be titled "Without Respect," has been fashioned around Ada Huxtable's report.

Some years ago, Jim Green, a millwright and trade-union leader, affirmed his craft's considerable skill by relaying to me a saying he recalled from his own apprenticeship days: "Son, we can fix anything except the crack of dawn or a broken heart." He knew it to be traditional and enjoyed its poetic imagery, but had no need to elaborate this bit of pithy speech into an extended story. Nor had Green heard other millwrights turn this aphorism into a lengthy narrative. Much job wisdom comes in scant packages.

In 1992, I heard a joke built into a tale at a verbal swap session. Walter Johnson, secretary of the San Francisco Labor Council,

asked, "Have you heard the joke about the unemployed union organizer?" Expecting a quickie, I shook my head, No. He began:

> Falling on hard times, the organizer tracked a lead to a pub-
> lic-service job. The personnel clerk gave him a long form to
> complete that included these questions, "Are your parents
> alive? If not, what was the cause of death?" The union man did
> not wish to answer, for his radical father had been hung for
> sedition in the Old Country.
>
> Needing the job, the organizer thought for a long while, then
> wrote, "My father suffered an honorable end at a public cere-
> mony when the platform upon which he stood gave way."

We remain free to identify "Father's Death" either as a sly joke
or as a traditional tale, to search for antecedents, and to extract its
meanings. Does it bring laughter because of the organizer's flowery
reply, or out of revulsion against corporate questions that pry too
deeply into private life? Does it evoke the response of cool or corn?

All working people hear one-liners, put-downs, hyperbole, jests,
riddles, aphorisms, and proverbs that under some circumstances
metamorphose into elaborate stories. As listeners, we can focus on
fundamental themes within different settings by overlooking matters
of structure. Alternately, we can direct our attention to plot additions
and convolutions that connect saying to tale to legend to epic.

Regardless of our choice in responding, we learn that basic motifs within tales reappear in other literary, musical, visual, or dramatic presentations. Professional scholars pursue analogies by the numbers; this is their choice and burden. Other readers remain free to
search for "twin" stories, to delve into background material, and
indeed, to record, assay, and distribute their findings.

A few puzzles need unraveling. For a century, many partisans
have issued labor songbooks. The Knights of Labor, Socialist Party,
Communist Party, and Industrial Workers of the World all gifted
their members with pocket- and pamphlet-sized songsters. In 1935
the International Ladies Garment Workers Union released two 12-
inch phonograph discs, the first sound recordings by any American
union. Before World War II, the Almanac Singers linked folksong
to polemical messages for union audiences.

Why do we lack booklets, recordings, and analysis of occupational
tales comparable to critical material directed at labor song? Count-

less more workers hear and tell stories than compose or sing songs. When will union educators, and their colleagues, accept responsibility for guarding narrative lore in the same way they have treasured music?

In considering these questions of heritage, we face a series of parallel problems touching thorny issues of race and sex. Plainly put, some work tales treating gender, personal behavior, or ethnicity reflect past codes that we now find repugnant. To illustrate: folklorist Manuel Peña has shared the experience of undocumented Mexican workers in the orchards and packing sheds at Fresno, California. He has encountered an ocean of *charritas coloradas* (red jokes) that carry *machismo* messages degrading to women. Do we ask Professor Peña to discard or bowdlerize such material?

No job frees itself easily of sexual lore—raw obscenity, predatory aim, voyeuristic impulse, cruel infidelity, erotic fantasy. Anxiety-based vulgarity intertwines with bawdy humor as both cross ethnic, regional, and religious fences, for no particular workers' cadre monopolizes the domain of Venus. Stories arise to substitute love for work, denigrate deviants, extol Amazons, perpetuate scandal, cheapen mates. Yarns of sexual acts told on one job may have been heard on previous days involving "shines," "spades," "rednecks," or "ridgerunners"—the list runs endlessly.

Laborlore enthusiasts have an uneven record in facing the gargoyles of race and sex. Where is the woven screen to wall off terror? Who fabricates the escape hatch? Some collectors will not record or publish stories denigrating women. Similarly, some avoid material retaining Stalinist lines; others delete tales hinging on ethnic status; still others avoid sexual imagery of any color.

While gathering tales for this book, I cast my nets widely, attempting to place each item in its time/place frame. Ultimately, wood hewers and water carriers conflate issues of race, class, and gender. Creators weave strands of satire, timidity, delusion, aggression, cruelty, trauma, and wit into their yarns. To demystify an offensive item—whether a shaggy-dog sketch or a bawdy jest—deflects its force in inflicting pain. We measure our personal growth by the leverage we gain over language and literature.

A few words on the format of my book may help open these pages. With listening and reading behind me, I have chosen 66 tales, many with variants, for a total of 116 discrete items. These do not march in sequential lockstep geared to chronology, travel, motif, utility, or meaning. Rather, my choices meander, pause, or stare left and right. "Calf's Head," a story shared in labor, ethnic, and regional communities for more than a century, begins our journey. "Stick Together" and "Quarrelsome Boys," twins from *Aesop's Fables,* close our volume.

Between the first and last piece, I have scattered items arbitrarily, seeking to replicate the experience of actually hearing tales "out of order"—before the morning whistle, on the lunchtime lumberpile, at the strike meeting, during the memorial service for a friend. For each selection, I have paired personal and academic questions. Do I find the tale appealing? Does it live in memory? Has it moved over time and place to show alteration among variants?

Most of my book's tales will meet conservative norms, although some readers may balk at the radical or erotic contents of a few stories. Other critics may question whether everything included here meets the test of traditionality. Not all bright anecdotes automatically become folktales. We constantly hear individual accounts that sputter and wheeze or remain leaden, unable to rise from fact to fiction, to move beyond personal authority.

Many workers fall back on bits of colloquial language to lubricate a recalled event, yet such speech fragments do not necessarily cohere into an expressive tale. I include a few work narratives that illustrate talk "en route" to story—verbal material waiting to find form, as the log awaits the carver's chisel.

Over the years, I have searched some arenas anticipating pointed labor tales on certain themes, only to be puzzled at my lack of discoveries. To illustrate: Scholars have long detailed efforts by the Industrial Workers of the World to organize farm migrants—wheat threshers, fruit tramps, straw cats. Wobblies were especially energetic in guarding crews against criminals who infested railway boxcars and jungle camps.

In 1915–16, IWW speakers and writers either coined or borrowed the locution *hi-jack* (possibly from Oklahoma oilfield hands) to name human parasites who "harvested the harvesters" by robbing them of their meager earnings. To my knowledge, no traditional tale emerged to explain the word *hi-jack*'s origin comparable to those yarns rationalizing the comedic *scissorbill* or the ideological *Wobbly.*

Not finding a tale elaborating *hi-jack* represents but one gap in our studies. Another results from hearing a tale and neglecting to write out its text. For example, during a 1959 meeting in Wisconsin, Mark Starr, education director of the ILGWU, told a story about a woman with a wig and wooden leg who couldn't be saved by a lifeguard because she wouldn't stick together. Starr attributed "Gotta Stick Together" to James Maurer, the Socialist Party vice-presidential candidate in the era of Calvin Coolidge.

Many in Starr's audience enjoyed his droll English-pub delivery and accepted the lesson—virtue in unity. In time, his story dimmed in my memory. Because it resembled the hillbilly ballad "Old Maid and the Burglar," I assumed that I would have no trouble in meeting someone who recalled its full labor treatment. IWW historian Fred Thompson contributed a tantalizing clue during my 1963 visit to his home, telling me that the tale reminded him of the aphorism about bananas, "Stick with the bunch or be skinned."

Joe Glazer, in a conversation with me, noted that Mark had also used this message in a union poster showing skinned bananas. I continue to look for Starr's "Gotta Stick Together," as well as for the ILGWU poster it inspired. Surely, a reader will be able to conclude this search, for I am convinced that every tale in my book can be complemented by variants known to storytellers beyond my reach.

Engaged in tale hunting for this collection, I sought parallel graphics—cartoons, prints, illustrations—and selected a set with strong narrative content. Over the years, artists have viewed work and workers from diverse angles of vision: vignettes of events highlighting labor history; job tasks intrinsically dramatic such as jackhammering or railway tie-tamping; bridges and skyscrapers under construction lending themselves to abstraction; scenes of struggle against physical and social forces. Within such breadth, I have cleaved to pictures tied in spirit or setting to the stories presented in this book.

Among the graphics scattered throughout my book, I have included a few drawings originally designed to complement specific tales. For example, Doug Bugge drew a "Boomer's Letter" to grace a Frank Lynch Labor Day column in the *Seattle Post-Intelligencer* (August 29, 1958). I include it with the railroad classic, "Service Letter." On March 5, 1937, the *Richmond Times-Dispatch* ran a cartoon by Fred Seibel of coal-mine leader John L. Lewis, "Like Davey Crockett's Coon." Although the account of Crockett, gun in

"Like Davey Crockett's Coon."

hand, grinning raccoons down from a tree is common, I have not found a coal-mine or trade-union repeat of this folktale. By reproducing and contrasting the Bugge and Seibel items, I hope to spur readers to keep their eyes peeled for, and to reflect upon, visual art matching verbal art found in *Calf's Head and Union Tale*.

I am aware that my book will raise hackles among some critics. Naysayers bray that workers who are glued to computer screens have shelved their expressive legacy in order to advance beyond craft or shop-floor lore. Cynics assert that folktales—instructive and amusing for a millennium—no longer serve in the realm of interactive multimedia, fax, and CD-ROM. I disagree heartily and offer this set of tales to all who continue to savor stories about work.

Radical colleagues tell me that old folkways impede progress or gloss oppressive hegemony, and they decry the hegemonic term *folk* for masking imperial designs to subordinate the weakest members in society. Modernists challenge that we have set the folk apart only to grind it down! Aware of such cloistered polemics, I remain unconvinced and unreconstructed—optimistic, unafraid of antiquarian labels.

I do not exaggerate the role of collectors and commentators drawn to laborlore's buried treasure. Rather, I ask that workers' songs and stories, customs and beliefs, be assayed, displayed, and utilized with deep respect. In recent decades, labor historians have engaged in internal debate on their discipline's fundamental concepts: class, culture, consciousness, identity, direction, spirit. Some assert that attention to folk-narrative tradition and related imaginative expression detracts from the basic realities in class formation and purpose.

As historians and folklorists meet, a second source of tension arises out of different understandings of "truth" in folktales. Although my book holds stories by and about Gene Debs, Mother Jones, Sam Gompers, and similar figures, I have not scoured biographies to "verify" tales humoring or enlarging their lives. In short, windies and whoppers about famed persons contain ethical and esthetic meanings despite their departure from or twisting of hard fact.

A related problem concerns events "firm" in history books but "distorted" or "absent" in folk narratives. To illustrate: To gain wages in line with war-years cost-of-living increases, Chicago switchmen struck in April, 1920. Then, John Grunau emerged as head of the rank-and-file Chicago Yardmen's Association, an insurgent group threatening the established Brotherhood of Railroad Trainmen and other dominant unions, as well as local and national employers and federal agencies. The strike spread like prairie fire beyond the Midwest and across craft lines (Love).

In July, the strikers projected an industrial union, the United Association of Railway Employees of North America. Both the CYA and the UA failed as BRT president Bill Lee recruited scabs to replace outlaws. Ultimately, the major brotherhoods, rail carriers, and government colluded to weed out rebels with "individual applications for re-employment." In the face of massive power, the defeated strikers gradually drifted back to work (Perlman and Taft 452–56).

Very likely, this bitter strike of 1920 spawned considerable lore, some of which may have been caught by reporters in the "uptown" and labor press. Yet, to my knowledge, no CYA stories have been reported by historians or folklorists. In March, 1995, Luis Kemnitzer, a former railroad brakeman in California, told me a CYA blacklisting story and a related "old joke." I include his two contributions as variants of "Service Letter" and "Word Play." Here, I note the gap of seventy-five years from event to tale recovery, as well as the erasure and alteration of historical detail about the Chicago insurgents' strike revealed in folk memory.

I dwell on this recent finding of a splinter of CYA lore and its ephemeral nature because I am convinced that many tales included in my book can be related in some way to historical events, persons, or causes. The challenge remains great for labor historians and their allies to get "underneath" the authority of formal documentation, to explore how factual events and fictive tales complement rather than contradict each other.

Finally, a retrospective note: When I was a child, my father told stories of becoming a skilled Old World harness maker and migrating from the Ukraine to the New World. Seeking freedom in a Hudson Bay forest camp, he met French-Canadian ox drivers and Cree Indian loggers. Striving to comprehend their exotic speech and intimate legends, he added several of their narrative arrows to his quiver.

Sad to say, like many youths, I neglected to record my father's tales. However, as a teenager, I heard Louis Adamic "lecture" at a Depression-born forum in Los Angeles. His stories of class-war prisoners at San Quentin, union dynos (dynamiters) and skid-road winos, penniless boomers and smug homeguards, and San Pedro Dalmatian fishermen bonded with my own family's legacy to win me over to labor history and laborlore studies.

Beginning work on the San Francisco waterfront in 1941, I listened to shipwrights, sailors, stevedores, bar pilots, and pile butts shift moods as they griped about tough times and boasted about strike valor. I felt privileged to enter their realm of skill and cause; their anecdotes became pennants marking my growth. These mechanics peer out of every nook in *Calf's Head and Union Tale.*

During the mid-1950s, I absorbed bountiful Wobbly lore from machinist John Neuhaus; a few of his stories also rest in these pages. Peter Tamony, Celtic bard and San Francisco word wizard, encouraged me by homily and example to link language to lore, occupational practice to arcane theory. From his own resting place, Peter looks down and smiles with this book's readers.

In 1957, an open-sesame voice commanded me to keep school-binder notes on tales I had heard, read, or told. The initial "Calf's Head" has moved literally from an early binder to these pages— pages displaying variety in voice and value, as well as in scattered sources. Need I again urge readers to record or write out their own stories and those of friends?

Cassette tape recorders, stubby pencils, pocket notebooks, and library anthologies become marvelous tools in conserving and interpreting our legacy. Like other instruments, the collector/commentator's tools must be kept "honed and oiled." *Calf's Head and Union Tale* both hews and marks a work-tale trail.

The words we call upon to compress and extend job practice wax and wane with the moon, advance and retreat with the tide. We celebrate the rainbow hues of language; we stand in awe at the thundering power of speech. Treasuring labor's traditional narratives, we journey into the realm where working people jabber and jive, moan and groan, whisper and roar, as they pour their experiences into random anecdote and structured tale.

"Union Meeting."

1

Calf's Head

A. Striker's Wife

The iron ore miners were on strike up in Minnesota. It was a long, hard strike but the men held out pretty good. A lot of them were Finns—Finns believe in solidarity. One day a striker's wife was about out of money. She went to the butcher shop to try to buy some cheap cut of meat that might last the family for a week.

She saw a calf's head in the case and figured it would make lots of soup. So she asked the butcher, "How much?"

He said, "One dollar."

That was too much so she started to leave. But just as she got to the door, she asked again, "Is this a union shop; is your meat union?"

He was surprised, but replied, "Sure, I'm a member of the Amalgamated [Meat Cutters and Butcher Workmen of North America]. I cut my meat by union rule; see my shop card in the window."

The lady said, "Well, I don't want any union meat. Don't you have a scab calf's head?"

The butcher was stumped but he was smart. So he said, "Just a minute, Ma'am," and he took the calf's head into the room back of the shop. Pretty soon the lady heard a lot of clatter. The butcher came out of the room and handed her the wrapped package.

He said, "That'll be seventy-five cents, Ma'am."

She was very pleased at the saving, paid up, and started for the door. But she was curious, so she asked, "Isn't this scab calf's head the same as the union head you tried to sell me for a dollar?"

The butcher said, "Yes Ma'am, it is. I just knocked out two bits worth of brains!"

B. Sheep's Head

Many women, during the 1916 Iron Range strike, took in boarders to supplement the earnings of members of their households. One woman went to the butcher to get something cheap as money was running out in the strike, and she had so many to feed. The cheapest thing she could find was a sheep's head. She figured how she could make soup with it, and perhaps some headcheese, but it was still too expensive.

The butcher tried to cajole her by saying butchers had to make a living. This was a good union sheep killed by union butchers; he couldn't sell it any cheaper. The woman said she had eight men to feed, and simply didn't have that money.

So the butcher said he had a way to fix that up. He took the head into the back of the shop, brought it out again, and sold it to her for what change she had in her hand. She wanted to know what he had done, for the head looked the same.

"Oh, that was a union sheep's head before, but I made it a scab— I took its brains out."

C. How He Made It Non-Union

On one occasion a non-union man entered a butcher shop to purchase a calf's head. As the butcher was about to wrap it up for him, the customer noticed the union shop card.

"Say, is that a union calf's head?" he asked.

"Yes Sir," answered the butcher.

"Well I am not a union man and I don't want union meat," said the customer.

"I can make it non-union," said the meat man, picking it up and retiring to the back room. He returned in a few minutes and laid the head on the counter with the remark, "It's all right now."

"What did you do to make it non-union?" asked the prospective buyer.

"I simply took the brains out of it."

D. Non-Union Sheep's Head

A good story is none the worse for being twice told, and the following one is worthy of repetition:

The boss butchers of one of the large cities resolved to hire only union butchers and placed a sign in their meat stores which read, "None but union meat sold here."

A non-union man who lived near one of these stores sent his wife to buy a sheep's head. The butcher wrapped up a sheep's head and handed it to her. Seeing the union sign, she said:

"I don't want that one. I want a non-union sheep's head."

The butcher took the sheep's head, unwrapped it, took his cleaver, chopped it in two, scooped out the brains, and handing it back to her, said:

"Here, madam, is a non-union sheep's head."

Sources

A. John Neuhaus told this tale at my home, San Francisco, about 1956. I wrote out his text from memory for "The Workers in the Dawn," in Tristram P. Coffin's *Our Living Traditions* (New York: Basic Books, 1968), p. 256. Reprinted without attribution in *The American Worker*, ed. Richard B. Morris (Washington, D.C.: Department of Labor, 1976), p. 56.

B. Fred Thompson (as told by George Speed) in letter to Saul Schniderman, Nov. 25, 1982.

C. *Industrial Pioneer*, Apr., 1924; reprinted, *Industrial Worker*, Oct. 25, 1961; reprinted by Joyce Kornbluh in *Rebel Voices* (Ann Arbor: University of Michigan Press, 1964), p. 87.

D. *Carpenter* 13 (Nov., 1893): 5. Reprinted by Dave Ransom as "Lesson in Unionism," *Carpenter* 113 (Nov.–Dec., 1993): 38.

Background

"Calf's Head," in spoken and written forms, exhibits internal variation surrounding a fixed trade-union belief—superiority to non-unionists, especially to scabs. The word *scab*, meaning a worker refusing to join a labor organization or engaging in active strike-breaking, dates to 1777 at Bristol, England, during a cordwainers' strike. Over the years, union activists have ridiculed their real and perceived enemies in song, story, skit, slogan, and speech.

In our four examples above, sheep and calf interchange, as the lead character shifts: striker's wife, boardinghouse woman, nonunion man, wife of notorious nonunion man. However, in all cases, the butcher remains constant, as does his act of scooping out, knocking out, or removing brains. Essentially, with a rhetorical scalpel, the storyteller cuts the scab to size, revealing the latter as brainless, spineless, or less than human.

Readers will enjoy another "Non-Union Calf's Head," told by Arthur Boose to Ben Botkin at Portland, Oregon. Boose treated the folklorist to an old-fashioned street-corner spiel (1957, 200). By placing the Portland text alongside those of Neuhaus and Thompson, we "hear" soapboxing from the heyday of the Industrial Workers of the World (Wobblies).

John Neuhaus, a San Francisco machinist and "double-header," held dual membership in the International Association of Machinists and the IWW, thus blending pragmatic and idealistic values (Green 1960a, 189–217). IWW exemplar Fred Thompson left a modest personal autobiography, *Fellow Worker,* edited by David Roediger.

During the 1960s, while telling John Neuhaus's "Striker's Wife" in labor-education gatherings, I had identified it as a Wobbly tale. Thus, I was excited to learn that I had erred in this attribution when I found, at the end of 1993, a pre-IWW (organized 1905) sheep's-head variant that had appeared as a filler in an 1893 issue of the *Carpenter,* the magazine of the United Brotherhood of Carpenters and Joiners of America.

It seems likely that *Carpenter* editor Peter J. McGuire included this account of a butcher creating a brainless scab while the tale circulated among nineteenth-century craftsmen. We can only speculate about McGuire's source for the "twice-told" story, and its prior appearance in the repertories of trade unionists. Below, I touch matters of origin for "Calf's Head" in comments upon a related narrative, "Writer's Brains, Producer's Brains."

2

Writer's Brains, Producer's Brains

"So," she said, "this man went into a butcher shop, *and?*"

"Do you really want to hear the joke?"

"But of course."

"Well. He goes into the butcher shop and he sees two signs. One sign says: Writer's brains, nineteen cents a pound. The other sign says: Producer's brains, seventy-nine cents a pound."

"Really?"

I waited. She sipped her drink.

"Now you are supposed to ask me," I said patiently, "why producer's brains cost seventy-nine cents a pound and writers brains only cost nineteen cents a pound."

[Repartee between man and woman in bar. She asks; he answers.]

"Well, the butcher said, do you know how many producers you have to kill to get a pound of brains?"

Source

Joke within dialogue in Alfred Hayes, *The End of Me* (New York: Atheneum, 1968), p. 75.

Background

In his novel *The End of Me,* Alfred Hayes introduces a Hollywood screenwriter, Asher, who, facing a declining career, falls in love with youthful, appealing, evasive Aurora. In turn, she leads him to his doom. I have extracted a bit of wry occupational humor from a di-

alogue sequence between them: Writer denigrates "bossy" producers by mocking their lack of brains.

Hayes may have heard an on-the-job joke about writers/produc-
ers, or he may have zipped his own craft into a traditional story involving similar comparisons or rivalries. Laborlore enthusiasts know
Alfred Hayes not as a folktale enthusiast but rather as the author
of the popular elegy "Joe Hill." (See "Singing Joe Hill" in Green
1993b.)

"Writer's Brains, Producer's Brains" shares a verdant family tree
with numerous missing-brain tales. In 1957, General Alfred Gruenther, American Red Cross president and former NATO command-
er, addressing the AFL-CIO convention, opened with a yarn about
one of Napoleon's colonels with a brain tumor. While in surgery, the
latter received a promotion to general. Instantly, the patient replaced
his cranium and started off the table. The surgeon remonstrated,
"You can't leave. You don't have your brains." The colonel replied,
"Don't worry; I don't need brains any more. Now I'm a General"
(1957, 106).

Other variants take different forms such as one involving Missouri
pioneers in Idaho, where Silver Creek ranchers hold in low esteem
their neighbor Happy Jack Shipton, a backwoods fiddler from Arkansas. After being ridiculed about going barefoot back home, Jack
narrates a boyhood adventure: Pap had sent him hunting for a hide
to make shoes, warning Jack to bring back the brains of anything he
shot—brains to tan the hide. Sighting a squirrel, the young hunter
blew off its head, scattering brains throughout the forest. Afraid of
a "wallopun" from Pap, Jack remembered a Missouri settlement over
the hill. Going there, he shot a mess of settlers and returned home.
When a skeptical auditor doubts this Arkansas windie, Jack, clinch-
ing it, replies: "Say you know I had to kill nine of them-there Mis-
sourians to get enough brains to tan that hide" (*Idaho*, 393).

Vance Randolph, in "Brains for a Tanner," places a related tale
in the Ozark Mountains during the Civil War. Seven bushwacking
Yankees kill Johnny Hutchinson. Young Jim Hutchinson gains revenge. As he slays the last Yank, a fool woman questions his action.
Jim replies, "I'm tanning a groundhog hide, ma'am, and it takes
three or four Yankees to furnish the material." Storyteller Price
Paine had heard this near Elk Springs, Missouri, about 1898. To
explain it to Randolph, Paine added: "We all tanned our leather

Choctaw style, in them days. You just scrape the fat off, and rub a spoonful of fresh brains into the flesh side of the skin" (1957, 89).

Dane Coolidge also used this theme in a joshing duel among Texas cowboys who rag two Mormon riders. Bishop Greenhouse and Kinch Talley fight back as best they can. Bishop explains that aversion to hard work and lack of good sense bar most Texicans from Mormon towns. He continues with a yarn: Grandpaw sends Paw after a gray tree-squirrel, "Be careful not to shoot him in the head, because I want the brains to tan the skin with." Paw messes up the chore. The indulgent old man sends his son out again to nab a Texan. Bishop winds up: Paw had to kill six Texicans to get enough brains to tan the skin. "That's why they [Mormons] won't take 'em into the Church" (1937, 151).

In February, 1962, at a union conclave in Detroit, I told John Neuhaus's "Calf's Head" to the assembly. Andy Brown, active in the United Automobile Workers, indicated that he had heard this Wobbly story as a boy in Scotland, but that it concerned Englishmen with their brains knocked out. Andy knew it as a lesson in national-identity inversion: They may rule us but we are more intelligent than our rulers.

Jokes about lost brains either by design or accident continue to move about America. In recent years, Wisconsin folklorist Jim Leary has gathered anecdotes barbing Norwegians (a Swede with his brains knocked out). No doubt, similar stories touch members of many groups. With such material at hand, we trace a tale's zigzag travels from Scottish patriots to Napoleonic soldiers to Ozark rebels to Arkansas hunters to Mormon cowboys to Midwest Norwegians to American trade-unionists to Hollywood writers. Surely, other elements—ethnic, regional, political, occupational, ideological—mark our tale's long journey.

3

How to Get into Heaven

There was a fellow went to heaven one time. He was a millionaire. When he got up he wanted to sneak in, without answering questions.

Peter stopped him.

"What did you do when you was down below?"

"I was a millionaire!"

"Did you work for it?"

"No."

"Did you rob and steal from laborers to get that million?"

"Yes."

"Never done no work in your life?"

"No."

"You gotta do some work before you get in here. Go over there to that storeroom and get a bucket. Come back and see me. You see that lake down there?"

"Yes."

"Fly down and bail out that lake and when you have done it come back and see me!"

Took him 200 years. Well, he come up and reported.

"Nothin' doin'; you can't get in yet! Hang onto the pail. Go over to the boy in the storeroom and get a pick and a shovel. Come back and see me! See that mountain down there?"

"Yes."

"Take that pick and shovel and pail and go and dig that mountain down. Throw it into the lake where you bailed the water out of it. Come back and see me."

That took him 500 years. That was 700 years. He went up.

"Go and put away your tools in the storeroom and come back and see me."

"Ascending Heaven."

Peter looked down at the job he had done for 700 years and was very well satisfied with it. A good worker.

"You won't have to do any more hard work but you can't get in yet! Go down to the Labor Temple on 84th Street between Second and Third Avenue. There's a fellow named Fred Kitilson owns a saloon there and stand with your belly up against Kitilson's bar 'til that squarehead son-of-a-bitch buys you a drink, and then I'll let you in!"

Source

Mike Ryan, interview with Marion Charles Hatch at Local 40, International Association of Bridge, Structural, and Ornamental Ironworkers, New York City, 1939. Text from WPA Federal Writers' Project in B. A. Botkin, *Sidewalks of America* (Indianapolis: Bobbs-Merrill, 1954), p. 284.

Background

Mike Ryan tapped into a set of intertwined traditional themes: rich man's ascent to heaven; judgment at heaven's gate; Peter assigns three difficult tasks to rich man. Ryan polished his old story's ending with two unusual details: a closing barb touching ethnic tension in occupational communities—the squarehead (Scandinavian) saloon owner never offering free drinks; and a realistic touch—specifying the location of Kitilson's saloon at the uptown Labor Temple.

This reference may have signaled a private joke among ironworkers, for, in 1939, Manhattan housed two downtown labor temples: the Central Labor Council headquarters and the Methodist Mission for indigent workers. Although union halls frequently shared space with bars, it seems unlikely that a religious charity would do so. With two separate temples, and their respective moves before 1939, what prompted Ryan to hark back to the East 84th location? Did Fred Kitilson, also in Local 40, own a building-trades bar, or did Ryan deliberately disguise the name and site of one frequented by ironworkers present in a storytelling session with collector Hatch?

My internal questions on Kitilson's saloon do not alter value in "How to Get into Heaven." Rather, the matter of location illustrates difficulty in grasping a tale's full meaning decades after it has been told. In 1994, labor historian Joe Doyle interviewed New York ironworker business agent Bill Colavito (Local 455) who started at the trade in the early 1930s. He had never heard of Marion Charles Hatch, and was surprised to learn that the WPA collector had gathered a rich harvest in Local 40's old hall.

Neither Doyle nor I have found notes by Hatch. It was unusual in 1939 (as it is now) for folklorists to seek out workers in union halls. Fortunately, Ben Botkin then encouraged Hatch, Herbert Halpert, Ralph Ellison, and other WPAers to collect "living lore." With luck, we may yet unearth the details of Hatch's visit to Local 40, and his response to Ryan's tale's compelling moral: millionaires who cheat workers never enter heaven!

We affirm the traditionality of "How to Get into Heaven" by comparing Ryan's account to related tales heard by Halpert at Lake Louise, Canada, and along New York's East Branch of the Delaware River (1945, 46; 1946, 92). In each, St. Peter assigns three tasks, certain that the entrant will fail the third (entering a saloon to cadge a free drink). We enjoy tales by ironworkers—often at skyscraper heights—who "put down" rich men; we marvel at links in the high-steel-story chain.

4

Daniel O'Connell's Duel

[James Murtaugh, at the first IWW convention, related "a little story" on "strife-makers" who needlessly criticized the AFL.]

In the old days Daniel O'Connell was challenged to fight a duel, and he accepted the challenge. His opponent was going around the country shooting the heads off from the roosters. O'Connell's friends came to him and reported this fact to him, saying that his life was in jeopardy on account of the marksmanship of his opponent.

O'Connell said, "Have the roosters got pistols to shoot back with?"

Source

James Murtaugh, portion of remarks at first IWW convention, *Proceedings,* 1905, p. 130.

Background

Murtaugh's "little story" calls for analysis involving its origin in Ireland, as well as the speaker's didactic purpose in recalling it from memory during the give-and-take of floor debate at a labor convention. Daniel O'Connell (1775–1847), a great patriot, political leader, and lawyer, engendered considerable lore, some of which reached the New World after the Great Famine. In folk tradition, O'Connell outwitted his enemies whether they appeared in the guise of blowhard marksmen, oppressive landlords, or treacherous Englishmen. (For parallel O'Connell stories see O'Sullivan 1966, 81–82.)

When founding delegates at the IWW's initial convention faced the issue of breaking sharply with craft unionists or, somehow, accommodating to the American Federation of Labor, the majority favored revolutionary industrial unionism. As the debate progressed, James Murtaugh identified himself as occupying an anomalous position, "a radical among conservatives and a conservative among radicals."

Murtaugh further revealed his labor credentials as both a craft- and class-conscious molder who believed in industrial organization. He held membership in the Iron Molders International Union, AFL, and had worked at New Decatur, Alabama, in the L & N Railroad shops, when Eugene Victor Debs organized the American Railway Union. Murtaugh joined the industrial ARU, serving as the New Decatur branch president. He explained his dual loyalty pragmatically: "While we were in that particular instance working for a railroad company, absolutely impotent to bring about better conditions for our craft [we joined the ARU], yet the majority of us working in foundries throughout the country were able to better our conditions as [Molders] craftsmen in those foundries."

In telling the O'Connell tale, Murtaugh made his own point clear, "the moral of this story is in the application of it." He viewed IWW "strife-makers" as a "discordant element" of super radicals, righteous in command of theory, and analogous to boastful hunters shooting unarmed roosters. Murtaugh's views did not prevail at the IWW's gathering among delegates determined to break with conservative craft unionism. In short, the Irish story alone could not counter the convention's majority sentiment. Despite this failure, I cite "Daniel O'Connell's Duel," caught "live" by a stenographic reporter, to reveal the actual circumstance of a folktale put to use within a labor-union setting.

5

Kelly Girl

The CEO in a company downtown needed some short-term help. He called the Kelly Agency and asked for a temp who would enjoy a modern office. The Kelly manager said she'd have a very good worker there at 10 A.M., the next morning.

That day the CEO was ready at 10. He was surprised to hear a scratching at the door. He opened it, and in jumped a dog—nice brown hair, soulful eyes, trim legs. Pausing to catch his breath, the boss asked, "Are you the Kelly girl?" The dog barked, "Bow-wow."

Not knowing what to do, the man asked, "Can you type?" The dog jumped into the chair at the desk, hit the keys with its paws, and barked, "Bow-wow." Next, the boss asked, "Can you make coffee?" The dog trotted over to the corner, heated up the Silex, handed the man a steaming cup, and barked, "Bow-wow."

Worried about what to do, the boss asked, "Do you use the computer?" The dog hunched up to the keyboard, flicked a switch button, waited for the screen to light up, and barked, "Bow-wow."

The CEO, amazed, had only one card left. He asked, "Are you bilingual?" Pleased as punch, the dog purred, "Meow!"

Source

Charlie Chavez, proprietor of El Manito Barber Shop, 3112 Twenty-fourth Street, San Francisco, told me this story, June 16, 1993. I wrote out his text the next day.

Background

"Kelly Girl" may have derived from a shaggy-dog story, but I have found no printed analogs. Told in San Francisco's barrio by a Mexican-American barber, it blends views of downtown office routines with ironic concern for present-day multicultural issues. Whether or not other storytellers stressed different strands of ambiguity within this tale, I do not know. Charlie had heard "Kelly Girl" from another customer some weeks before he passed it along to me, but offered no special evaluation of the previous jokester's status or politics.

"The Typist."

6

Hand on the Jailhouse Wall

[Alex Campbell, active in the Molly Maguires, a Pennsylvania anthracite miners' secret order, had been tried as an accessory to
murder in Mauch Chunk, Carbon County, after identification by
James McParland, a Pinkerton detective/labor spy.]

Several months later, when [Campbell's] appeals for a new trial
had been denied by the higher courts, [he] heard the sheriff read
his death warrant. Then he rose to his full height—he was a big,
powerfully built man—and declared: "It's hard to die innocent, but
I shall not be the first to die thus. God knows that I am innocent of
any crime, and the people know it, and the Commonwealth knows
it."

More months passed and then came the dawn of Black Thurs-
day—June 21, 1877. Campbell was up early that morning and as he
fingered his rosary his lips moved in prayer. He dragged his ball and
chain closer to the oblong-shaped chink in the wall representing a
window and with weary eyes sought to catch a last fleeting glimpse
of the patch of blue beyond.

In the jail corridor there was a murmur of hushed voices—many
spectators had assembled for the hangings.

Suddenly the heavy cell door was opened with a clang. It was the
sheriff. The zero hour had arrived. As the door stood partly opened,
Campbell caught sight of the scaffold in the narrow, somber corridor, and a shiver must have run up and down his spine.

As the sheriff approached him, Campbell said brokenly, but with
evident deep sincerity, "I am innocent. I swear I was nowhere near
the scene of the murder—"

And then, as if to impress the sheriff with the truth of his pro-
test, Campbell bent over, ground his right hand in the dust on the

cell floor, and dragging his ball and chain with him, took a long stride toward the wall. Then stretching himself to the full height, he smote the wall with his large hand.

"There is the proof of my words," he shouted. "That mark of mine will never be wiped out. There it will remain forever to shame the county that is hangin' an innocent man."

They hanged Campbell that morning, but the imprint of his hand stood out from the wall like truth itself. In vain did the sheriff try to remove it. Succeeding sheriffs also failed. Campbell apparently was right.

Source

George Korson, *Minstrels of the Mine Patch* (Philadelphia: University of Pennsylvania Press, 1938), pp. 251 and 307.

Background

George Korson, an anthracite region newspaperman, began collecting mine lore in the mid-1920s, thus helping elevate work as vital in understanding American tradition. (Angus Gillespie has detailed his immense contribution.) Korson gathered several variants of the jail-wall legend, collating them to complement the industrial ballads he had encountered. In an evocative film from 1970, *The Molly Maguires*, Sean Connery brought fresh attention to the organization so feared by mine owners more than a century ago.

Curious about the traditionality of the Mauch Chuck legend, Korson added a sketch on the handprint motif's use in sixteenth-century India and twelfth-century Germany. We find a parallel belief in Mormon lore—the ineradicability of Joseph Smith's bloodstains after a mob murdered him in a Carthage, Illinois, jail on June 27, 1844 (Fife 1942). In tradition, these stains have lasted to the present day.

Korson also reported hearing cynics scoff at believers' claims regarding the Mauch Chuck handprint narrative. Some branded it a deliberate hoax. Other naysayers advanced a "rational" explanation for the jail mark's genesis and persistence despite attempts by sheriffs to cover it with whitewash or to scrape it off the wall. Few folk certainties remain free from skeptical assault.

Rosemary Scanlon, a coal miner's granddaughter, knew the tale from childhood as part of her family's heritage. In a case study, she returned to the Mauch Chuck legend with a remembrance from her mother of the "supernatural sign, a testimony to the innocence of a condemned man." Scanlon noted that this quasi-religious belief had been kept alive by a diverse set of bearers: tourist visitors to the jail; unionists honoring Campbell and the other Molly Maguires as pioneers in labor's cause; Irish-Americans reaffirming ethnic roots (1971, 97–107).

As I neared this book's end, writer-historian Charles Stumpf of Conyngham, Pennsylvania, a coal miner's son, shared with me a score of newspaper clippings on the Molly Maguires. Such local-color reports, collected between 1975 and 1995, give evidence to the complex layering of a tale after decades of attention by historians, journalists, promoters, preservationists, filmmakers, and dramatists. In short, the "Hand on the Jailhouse Wall," told initially within the anthracite community and in the 1920s by miners to George Korson, now appeals to diverse narrators.

In 1954, Mauch Chuck residents renamed their town Jim Thorpe. Some dwellers then hoped for a giant museum/sports arena honoring the famed Indian football hero. Others, unreconstructed, clung to the original name as it invoked both coal and Molly Maguire lore. In the latter camp, local preservationists in 1975 succeeded in adding the Carbon County Jail (with its intact handprint) to the National Register of Historical Places. In 1978, Pennsylvania governor Milton Shapp, spurred by labor historians, issued a proclamation asserting injustice in the Molly trials and hangings.

Carl Larson, in a feature article (1980), attributed the handprint to Tom Fisher, executed on March 28, 1878. Further, Larson reported that the miner's mother was Irish and father, Pennsylvania Dutch. Their "boy had been raised with hexerei, the sometimes mysterious power of hex signs." Thus, an "ethnic" belief somehow animated the death-cell sign left by Fisher in Mauch Chuck. Strangely, Alex Campbell disappears from this story: however, hexerei witchcraft appears as "Dutch" legends merge with labor tradition.

On June 21, 1980, the Pennsylvania Labor History Society joined hands with Schuylkill County officials and Commonwealth preservationists to place a plaque, "Hanging of the Mollies," at the Pottsville Jail. The bronze marker looked back at the judicial executions of 1877–78 as "part of a repression directed against the fledgling mineworkers' union of that historic period," and named Jack Kehoe, a Molly leader hanged in Pottsville. Previously, Governor Shapp had issued a posthumous pardon for Kehoe.

In August, 1980, the New York Theater Caravan brought a stage production, *Molly Maguire* (written and directed by Marketa Kimbrell), to anthracite country. Its sympathetic audience included descendents of the original Mollies (Walentis). With Molly interest stimulated by film and play, Joseph Wayne, great grandson of Jack Kehoe, salvaged parts of the Schuylkill County Prison, in 1984, for display in his Girardville tavern. Wayne knew that history buffs visited his area in pursuit of coal-mine folklore (Texter).

Patrick Campbell, Alex Campbell's grand nephew, heard Molly stories in childhood. After seeing *The Molly Maguires,* and disappointed at its omission of Alex, Patrick undertook a personal odyssey to recover family tradition. In 1992, he published *A Molly Maguire Story,* adding detective-like details to an unending and ambiguous narrative (Christopher).

An architectural/curatorial detail adds to our overview of an endless tale. In January, 1995, Tom and Betty Lou McBride bought the former Carbon County Jail, turning it into the Old Museum Jail and Heritage Center. The structure—rusticated stone, massive walls, elevated guard turret—stands as a visual reminder of many local Bastilles. Tony Greco's report on the McBrides' effort includes a photo of Campbell's handprint of 1877 in cell 17, an eternal sign of his innocence.

In October, 1995, Marigrace Heyer expanded Carbon County jail lore with a feature article, "Restless Spirits." After touring the old prison, visitors wrote the McBrides noting strange feelings of apprehension, invisibility, or sadness. Poconos psychic researcher Chip Decker "explained" to Heyer that Molly Maguire ghosts lingered at the jail seeking peace to expiate the traumatic hangings of 1871.

Opening with George Korson's "Hand on the Jailhouse Wall," and closing with local-press anecdotal details, I touch the interplay of oral tradition, paranormal behavior, folkloric scholarship, regional journalism, labor history, historic preservation, and commercial tourism. Individuals in such endeavors do make strange bedfellows, yet we must evaluate their varied efforts if we wish to extract full meaning from laborlore legends and landmarks.

7

Service Letter

A. *Crane with a Broken Neck*

After the [American Railway Union] strike of 1894, the GMA [General Managers Association] refused to let the strikers return to their old jobs, instituting the most effective blackball system known in railroad history. . . . The GMA action . . . [involved] revenge, coupled with fear of what might have happened if the strike had succeeded. . . . ARU men seeking employment . . . were stymied because their bosses refused to verify the extent of their railroad experience.

This obstacle was overcome by one of the victims, who sued a railroad company to get a service letter. The fellow won his case and was awarded damages as well as the letter. Thereupon the GMA roads saw the light. Any erstwhile employee requesting a clearance could get it. The letter set forth his record, ending with these words, "Left the service of his own accord." But there was a catch in this sudden change of heart. The trick was revealed to me [Freeman Hubbard] years ago by several old-timers who had been through the Pullman strike. One of them, a retired boomer named William F. Knapke of East St. Louis, Illinois . . . put the situation as follows:

Two young brakemen, Smith and Jones, both of whom had been strikers, walked into a trainmaster's office looking for a job. Smith asked the trainmaster's clerk, "Hiring any brakemen?"

"Let's see your service letter," was the noncommittal reply.

Smith handed him the clearance. The clerk took it into the next room, returned in a few seconds, and handed it back, saying "Sorry, can't use you."

The same process was repeated with Jones, except that the clerk said to Jones, "Come back this afternoon and fill out an application."

Since both brakemen were about the same age and had about the same length of railroad experience and both service letters read very much the same, the applicants naturally wondered why Smith had been rejected and Jones hired. They puzzled over this matter for quite some time. At length, in comparing the two letters, one of the men happened to hold them up in front of a strong light, and the mystery was solved. He noticed watermarks in the paper. Both depicted a crane; but Jones's bird, the trademark of a famous paper company, stood proudly with head erect, while Smith's had its head hanging down as though with a broken neck.

"Crane watermarks appeared on *all* the clearances of some roads," according to Bill Knapke, "but 'head-up' letters were given to those men, whether strikers or not, who had not been ARU leaders, agitators, or saboteurs. This symbol said, in effect: 'If you want to hire this applicant, it's all right with us.' But in the case of strikers who, like Smith, had been too active to please the brass collars, the 'crane with a broken neck' constituted a warning to prospective employers that his services were undesirable."

Other strike veterans tell me [Hubbard] that the droopy-necked bird was used for *all* American Railway Union members, regardless of their conduct during the early summer of 1894. Among those who take this view is Arthur B. Clark, a boomer now living in retirement at Stockton, California.

"The black-listing watermark was all too real," he says, "as many an old ARU man will testify. It was pointed out to me by my brother-in-law, E. W. Waddell, master mechanic on the Rock Island at Fairbury, Nebraska. Waddell died some years ago. The 'crane with a broken neck' was then dim but could be discerned by holding the service letter to the light. I had been in the Pullman strike myself and carried one of those letters in my pocket for months, until I learned from Waddell that it was my death warrant insofar as getting a railroad job was concerned. Then I disposed of it in short order, as did other strikers branded with the same outlaw stigma when they learned the truth."

Is such a letter now extant? If so, it should be preserved. It belongs in the permanent museum of railroadiana. . . . I myself [Hubbard] have never seen this odd watermark. I cannot even produce indisputable evidence that it actually served as a blackball device. . . .

We now hear from Charles Anthony Roach, nicknamed Silent

Slim. . . . "As one victim of the American Railway Union strike in 1894, I will testify to the validity of those service letters watermarked with a crane whose neck appeared to be broken. I was working as a switchman for the Louisville & Nashville out of East Nashville, Tennessee, at the time the strike order was issued; but instead of walking out with the other ARU members, I reported sick and did not show up in the yards again until I knew the cause was lost. The general yardmaster, Billy Yater, said he would not put me back on the pay roll until I got a clearance from Nashville. I knew what that meant."

"After shoving my sox into a bundle and putting on a thousand-mile shirt, I applied for a service letter. Well, they gave me one. I toted it around for nearly a year, until I met another boomer in Springfield, Illinois, at a hobo jungle fire. . . . I showed my companion the service letter and mentioned the negative results. . . . I passed [the letter] over. Holding it to the light, he grunted, 'Just like thousands of them. Look at this, Slim!' Then he showed me, through the firelight, the faint outline of a broken-necked frog catcher."

After the order had gone forth, "No jobs for ARU strikers," and apparently had been backed up by the "crane with a broken neck," thousands of good railfaring men quit the steel highway forever; but there were other thousands to whom railroading was the one job they knew best and liked most, and these managed to get back on the rails by one subterfuge or another.

Harry K. McClintock, known as Haywire Mac, who was still switching cars at San Pedro, California, [commented]: "The benevolent old gent who owned the Missouri & North Arkansas Railway was a tower of strength for the boomer. . . . His pike was called the 'Clickety-Bang.' A man could brake for a month or two on the M&NA and get himself a service letter that would cover the 1894 strike. As late as 1912, I saw boomers hiring out on Clickety-Bang letters, and such references were always okayed by the friendly old gent who owned the streak o' rust."

B. Headless Goose

[Seattle Wobbly Thomas Nash tells newsman Frank Lynch about W. F. Moudy—"Old Mutiny."]

"Old Mutiny was a railroad man, a 'shack,' a brakeman. He was converted by an up and coming rabble rouser, one Eugene V. Debs. Think of that.

"Old Mutiny went out on a strike in the 90s and the slaves lost that one. Old Mutiny considered himself on strike against the railroads personally until the day he died.

"Did you [Lynch] ever hear of the 'headless goose?' Old Mutiny told me [Nash] that one.

"Most of the railroaders of his day were 'boomers.' Went from one line and the end of the land to another. They had to have a letter—a certificate—to establish experience.

"The letters were similar—exactly alike, for that matter, except for the details. When the boomer presented the letter, he got something like this—

"'Parm me—parm me. Have to go to another room to check.'

"Simon Legree, he took the letter to another room. Held it against a window.

"There was a watermark on the letter—see—a crane. If the entire crane showed, the man was a 'punk,' a 'scissorbill,' a devoted and loyal worker.

"If the head of the crane was gone the bearer was a 'Wob,' a believer, a worker for the One Big Union. He went out on his hind end."

C. Pop's Choices

Pop [an ARU striker] couldn't get a job with any of the lines that were in on the blacklist [after 1894]. He had three choices. He could try to go into some other line of work. He could try to conceal his identity. Or, he could look for little jerkwater rail lines that didn't subscribe to the blacklist—not necessarily because they didn't believe in it, but more likely because they couldn't afford to pay the blood money the list promoters were asking.

Pop had too much pride to let them hound him out of his trade. He had spent years learning all there was to know about shunting locomotives and railroad cars from one track to another, on main lines, spurs, freight yards, wherever it needed to be done. He determined to stick to his trade 'til they carried him out in a pine box. That meant he sometimes had to use a fictitious name.

There wasn't too much mileage in aliases, however, when it came to working for the major companies. They had lots of spies. And if you wanted to move from one job to another, they required a letter of recommendation from your former boss. They had a special trick for weeding out people. There were two types of stationery. On the surface, they looked the same, but they had different watermarks. One meant you were okay. I [Joe Murphy] can't remember what that watermark looked like—maybe an American eagle or the Liberty Bell.

Pop told me [JM] about the other type. He had personally seen them being used against him. If your letter of recommendation had the watermark of a crane, it meant you were not to be hired no matter how much the letter might seem to praise you. All the employer had to do was hold the paper up to the light. If he saw a crane, it meant you were suspected of being a union sympathizer, or some other high crime, and you were out on your ear. I have no idea why the mastermind behind this scheme chose the symbol of a crane.

The third choice was the one Pop usually fell back on. He went around the country looking for tiny rail lines that weren't in on the business of stationery watermarks and labor spies. They only asked that you knew your job and could show up reasonably sober a good percentage of the time. The trouble was that these little lines often went busted or were gobbled up by the big ones. So Pop's job sometimes lasted only a few months. Then he'd have to hit the road again and find another line.

Sometime late in 1903, or early in 1904, Pop was out of work again. He heard by the grapevine that there might be something available on a short line operating between Frisco and Half Moon Bay about twenty-five miles down the coast [from San Francisco]. He got the job, rented a house, brought the family out, and that's how I happened to be born in Frisco rather than Flagstaff, Fargo, or some other place.

D. Snake on a Card

There was a big strike around 1920. I [Tony Rosic] don't know exactly when. Everyone went out. The company, maybe the Burlington, was the scabbiest outfit. It fired the guys, wouldn't take them back. These guys had a lot of time in service, twenty or thirty years.

Being out of service, they had to find other jobs. As I recall, before the unions you could get a job anywhere. You know, the boomers. These boomers couldn't get jobs because of the scabs working.

Then, the company started a blacklist. They put a little snake on a card. The boss would hold the card up to the light. If the trainmaster saw the snake he wouldn't hire the good union men. The only guys who had the snake on the card were the men who had gone out on strike. The scabs didn't have snakes on their cards.

E. CYA Fugitives

When I [Luis Kemnitzer] was braking on the Southern Pacific Western Division, 1952–62, mandatory retirement hadn't been invoked yet. A few veterans of the Chicago Yardmen's Association 1920 strike were still working in California and telling tales. The mainstream railroad unions called the CYA a "rump union," that is, independent—not part of the union establishment; not a party to official contract negotiations. Rumors of Wobbly influence in the CYA were undoubtedly true. One of the old "rails," a CYA fugitive who told me about the strike, claimed that he had been a Wob in 1920.

Although the strike started as an action on the Chicago belt lines, so many grievances had built up on so many properties since the reprivatization of the railroads in 1919 [the federal government had controlled the lines during the war] that job actions broke out all around the country.

Also, since CYA success threatened mainline unions, they, especially the Brotherhood of Railway Trainmen, according to these old "rails," cooperated with the carriers in recruiting scabs. At any rate, brakemen and switchmen, with spotty success, wandered all over the country looking for work.

These veterans, CYA loyalists, told me that the railroads had a secret blacklist to keep strike sympathizers off the properties. Any time an experienced man applied for work, he had to show a service letter from the last job certifying that he had worked for a certain length of time, and that he was laid off without prejudice. When the man applied and showed his service letter, the employer would disappear into the next room, and then come back and tell him whether he was hired or not.

The letter was written on stationery with the watermark in the shape of a crane on it. If the man had a "clean" record, the crane was healthy. If the man was suspected of "rump union" activity, the crane's neck was broken. My "teachers" swore that this was true and that it had happened to them, although none had a copy of the broken-neck-crane letter. Four or five men told me variations of this story.

Knowing of the blacklisting practice, many men "flagged" or "worked under a flag"—under assumed names. One CYA fugitive told me that he had applied for work "under a flag" at the Pacific Electric [Big Red Cars] in Long Beach claiming to be a good and loyal BRT member, not knowing that at that very time the BRT had threatened a strike at the PE. The old timer never got the PE job.

In fact, during the 1950s, the remaining CYA boomers came to the ends of their working lives. These men then struggled through bureaucratic procedures to claim Railroad Retirement Act benefits accruing under all their separate aliases. By "unflagging" themselves, they beat the old watermarked service letter.

Sources

A. Freeman H. Hubbard, *Railroad Avenue* (New York: McGraw-Hill, 1945), p. 178. Reprinted in B. A. Botkin and Alvin F. Harlow, *A Treasury of Railroad Folklore* (New York: Crown, 1953), p. 168.

B. Frank Lynch, "You'll Get Pie in the Sky When You Die," *Seattle Post-Intelligencer,* Aug. 29, 1958, p. 17.

C. Joe Murphy, reminiscences collated by Henry Anderson from visits with Murphy at his home in Occidental, Calif., 1955–87.

D. Tony Rosic told me his story at Champaign, Ill., Feb. 20, 1959. I wrote out his account as he talked.

E. Luis Kemnitzer told me his story at my home in San Francisco, Mar. 7, 1995. Subsequently, he added details in a letter and phone calls.

Background

The crane-watermark service-letter tale, in all its forms, touches a railroad-union legend with a long life in tradition. The Pullman Strike of 1894, and its leader Eugene Victor Debs, have been treated extensively by historians. Yet no scholar or rail fan has found an actual blacklisting letter.

Initial reports of the "Crane with a Broke Neck" came from Free-

"Winter Brakeman."

man Hubbard, long-time editor of *Railroad Magazine.* In extensive travels, he met the great boomer storytellers of the 1920s and 1930s. From Bill Knapke, Art Clark, Charlie Roach, and Mac McClintock, editor Hubbard carefully pieced together a colorful account of the demise of the American Railway Union, the scattering of its loyalists, and their imaginative explanations for job loss.

Hubbard hazarded no guess as to the natal day of the watermark letter legend—presumably, a few years after the strike's end. We learn of such a yarn's origin only after it surfaces to turn historical event into fictive adventure. We can but guess at how long a tale lives in the hearts and memories of its believers. Possibly, "Service Letter" originated in another industry prior to the ARU strike. If so, no evidence has appeared and no collector, prior to Hubbard, printed a variant hinging upon watermarks as anti-union tools.

For a Labor Day feature column in 1958, Frank Lynch saluted Tom Nash, one of the last guardians of the Seattle IWW hall. Nash reminisced about "doing time with the Centralia boys," Joe Hill's songs, and brakeman Moudy's "Headless Goose." Curious about this account complementing Freeman Hubbard's findings, I wrote to ask if Lynch had ever read the crane-letter tale. Lynch replied negatively; railroader Moudy, out of personal experience, had told Nash the story, and the Wobbly had passed it along to the newsman.

We observe that some Wobblies adopted the ARU "Service Letter" narrative as their own, although the IWW had not organized until a decade after the Pullman strike. Of course, ARU veterans became Wobblies, consequently merging lore of the two unions. Good tales jump lines of formal affiliation as well as of skill jurisdiction.

Joe Murphy, an active Wobbly in the 1920s, had no need to merge ARU and IWW lore. He knew the watermark tale as part of family tradition in that his father had been an ARU striker in 1894 as well as a devoted follower of Gene Debs. Joe's account parallels those gathered by Freeman Hubbard from other Pullman veterans, except for the choice detail of an American eagle or Liberty Bell letter symbolizing a safe employee and a crane, a subversive worker.

Henry Anderson's seemingly casual treatment, quiet and conversational, in "Pop's Choices" holds great meaning as it touches a pulse in storytelling art—its revelation of the manner in which labor history and job-site legend may combine to buttress autobiography. In this case, Joe Murphy used the blacklisting letter and his father's temporary employment on a railroad short line to explain Joe's birth in San Francisco. As a disciplined unionist, Murphy prided himself on labor-history knowledge. As a superb raconteur, he wove personal experience into society's large chronicles.

Tony Rosic's fragmentary account from 1959 may represent one closing path in our story's journey. A locomotive hostler, Tony picked up "Snake on a Card" at the Burlington Line's Chicago yard about

1954 from yardmaster "Old Man" Gaffney. Apparently, Gaffney had learned the tale from a companion who advanced the strike date from 1894 to 1920, meanwhile converting the crane letter to a snake card. Such changes demonstrate the role of word-of-mouth circulation in oral tradition's extensive domain.

While completing *Calf's Head and Union Tale,* I visited an old friend, Luis Kemnitzer, an anthropologist at San Francisco State University. Working for the Southern Pacific through the 1950s, he absorbed considerable rail lore. His "CYA Fugitives" is especially welcome for its reflection of union rivalry—independent organization versus established brotherhoods. Also, its ending on "flags" and retirement benefits brings into focus the ceaseless efforts by many workers to deflect blacklisting and related discriminatory actions.

Does it seem strange that a story spawned by the nationwide ARU strike (1894) ends with a Chicago CYA strike (1920) and the latter's (1950s) California fugitives in their strategies of "undoing" broken-crane letters? It is possible that additional variants of "Service Letter" can be located to alter my findings. Welcome to the hunt!

In my book's introduction, "Tales Heard and Told," I sketched key CYA events in order to comment on relationships within the academic disciplines history and folklore. Beyond such attention, we ask whether Joe Murphy's reminiscences and Luis Kemnitzer's tale mark the trail's end for "Service Letter" lore. Shall we continue to find similar stories in current employment practices? Perhaps a computer wizard will create a broken-crane device to be transmitted via Internet. Perhaps new yarns about devious job-firing techniques already circulate.

"Boomer's Letter."

8

Hitting the Dutchman

A. Intermountain Pressroom

The pressroom of the *Evening Intermountain* in the early days was in the basement of a building on North Main Street [Butte, Montana]. Next door was the basement of a large saloon where the beer kegs were placed and kept cool. For some reason, perhaps through an error in construction, it was necessary to run the beer lines of the saloon across the ceiling of one corner of the composing room. The pipes had been there for some time when one day an inquisitive printer discovered that the pipes contained beer. A hand drill was obtained, a hole was bored and corked tight with a small steel plug known as a "dutchman." From then on, it was one continual party for the *Intermountain* printers.

The bartenders in the saloon above thought that something was amiss, but on investigation failed to see the tapped pipe, as the printers had it well camouflaged. They didn't dare press the search too closely for fear that if the printers hadn't discovered the beer lines, any suspicious action might disclose the secret to the ink slingers.

Just after the Butte-Anaconda printers' annual mulligan, a moist affair that lasted several days, many of the boys suffered from parched throats. As a result, they began "hitting the dutchman" pretty heavily, and soon several of them were laid out in varying degrees of drunkenness. One printer either forgot to replace the plug or didn't screw it in tight enough with the result that the beer leaked out onto the floor of the print shop. Soon the kegs in the saloon ran dry, and the investigation showed where the beer had been going.

Before the discovery of the tapped beer line, however, the printers had magnanimously acted as host at a beer bust for the owner of the saloon, recently elected as county commissioner. The commissioner, not to be outdone, reciprocated with a party of his own. Later, to his chagrin, he discovered that he had been treated with his own beer.

B. *Detroit River Telephone Cable*

The telephone company had a cable runnin' through the railway tunnel under the St. Clair River between Sarnia and Port Huron. It was hung on a seven-strand steel messenger. The damp air in the tunnel rusted this messenger an' it broke in several places. A freight was goin' through an' the engineer, while leanin' out of his cab, got hurt pretty bad by a broken end strikin' him on the head.

The telephone company had iron hooks bolted onto the flanges of the steel sections of the tunnel. The company sent Terry an' me [Casey] an' two other hikers down there by train. Our job was to lay the cable in them hooks, take down the old messenger, coil it up an' ditch it outside somewhere. . . .

Another job Terry an' me was sent on was to help repair a big, steel-armored telephone cable laid in the bed of the river between Detroit an' Windsor. [The foreman] chartered a tug an' loaded on all the supplies needed, including grappling hooks an' a big reel o' the same kind o' cable that was in trouble. . . .

The river was jus' lousy with boats. . . . One o' the Windsor fellers was tellin' us how, a little while before, a boat pulled up a lead pipe on 'er anchor. The crew put a hole in it an' found it was full o' whiskey. This feller explained that a big Canadian brewery had laid this pipe across the river an' was usin' it to pump whiskey through to a warehouse in U. S. free o' duty, an' he said, "If them d——n fools on the boat had any sense they would o' kept their yaps closed an' went to the brewery man an' he'd paid them a mint o' money to keep quiet, but what did them d——n i'juts do?

"They took everything on the boat, that would hold water, an' filled it up with whiskey an' they all had one glorious, free drunk." It didn't take the U. S. Officers long to get onto what this pipe was used fer an' where it come from, an' I guess it cost the big brewery man a good many thousands o' dollars to get the thing squared up.

Sources

A. WPA Writers Program [William Allen Burke], *Copper Camp* (New York: Hastings House, 1943), p. 93.

B. Shappie [Frank Shapland], "Casey's Chronicles of the Work World,"
Journal of Electrical Workers and Operators 35 (Jan., 1936): 24.

Background

In these related accounts of printers and electricians tapping into
beer and whiskey lines, we sense the sheer pleasure workers took
in "free drinks," coupled with knowledge that carelessness or greed
would eventually end their sprees. While some lucky souls did stumble onto liquid treasures at work, many others had to take such joy
vicariously in song and story. I do not know how many times these
tales reappeared, localized to particular trades and sites.

The term *dutchman* as a patch, plug, or insert to hide or fill a flaw
in stone, metal, or wood has been used widely by skilled mechanics in many occupations since 1859. I have traced this usage in
American Speech (1960b); J. E. Lighter treats it fully in his current
slang dictionary (1994).

Our two variants of "Hitting the Dutchman" come from the
memories and pens of William Burke and Frank Shapland. Burke
(1893–1969) edited *Copper Camp,* one of the best of the New Deal
grab-bag guidebooks holding regional and occupational lore. A Butte
newsman before his WPA stint, he offered many of the anecdotes
such as "Intermountain Pressroom" without direct attribution to
fellow workers.

"Shappie" (a pen name for Frank Shapland, a lineman and charter member of IBEW Local 203, Victoria, British Columbia) contributed lengthy "Casey" features to the IBEW journal through the
1930s and early 1940s. His stories touched all aspects of electrical
skill, including "Mother Bell" telephone work. "Shappie" identified
his Detroit River whiskey-adventure source as a "Windsor feller,"
likely a Canadian on the cable-repair job. For the large setting of
unionism and craft skill in which Shapland set "Casey's Chronicles,"
see Grace Palladino, *Dreams of Dignity.*

For many years, union magazines and papers served as outlets for
members such as Frank Shapland who put their thoughts into creative writing. Some had a keen ear for vernacular speech, combin-
ing it with technical detail to record occupational tales close in spirit
to folkloric narratives within ethnic and regional communities.

9

Public Works

A. San Berdu Courthouse

San Bernardino [California] was especially well-known among the migratory workers as a place where they would be picked up on sight. Fellows would go hundreds of miles out of their way just to miss San Berdu. Then suddenly the word began to spread among the fraternity that San Berdu was "good"; it was no longer "hostile."

The story got out that an officer had picked up two hobos and hailed them into court. The hobos gave the judge the usual story that they were looking for work. The judge turned to the officer and said, "I believe you've made a grievous error, officer. Take these two gentlemen out to breakfast and see that they get fifty cents each."

The same incident occurred several times. When the word spread among the traveling fraternity, several hundred congregated in the railroad yard. The officers then arrested the entire lot. "That," says Dan Buckley "is the way San Berdu built its courthouse and its schools."

B. Baltimore City Jail

As my [H. L. Mencken] memory gropes backward I think, for example, of a strange office that an old-time roundsman named Charlie had to undertake every Spring. It was to pick up enough skilled workmen to effect the annual re-decoration and refurbishing of the Baltimore City Jail. Along about May 1, the warden would telephone to police headquarters that he needed, say, ten head of painters, five plumbers, two blacksmiths, a tile-setter, a roofer, a bricklayer, a carpenter, and a locksmith, and it was Charlie's duty to go out and find them.

So far as I can recall, he never failed, and usually he produced two or three times as many craftsmen of each category as were needed, so that the warden had some chance to pick out good ones. [Charlie's] plan was simply to make a tour of the saloons and stews in the Marsh Market section of Baltimore, and look over the drunks in congress assembled.

He had a trained eye, and could detect a plumber or a painter through two weeks' accumulation of beard and dirt. As he gathered in his candidates, he searched them on the spot, rejecting those who had no union cards, for he was a firm believer in organized labor. Those who passed were put into storage at a police-station, and there kept (less the unfortunates who developed delirium tremens and had to be handed over to the resurrection-men) until the whole convoy was ready.

The next morning Gene Grannan, the police magistrate, gave them two weeks each for vagrancy, loitering, trespass, committing a nuisance, or some other plausible misdemeanor; the warden had his staff of master-workmen, and the jail presently bloomed out in all its vernal finery.

Sources

A. Dan Buckley, interview with Hyman Weintraub at Los Angeles, 1946. Text transcribed by Weintraub in "The I.W.W. in California, 1905–1931" (M.A. thesis, Department of History, UCLA, 1947), p. 279.

B. Anecdote in Henry L. Mencken, *Newspaper Days* (New York: Knopf, 1942), p. 206.

Background

These two accounts from opposite ends of the continent hinge on the same plot line—law officers use migrants/drunks to construct or maintain public buildings. Upon my initial reading of Mencken's account, I sensed its traditionality, but could not confirm it by reference to Baltimore histories. Would wardens and magistrates have admitted to this practice?

Reporter Mencken may actually have witnessed roundsman Charlie seeking and favoring drunks with union cards, or have been in court when magistrate Grannan meted out "justice" to unlucky craftsmen. Ted Schuchat, a former Baltimore newsman, has suggested to me that Mencken may have received this tale from Jim Tully,

"Rebuilding the City Hall."

James Stevens, or Louis Adamic—writers who had contributed hobo and labor material to the *American Mercury*.

Dan Buckley arrived in California in 1900 via a side-door Pullman (boxcar), and served in Leavenworth Prison after World War I on criminal syndicalism charges. He spent his senior years at Pershing Square, Los Angeles, expounding Wobbly doctrine. In talks with Weintraub, Buckley connected the practice of rounding up workers for civic tasks to "social salary"—hoboes provided livelihood for public officials directly: "For every bum that was picked up, the officer got fifty cents, the judge who convicted them got a few dollars, and the sheriff got sixty-five cents a day for feeding them."

10

Horace Greeley's Editorial

Horace Greeley had terrible handwriting—the world's worst. Only one compositor on the *Tribune* could read the editor's scrawl. This old hand did not let anyone else set the daily editorial. One day, the other printers became tired of the old hand's boasting. They went out, found a young chicken, and brought it back to the composing room. The men dipped the chicken's claws into an ink pot. Then they let the chicken walk all over a page of Greeley's foolscap.

Then, they gave this marked foolscap to the old compositor. It did not phase him. He just stood proudly at his case, read the chicken-claw marks, and set the type for a thundering editorial on slavery. It ran the next day like any normal editorial. Greeley never let on that he had smelled a joke. But the printers ragged the old hand about his reading skill. Finally, the laughter got to him, and he quit.

Source

Paul Aller told me this tale in San Francisco, 1941. Carrying it in memory, I shared it with Maggie Holtzberg-Call for *The Lost World of the Craft Printer* (Urbana: University of Illinois Press, 1992), p. 192.

Background

Paul Aller (1902–78) worked fifty years as a printer in San Francisco, including a long stint at Johnck & Seeger. Among memorable achievements, he helped produce several fine Grabhorn Press books. His peers in Local 21, International Typographical Union, knew him for shop playfulness. Aller composed poetry directly at the type case, and issued a constant stream of ephemeral comic broadsides, invitations to imaginary meetings, membership cards in nonexistent organizations, absurd wall mottoes, and spurious newspaper ads.

I met Paul when I was new to the shipwrights' trade, gaining a sense of its antiquity. He impressed me with his respect for printing traditions, as well as for the similarity in his feeling for typography to that of the artisans who guided me into the maze of shipbuilding lore. Despite the tremendous difference in our crafts, we united in extolling the importance of each.

Paul Aller's "Horace Greeley's Editorial" inverts the usual shop-floor prank directed at raw apprentices in that the *Tribune* printers tricked and humiliated the senior member on their floor. I have long assumed that this tale appeared in a biography of the noted editor. However, I have failed to find it in published form. This lack seems unusual in that "typos" have been particularly zealous in preserving their lore.

11

Cormorants

Many years ago a Japanese fisherman held up a shiny ring to get the attention of a cormorant that was diving after fish very successfully. The silly bird let him put the ring on her neck, and he tightened it, and also put a cord around her foot. Thereafter he let her go fishing, but since with the ring she could no longer swallow the fish she caught, he kept them, feeding her the less salable parts—in short, set up the wage system.

Other fishermen enticed other cormorants, put rings around their necks, cords on their feet, and let them do their fishing for them, paying them with the unsalable portions of the fish they caught.

After many years some cormorants, hearing of successful strikes by human beings who were in a situation much like their own, decided to strike. They refused to fish. This meant too that they got nothing to eat, so after awhile they had to settle their strike. A smooth-talking fisherman agreed henceforth to treat the cormorants just like human beings, pay them wages, and sell them food later on as they spent those wages.

Each cormorant got a small pebble as it brought in a fish, and stored that away. At the end of the day they took their pebbles and went shopping to the fishermen. They found all they could get for their pebbles was the same old heads and tails and innards that they had got before. But their Protective Association of Cormorants (PAC) felt that they must stick to their agreement.

Some very dissatisfied young birds went on an outlaw strike, and, as it spread, the public relations department for the fishermen explained that with the rising cost of the cords that they put on the cormorants' feet and the high prices charged for the rings they kept around their necks, this was the best the fisherman could do. A Left

Caucus in the birds' union insisted they didn't want any cords around their feet or rings around their necks, but they were denounced as dangerous idealists. So the cormorants still work for heads, tails, and livers.

P.S. There is a rumor that lately some cormorants try to open the rings on other cormorants' necks, and peck the cords on their feet to tatters, but on a piece-work basis they haven't much time for this.

Source

Fred Thompson, "Soapbox Story," *Talkin' Union* issue 5 (Nov., 1982): 7. For parallels in print see:

1. Gaylord Wilshire, *Hop Lee and the Pelican* (New York: Wilshire Book Company, ca. 1902) (12-page illustrated leaflet).

2. Meyer Emil Maurer, "Ring around a Rosy," column in *New Leader,* Oct. 24, 1936 (short revision of Wilshire's tale).

3. Maurer's story reprinted with title, "Hop Lee Gives the Pelican a Job," *Industrial Worker,* Dec. 5, 1936.

4. [Fred Thompson], "Cormorants, Revolt! A Old Fable Brought Up to Date," *Industrial Worker,* Sept. 20, 1947 (tale expanded to 2400 words).

5. Fred Thompson, interview with Stewart Bird and Deborah Shaffer at Chicago, July, 1978, for film *The Wobblies.* Untitled cormorant text transcribed by Bird and Shaffer; edited by Dan Georgakas for Stewart Bird, Dan Georgakas, and Deborah Shaffer, *Solidarity Forever: An Oral History of the IWW* (Chicago: Lake View Press, 1985), pp. 216–17.

Background

Fred Thompson's labor parable stems from descriptions by travelers and naturalists of cormorants in the Orient. I do not know who first drew an analogy from fishing birds to exploited wage slaves, but I have traced variants back to Gaylord Wilshire, flamboyant socialist, at the turn of the century.

When Joyce Kornbluh gathered material for *Rebel Voices,* she and I visited Thompson at home in Chicago (June 22, 1963). In a taped interview about soapbox techniques and messages, he recalled two oral sources for his cormorant tale. He first heard it told by IWW organizer-orator James P. Thompson in Seattle (probably in the mid-1920s). A decade later, Fred heard it again from John Keracher (Proletarian Party) during a strike at the Jones & Laughlin Steel Works in Cleveland. Thompson—enjoying Keracher's wordplay,

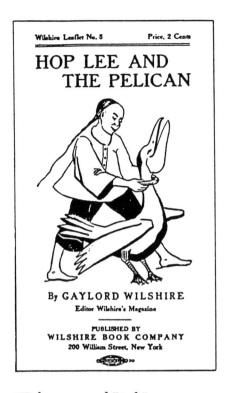

"Fisherman and Bird."

Protective Association of Cormorants, on then-popular union PACs (Political Action Committees)—elaborated the story in the *Industrial Worker* (1947).

We can believe that variants of "Cormorants" other than those cited above can be found. For example, Tom Walker, in correspondence, has noted an intriguing fork in the trail: During 1914–15, Eunice Tietjens visited Wusih, China, turning impressions into a book, *Profiles from China,* which included "Cormorants," a stormy poem about tamed sea birds in servitude. Previously, when her poem had appeared in the *International Socialist Review,* the editor added a headnote: "A bunch of 'wobblies' read this one night in a place called the Dill Pickle, on the North Side of Chicago. They decided that all scabs, strikebreakers, detectives, spies and spotters are human cormorants, who 'grow lousy like their lords.'"

I cannot demonstrate that any of the Dill Pickle crowd before 1916 had heard Wilshire's "Hop Lee" in any form. However, rebels hearing or reading either the poem or parable would have relished equations of cormorants with wage slaves, scabs, and spies.

12

Heaven's Gate

A. Drag Up

Five ironworkers get killed on a job, and St. Peter starts showing 'em around Heaven. They go around and see the Protestants singin' away, and that ain't for them. Then they see the Catholics, that ain't for them either, and the same with the Jews. So St. Peter puts 'em in a separate place in Heaven.

Pretty soon God comes by, so he asks Peter, "Why'd you put all them ironworkers in a separate place? We can't make a separate Heaven for the ironworkers." St. Peter says, "Well, God, there's no need to worry about it. They'll stick around for a few days and drag up, anyway."

B. Roughnecks in Hell

A roughneck died and found himself at the gate of Heaven. But he couldn't get in because there was a big mob of other roughnecks waiting for St. Peter to admit them.

So he started a rumor.

"Say, buddy," he told one of his fellow workers. "I hear there's a big boom on in Hell. Bringing in lots of wildcats and paying big money."

The rumor spread, and had its effect. All the oil workers turned and headed for the big boom in Hell.

As he stood there watching them run down the road, the old roughneck said to St. Peter:

"You know, the way they are taking off—there might be something to it."

And he ran off down the road after them.

And they say that's the only reason there are any roughnecks in Hell today.

C. Rumor in Heaven

A prospector from Fairbanks came to Heaven. He stopped at the gate, presenting his credentials to St. Peter who positively refused him admission. The man, however, argued the case saying that he had a good record and wanted to know the reason why he couldn't be admitted. St. Peter told him there was no chance at all; he already had a man in there from Fairbanks, that he didn't want anymore like him 'cause he had dug up the streets, dug holes everywhere.

This new fellow told St. Peter, "I'll make a deal with you. If you let me in, I'll get the man out of there in half-an-hour. If I don't, I'll go with my own free will." St. Peter thought that was a good deal, so he let him in.

The prospector wandered up the street. He didn't go far until he saw where a fellow was digging. Going up to the hole, he looked down. He said to the fellow in the hole, "Hello, there! How does it look?" "Oh," the fellow answered, "It's all gold—four walls of gold, bottom all gold. It's all the same everywhere."

"Well, that's fine," said the new arrival, "but say, have you heard of the new stampede down to Hell?" "Well no," came the answer, "Is there a stampede on to Hell?" "Sure is." With that the man came out of the hole and vanished in the direction of the gate.

Seeing that he had time to spare, the Fairbanks prospector took a little passey around to look the place over. Finally, deciding to notify St. Peter of his success, he headed for the gate. He didn't find anyone there but an attendant. The fellow asked where the old man was. The attendant answered, "Oh, he was here just a minute ago; he's around here some place. He talked a little while with a fellow, and then seemed to get into an awful hurry about something, and here he comes now."

And sure enough there St. Peter was with a big pack on his back. This fellow stopped him to tell of success in removing the first prospector. So he asked St. Peter where he was going. His answer was very brief, "Oh, hurraw for Hell! I'm off for the stampede, too."

Sources

A. Joe Downey joke told to Ronald Stanford, New York, May, 1971.

B. Mody Boatright, *Folklore of the Oil Industry* (Dallas: Southern Methodist University Press, 1963), p. 196.

C. Gene Nelson, interview with Herbert Halpert, Fairbanks, Alaska, May 31, 1944. Text in Halpert files, Memorial University, St. John's, Newfoundland. (Nelson, age sixty-four, attributed this tale to James Wickersham, Alaska's first territorial judge and esteemed raconteur; for his adventures see Wickersham, *Old Yukon*.)

Background

The "Heaven's Gate" title covers widespread variants of a "religious" tale that has circulated across occupational, ethnic, and regional boundaries. Ernest Baughman, in his motif-index compilation, uses several entries touching this complex: gate of heaven, arrival in heaven, and liar believing his own lies. An underlying bit of job wisdom runs through our three stories above: itinerant workers drag up (quit, draw last pay) to travel in response to seasonal weather, building booms, physical exploitation, wealth fantasies, inner wanderlust. As they move about, restless workers may delude themselves or victimize their buddies by spreading rumors and repeating tall tales.

Downey's joke asserts simply that ironworkers will not linger in Heaven long enough to enjoy its rewards. Boatright's oilfield hand, who starts a rumor to make a place for himself in Heaven, succumbs to his own deception. Halpert's Alaska sourdough uses the gold-strike-in-Hell "come-on" to fool a previous entrant digging up golden streets. Not only does the street-prospector drag up but St. Peter himself follows the fool to Hell.

Professor Halpert knows many stories similar to our three above; he'll comment upon them in a forthcoming article on Alaska tales. Here, I cite but one from East Chicago, Indiana, told in 1942 to William Hugh Jansen by a tankbuilder. (This demanding trade combined the skill and brawn of inside shopmen and outside erectors: fabricators, riveters, welders, riggers). A tankbuilder gets to Heaven. God tells Peter to get him out. Peter's helper whispers that the Devil's building "four eighties" in Hell. Unable to resist the lure of such a big job, four eighty-foot-high steel tanks, the tankbuilder heads below.

We sense the appeal of "Heaven's Gate" across boundaries of language and literature by noting a variant from Mexico heard by Riley Aiken in 1930. Herr Mensch, an Austrian miner in the Sierra Madre del Occidente, spins a detailed "Prospectors in Paradise." (I do not know whether Mensch told it in German or Spanish, nor whether he first heard it in Europe or Mexico.) He introduces Pepe Perancejo, who always sold his gold for a few bottles of tequila. In a blundering mood, St. Peter admits Pepe. Other prospectors follow who litter Heaven with deep shafts and slag heaps. Nuestro Señor orders Peter to get rid of all the prospectors. Pepe fakes a telegram on a gold strike in Hell. His fellow workers depart; none return. Pepe, now lonely, convinces himself that the ore below is finer than that above. He shoulders his pick and shovel and trots to Hell (Aiken 1964, 5–8).

In 1936, Carl Sandburg added to the "Heaven's Gate" complex with a brief plot summary within *The People, Yes*. Without hinting at a source, the poet opened as if he were on an oilfield crew: "One of the oil men in heaven started a rumor of a gusher down in hell" (90). Two related narratives appear elsewhere in this book: "How to Get into Heaven," told by a Manhattan ironworker, describes a millionaire's arrival in Heaven and the guardian's ruse to keep him out by assigning three difficult tasks. "Mother Carey's Chickens" touches yet another theme—sailors suspended between Heaven and Hell. Elsewhere, in a case study, "Marcus Daly Enters Heaven," I treated Harry "Haywire Mac" McClintock's tale of a copper-mine mogul's encounter with God and Jesus (Green 1993b).

Mody Boatright and Herbert Halpert are well known to students of American folklore. Here, I thank each for friendship over the years and for story swapping with me. In borrowing material from noted folklorists for my book, I "pay dues" to pioneers in occupational studies. By adding Ronald Stanford's contribution, I reiterate that laborlore belongs to those who create, absorb, or pass on treasured material.

During 1971, Ron had gathered jokes from ironworkers while preparing for their role in the initial and innovative "Working Americans" portion of the Smithsonian Institution's Festival of American Folklife (1971). His "Drag Up," in this book's setting, enlarges the "Heaven's Gate" corpus—ultimately, a set of wry commentaries on anxiety over the human condition. Shall we—regardless of craft or calling—reach or remain in Paradise?

13

Propwash

Back then you had so much more fun than you do now. Back in the old days everyone knew when you were new. . . . They have to get you when you're new because you catch on real fast. One of the things they did to me was, when we were in Atlanta, Georgia, heading back north, and I went up front and the crew says "Where's the propwash?" And I had no idea what propwash was and I said, "Well, I don't have it."

And I later found out that a propwash is nothing but air that comes off the back of a propeller, but in the meantime I have to walk through a full cabin of passengers, open the door, ask the mechanics for propwash, so they immediately take up the bite, they go and get this great big huge burp bag full of water clean to the brim, and I'm flying a DC3 which sits like this.

I don't know if you know the landing gear and there's a baby tail wheel and as I said you have to have a minimum of three-inch spike heels and I'm going up there trying not to spill one drop of this water which I think is propwash, hand it into the cockpit very carefully. With this they open the door, throw it onto the ramp and say, "Now we can go!"

Source

Jean, an airline flight attendant, interview with Jack Santino; time and place unspecified. Text transcribed by Santino in "A Servant and a Man, a Hostess or a Woman," *Journal of American Folklore* 99 (July, 1986): 315.

Background

Neophytes in many trades experience initiation pranks. Within an on-the-job ritual, an apprentice electrician may be sent to fetch a

"In the Air."

bucket of volts; a carpenter, a keg of toe nails; an ironworker, a pair of sky hooks; a salesclerk, a shelf stretcher. Such fool's errands occur regularly across lines of skill, region, gender, and ideology.

Jean, in conversation with folklorist Santino, elaborated an airline rite-of-passage into a full story. Details from dress code (three-inch spike heels) to work site (DC3, baby tail wheel) authenticated her account. Yet, she carefully moved her story away from present-day reality to the nostalgic past (old days, more fun).

14

Wilmington Trestle

[Patrick Connelly's] gang assisted the force of bridge builders and pile drivers in the construction of the trestle. As the structure neared completion, the inhabitants of both towns [Wilmington and San Pedro] planned a monstrous celebration, with everything good to eat and drink, on the grand opening of the railroad connecting the two towns.

At last the day of the big celebration was at hand and everyone was dressed in their best for the occasion. The train of flat-cars with benches made of planks was used to convey the workmen to the terminal at San Pedro where a barbecue was spread. Several temporary saloons were constructed with palms and branches of pepper trees. As the workmen left the train the engineer admonished them that he must now return the train to Wilmington before dark, and that he would whistle three times at three minute intervals as all must return to work at once or be left behind to walk around the west basin to their homes in Wilmington. Well, they painted San Pedro red.

When the warning whistles were blown many ran to the train in various stages of intoxication. Nearly thirty were left behind. I [Connelly] tried every means to get them aboard, and even had the engineer delay the train a few minutes, and tried to drive the slackers aboard, but without success. They returned to the festivities and stayed there until darkness enveloped them. Some proposed to walk the two-mile trestle, others to return by the Wilmington-San Pedro road and a loud debate ensued. Finally it was decided to walk the trestle.

I advised the road [Southern Pacific], and with great misgivings was obliged to go with the crowd. We could scarcely navigate the roads, much less the open trestle. It was to be a night of horror. Some had to be carried occasionally; they would bunch up and enter into loud discussions as to which gang had driven the most piles and greatest number of stringers and ties. More trestle was built that night than had ever been built in months before.

Mid-night found us half way across the trestle and another debate started as to where they had encountered the deepest water and mud in the pile driving. Some said it was here, others insisted it was there. One fellow, in pointing out the place, staggered and fell into the water. He floundered around in the mud and water for awhile and was actually drowning. Some had ideas of rescuing the victim and one suggested that as I was the most sober of the gang that they would hold me by the feet while I reached down and pulled him out of the mud.

My blood froze in my veins at the thought of these drunks dropping me head foremost into the mud from the trestle, but I consented and after several attempts caught the victim's hands and with much difficulty landed him on top of the trestle, apparently dead. After digging the mud and slime from his mouth and ears and giving him another drink the victim revived. The first words he uttered were: "You're right. Pat, that was the deepest spot. I was a long time coming up."

Source

Extract from "Wilmington Celebrates 75th Anniversary," *Wilmington (Calif.) Daily Press*, Sept. 22, 1933, p. 3.

Background

Patrick Connelly, a Southern Pacific Railway section foreman told this trestle-walk story to an unnamed reporter sometime before the Los Angeles harbor town celebration. "Wilmington Trestle" illustrates Connelly's personal experience narrated in his vernacular language, but modified by "outside" journalistic prose. I do not rank traditional speech patterns over news reports; both complement each other and share tasks in preserving/presenting work's heritage.

One perception of difference between Connelly's account and a folktale, conventionally defined, rests in our knowledge that work experience constantly flows into abundant speech. As listeners, we establish mental templates to distinguish various categories of personal narrative when related by others. A mate cleaves to the truth; another stretches happening into fiction; still another teeters between.

Frequently, we identify ourselves to others by naming jobs and describing tasks; talk about work enhances sociability. Yet even the most gifted speakers do not necessarily cast their stories in traditional molds. Nor do speakers, even in close-knit occupational communities, refine and pass on all they hear. I can well imagine that Connelly enjoyed a host of Celtic tales, that he knew the inside of both union hall and corner saloon, but have no way of knowing whether the anonymous journalist who talked to him in 1933 sensed any virtue in traditional tales beyond savoring and reporting one of the section foreman's adventures.

Bill Myers, an officer in Los Angeles Pile Drivers Local 2375, found "Wilmington Trestle" in yellowed print while gathering material for his union's history. Myers recognized that a Southern Pacific section foreman had touched a celebratory motif: "More trestle was built that night than had ever been built in months before." Who hasn't stowed tons of cargo in a dream, or composed brilliant poetry in the barroom? With this query, we hail Patrick Connelly for dressing a bare-bones work story in an imaginative cloak.

15

Fleas and Dobies

[Exchanging anecdotes on good union men, Terry Callan described his father-in-law's joining the IBEW.]

Back in Lincoln, Nebraska, my wife's dad, Charlie Peterson, as a young man started working in a furniture store. Electric washing machines were just getting popular. Every time a country gal bought an appliance, she needed a power hookup. Dad told Bud, the store boss, "I can hook up those back-porch machines, ten dollars a washer." Bud didn't know that Charlie could do home wiring, but he gave him a shot.

Dad just went out there and pulled "Okie rope through the woodpile." [I expressed surprise at this locution.] You know, they drill holes through the wood studs and pull Romex. They didn't bother with knobs and tubes [porcelain insulators]. Pretty soon, Bud became an electrical contractor; Charlie quit selling furniture and took up the electrician's trade. He bought Audel's and other books; he studied hard. Next, he joined Local 265 [International Brotherhood of Electrical Workers]. He was a good union man; he climbed the ladder.

The Local was poor but Charlie persuaded the reluctant members to buy an old abandoned dairy—all seventeen acres—on the outskirts of town. He said, "We'll remodel the dairy. Don't worry about the cost. We'll build ourselves a new hall with fleas and dobies." They did; built the nicest union hall in the state of Nebraska—plenty of high yard-lights to keep everything bright.

Source

Terry Callan told me this story during a visit to the Joint Apprenticeship Training Committee, Carpenters 46 Northern California Counties, Pleasanton, Oct. 26, 1993. I wrote out his text that day. Subsequently, I visited Charlie Peterson in Fremont, Calif., May, 5, 1994, obtaining additional details on "Fleas and Dobies."

THAR'S NOTHIN' TO IT MAW!
YOU GO RIGHT IN AND SEND
FOR THAT 'LECTRIC STOVE.

"Nothin' To It Maw."

Background

Like many in-group accounts, Terry Callan's depends on knowing construction practices, for example, the transition from slow "knob-and-tube" work to fast-installation Romex (insulated grounded wire wrapped in woven jute loom). Callan used the pejorative locutions, "Okie rope" and "woodpile," to illustrate how his father-in-law broke into the electrician's trade, thereby becoming an active unionist. In a right-to-work state, Charlie Peterson put his energy into building a hall, one that combined quarters for meetings, business matters, social affairs, and apprenticeship training.

Callan, delving into family saga, noted that in 1976 Charlie had received a wall plaque from Local 265 in thanks for his achievement. I include "Fleas and Dobies" within a collection of traditional items, conscious that it is not a folktale. Yet, it holds elements of form and style in common with many folk narratives.

Traditional tales serve diverse ends: to educate, entertain, maintain social cohesion, subvert authority, assuage pain, articulate folk wisdom. At times, storytellers incorporate these contradictory elements; often, the raconteur relies upon colloquial humor or esoteric speech to drive a point home. Callan's story highlights special language unknown beyond the labor movement.

Here, I offer brief etymologies to comment on Peterson's plan for obtaining a union hall. His usage *dobie* refers to an unsavory custom of charging excessive dues, assessments, or special work-permit fees paid by building-trades unionists moving from one jurisdiction to another. A business agent may ask the out-of-towner to pay his "dobie" before job dispatching, or simply demand that the traveler "dobie up."

Dobie holds many meanings, among them: adobe brick or dwelling; infantryman (doughboy); Indian (Asia) washerwoman or laundry boy (dhobie); to execute by firing squad (dobe-wall); California fifty-dollar piece coined in the shape of oblong adobe brick; Mexican silver dollar deemed of small value like an insubstantial adobe hut. Americans have used *dobe* and *dobe dollar* to name coins for more than a century (Lighter 1994; Mathews 1951).

This money trail leads to special trade-union usage as we infer from a short story by Roy Norton in 1910. In San Brigador, a fictional Mexican community, a soldier-of-fortune/mining engineer recounts trouble: "The next day while we were working, the General came again, and with him was the Chief of Police. They said, 'I had to pay five hundred dobie dollars before I went ahead with the work'" (4).

Workers returning from Mexican construction, mining, and railway-building jobs carried *dobie* north, extending it from the act of political payoffs or graft to union fees. During the 1950s, the National Labor Relations Board tried to outlaw or alter the dobie practice, yet it persists today in modified form. NLRB cases provide early examples: See Decision re H. K. Ferguson Company vs. Tuscaloosa District Council of Carpenters on dispatching millwrights to Demopolis job, 1956–57—"employee had to pay a 'dobie,' or foreign dues of $4.00 a week" (124 NLRB 70).

In Terry Callan's story, set in the years 1969–75, when fleas paid dobies to work in the Lincoln jurisdiction, local electricians reduced outsiders or travelers to the status of parasites, a strange reversal in that homeguards actually lived off boomers in regards to the hall construction. We ask: Who were the real fleas in Nebraska?

When I related "Fleas and Dobies" to my son Derek, a member of IBEW Local 6, San Francisco, he noted familiarity with both key words, having heard the derogatory tags *fleas* and *dobies* in 1975, while paying dobie dues on the Alaska pipeline. *Fleas* brought to the surface tension between Alaskan electricians and travelers from the Lower Forty-Eight. Derek added that his buddies were reluctant to discuss fleas, associating them with a secret fraternity fostering unwelcome practices.

Thus, I questioned several union electricians in Northern California. One recalled a bit of wordplay: *fleas* stood for "fun-loving electricians are sexy." We imagine fleas not in erotic acts but rather as travelers jumping from job to job, on seeing a T-shirt designed for the seventy-fifth anniversary of Oakland IBEW Local 595 in 1982. The front held the international's logo; the back joked about the pariah status of boomers with a map of the United States composed of all IBEW local numbers, and the motto, I'VE BEEN EVERY WHERE. This may have been inspired by Hank Snow's country hit, "I've Been Everywhere." A similar T-shirt featured Willie Nelson's song title "On the Road Again" above the union logo (front), and a massive five-column list of IBEW locals—1, St. Louis to 2330, St. John's—below the motto I'VE BEEN EVERY WHERE (back).

With yarns from Nebraska, Alaska, and California complementing each other, I continued my search. No one had a definitive story; no one admitted seeing any printed material actually issued by fleas. One retiree suggested that fleas had originated in Baltimore after a dispute between that local and the IBEW staff in Washington. Another called fleas "sea lawyers," experts in union constitutional and contractual matters. Still another old-timer recalled that fleas were men of great skill who flocked to difficult jobs such as the building of a giant taconite (iron ore) plant at Hibbing, Minnesota.

A journeyman wireman told me that industrial or factory workers organized by the IBEW became fleas in order to elevate their low status. A fellow worker contradicted this by asserting that fleas only initiated talented or militant men, those most loyal to union principles. An old-timer laughed at this latter characterization, for he saw fleas as agents provocateurs bent only on union disruption. Did fleas seek craft loyalists, or, conversely, industrial radicals; did outlaws flock together to increase their strength?

The difference between boomers/homeguards, linemen/wiremen, or construction hands/factory hands goes back to the earliest days of the IBEW. Indeed, such struggles have divided American workers in many trades for two centuries. I do not know whether fleas placed their codes in print, or in insignia on rings and belt buckles. To compound mystery, Charlie Peterson, upon talking to me, referred to bees and fleabees as similar to the fleas who had paid dobie dues in Nebraska.

Peterson shared a choice story from his last job before dragging up (quitting or retiring). In 1979, he ran work for the Commonwealth Electrical Company on a huge coal-burning power plant in Lincoln. Needing extra men, the contractor arranged with the University of Nebraska football coach to hire his team for the summer. Each player, securing a temporary permit, became a fleabee. Hence, All-American potentials appeared as lowly fleas in the eyes of Local 265's old-timers, who enjoyed ragging their state's athletic heroes.

In June, 1994, an electrician sent me a little booklet, *One More Tramp Guide* by Billy Craddock, published in 1978 by the BEE at Hookstown, Pennsylvania. This nontechnical introduction to basic labor law identified the Brotherhood of Electrical Employees as "a formally organized fraternity of traveling construction electricians" (50). Without using the nickname *fleabee,* Craddock suggested its origin in describing the FLE: "an informal fraternity of traveling construction electricians, based almost entirely on oral traditions. Its members assist each other in overcoming the hardships of the road. The history of the FLE is many decades long."

I have yet to locate a formal history of the FLE, let alone any example of its printed ephemera. Who can bring BEE, FLE, fleabee, and fleas stories to the surface? Billy Craddock's reference to "oral traditions" within a fraternity operating in the shadows of the fraternal IBEW calls for elaboration. Where do we enter this maze?

I have used "Fleas and Dobies" to illustrate but one path relating tale to word study. Terry Callan expressed appropriate pride in

Charlie Peterson's skill as an electrician, loyalty to union, and acumen in tapping funds needed to house his local. Also, the former gifted me with two special labor terms: *dobie,* familiar; *fleas,* strange. This conjunction, in turn, harnessed curiosity; thus building the Callan/Peterson personal narrative into a lexical commentary.

16

Philharmonic Committee

I [Meredith Willson] was on the Philharmonic Orchestra Committee by this time [1927], to meet with the Board of Directors once a year merely because, in high school, English was my very best subject and I made a noise like I was pretty smart. We were trying to get an additional five dollars a week per man for the summer season, and our ace in the hole was a viola player who greatly admired Bruckner, one of the master composers of the last century.

Now we are told that Bruckner, in spite of the great music he wrote, was very eccentric—didn't bother about bathing and wore a beard that collected things during the day: soup, coffee, tobacco. Our viola player had, as a sort of personal tribute to Bruckner, raised whiskers and he also ate chocolate most of the time because that collected noticeably in his beard and gave him a very Brucknerish look.

We had him waiting outside the board room and told the directors—Mr. Clarence Mackay, Mr. Otto Kahn, Mr. Triller, and a couple others—that many of our members couldn't live on the prevailing wage. In fact, "One viola player is practically living on chocolate bars," we said. We opened the door, brought him in as "Exhibit A" with his beard full of Hersheys, and got the raise without a struggle.

Source

Meredith Willson, *And There I Stood with My Piccolo* (Garden City: Doubleday, 1948), p. 95.

Background

We know Meredith "Music Man" Willson as a star in American popular culture rather than as a former member of the Philharmonic

Orchestra's negotiating team for New York City's Local 802, American Federation of Musicians. No one has ever vouched for the veracity of all of Willson's stories. His chocolate-candy ploy in collective bargaining makes light of a tedious, grueling process. Nearly every veteran of labor relations with management recalls some zany event which broke tension at a critical contractual juncture, or of a joker who won the day for brother and sister unionists.

17

Bringing in the Tools

A. Donkey Engine

A hooktender they had years ago up around the Puget Sound area someplace, around Tacoma, maybe. He was pretty wild and pretty rambunctious, and in the camp they had an old bucker—log bucker, cutter—that was a real nice old fellow and everybody in camp liked him. And finally, after a period of time, he decided he would quit and go someplace else. He left his tools setting on a stump or on a log or something for the next bucker to come along and use.

When [the old bucker] got down to the camp and the bullbuck [boss] asked him where the tools was, and he said he left them out in the woods for the next cutter to come along. The bullbuck got mad and just beat the stuffings out of him, knocked him down, kicked him and bruised him all up for not bringing the tools in.

The whole camp got to thinking about it; this one rigging crew got real mad the next day a-thinking about it. That night, just at quitting time, they come sliding in to the time shack with the donkey [engine] on the sled, and the foreman come running out, and he said,

"What the hell's going on here, whaddya mean bringing this donkey and all this rigging in here?"

You know, a two-hundred-ton machine, and the hooker said, "Well," he said, "We all decided to quit and we just brought our tools in."

B. Cold-Deck Machine

This Sam Rasmussen was there when it happened. And this guy had been cutting timber. That was with the old hand crosscut. Well, he came in and decided he was going to quit that night. And he went to the timekeeper to draw his time, and the timekeeper said, "Did you bring your tools in?" "Well," he said, "No. They're out there where I was working." "Well," he said, "We can't pay you off till you bring your tools in." So he had to wait through the weekend and go out there Monday morning, and work Monday and pack his tools in, and picked up his time and left.

A few years later he came back and he was tending hook. Same outfit. One Friday night he came in, he was tending hook on a cold deck. And he came in and he blew that afternoon for the rigging car and stuff, and he had moved that cold-deck machine down off the hill, stripped the tree, I mean loaded it on the car and brought it in—the setting wasn't done yet—brought it in to camp and came in, and the supe comes out and said, "Well, you all done down there?"

"No," he said. "I just quit tonight. And the last time I quit," he said, "they told me to bring my tools in, and here they are. I want my time." What could they say? They had to go rig the same machine up on the same tree again.

Sources

A. Eathyl Rotschy, Yacolt, Wash., May, 1986. Recorded by Jens Lund at a logging show, Lewisville County Park; transcribed by Lund.

B. Laurence Gaydeski, Forks, Wash., July 9, 1994. Recorded and transcribed by Robert E. Walls.

Background

Throughout this century, folklorists have collected songs and stories from woodsmen scattered from Penobscot River to Puget Sound. Books by Fanny Eckstorm, Franz Rickaby, Edward Ives, and their peers have helped move lumberjack artistry from bunkhouse to home parlor. In recent years, folklorists Jens Lund and Bob Walls have returned to the woods to treat logging lore touched by current environmental politics.

"Bringing in the Tools," in our two variants, hinges on resistance by crews and individuals to bosses who delay payment to footloose loggers, or otherwise challenge their independence. In the first instance, when a sadist beats up an old bucker, the whole crew retaliates. In the second, a lone hooktender handles the superintendent.

"Steam Donkey."

In both narratives, justice rests on acting out the initial command to bring in hand tools by extending the irrational order to heavy gear.

Readers unfamiliar with logging practices may be puzzled by references to donkey engines and cold-deck machines. Walter McCulloch glosses these extensively; I summarize: *Donkey,* originally, an upright steam boiler and a ship's capstain using manila lines (rigging) to haul or move logs to skid road, rail line, river edge, or sawmill pond. In time, gas, diesel, or electric motors and wire rope or steel cable replaced steam and manila. *Cold deck,* big pile of logs yarded up (moved) to a spar tree in the woods; *cold decker,* a gas-driven donkey engine with small drum capacity used to build cold decks.

The anecdotes heard by Lund (1986) and Walls (1994) have moved about in the Pacific Northwest since "camp days" in the 1880s. In 1975, Ed Gould printed one from British Columbia in which hooktender Ohlson used a locomotive to drag a donkey with its "snarl of shackles, lines and blocks" to the timekeeper's office steps (89). Have similar stories been told in Maine, the Great Lakes region, or Canada's maritime provinces?

Variants of "Bringing in the Tools" reported by Gould, Lund, and Walls mark shifts away from hand-held crosscut saws and double-bit axes to two-hundred-ton donkey engines, specially designed highway log trucks, helicopters, and computer-driven sawmills. These new machines simultaneously advance production and erode employment. Do they also reduce the wood worker's sense of personal freedom? We ask: Will the storytellers who shaped "Donkey Engine," "Cold-Deck Machine," and Ohlson's adventures be able to adapt their tales to cataclysmic changes in their industry and communities?

18

Steam-Shovel Red

I [Gilbert Mers] was wielding a bonus muckstick on the 1900 level of the C&A's Junction Mine [at Bisbee, Arizona] when I quit [1927] to come to Texas. Our local [copper] mine camp had its own tales of great feats on the job.

There was "Steam-Shovel Red." Red came out of the lead mines around Joplin, Missouri. They produced men in that lead country who could really fan that muck away with a shovel, you can take my word. Well, at some social function, a high mogul of the Copper Queen and a high mogul of the C&A got to talking shop. Turned out that each company had a mucker moving amounts you wouldn't believe.

It wound up with a bet between the two as to whose champion was the real champ. They began to plan for a public contest. Then, when each had ordered underlings to contact the prospective contestant, a records check revealed the champion of both companies to be one and the same man! "Steam-Shovel Red" was working day shift for one company and night shift for the other.

The regular day shift ran from 7:30 A.M. to 3:30 P.M.; night shift, 5:00 P.M. to 1:00 A.M. Eight hours total underground—"from collar to collar," the expression went—with a thirty-minute lunch break. The gap between day shift quitting and night shift starting was to give time for smoke and gases from day blasting to dissipate and allow breathable air for night shift workers. So you can see that the gap allowed time enough for a man to move from one mine to the other. When did Red sleep? Well, all day Sunday, maybe, after the six-day week. He darn sure didn't sleep on the job, not and turn out the amount of work that he did.

Any ordinary person would have been fired without recourse for working for two companies at the same time. Red was told he'd have to quit one job or the other. It would appear, from the story, that Red had lived up a lot of night life to help fill the vacuum that cutting his work career to one shift per day created. But he didn't last forever. Red broke down physically, drove himself past his limit, and never regained his former strength, the way I heard it. The company took care of him by giving him a "firebug" job, walking a designated area of the mine on the graveyard shift, checking for fires and fire hazards.

Source

Gilbert Mers, unpublished portion of autobiographical typescript prepared for his *Working the Waterfront* (Austin: University of Texas Press, 1988).

Background

While writing about "apprenticeship" copper-mining days prior to a lifetime as a Gulf Coast "rebel" longshoreman, Gilbert Mers sent me his extensive draft. Reading it with great interest, I suggested a few revisions, and recommended it for publication. With Gil's permission, I "salvaged" several of his unpublished tales from the original typescript.

"Steam-Shovel Red" holds special tall-tale interest in recalling a work contest, not as in the John Henry ballad between man and machine but rather a competition between two giants in the Paul Bunyan mold. Mers skillfully places the fantasy of limitless strength in a realistic frame of muscle and muckstick (shovel). His tale's closing message echoes considerable job belief: some workers can handle two jobs; despite such prowess, job athletes end dismally on scrap heaps.

19

More Than I Do

A. *Blew Your Tip*

Five rowdy black guys walked in the door and they went to seat themselves at table seven. I said, "Excuse me. You all got to wait to be seated." "We ain't got to do *shit*. We here to eat. . . ." So they went and sat down. And I turned around and just looked at them. And they said, "Well, I hope you ain't our waitress, cause you blew your tip. Cause you ain't getting nothing from us." And I turned around and I said, "You need it more than I do baby."

B. *Tom and the Waitress*

Tom, a high school physics teacher at Rice Lake, Wisconsin, was a slightly disheveled, bespectacled fellow who kept a plastic penholder and a slide rule in his breast pocket. He had been mentally grappling with some complex mathematical problem when inspiration came to him in a restaurant. Lacking paper, he began writing equations on a paper napkin while muttering to himself excitedly—oblivious to the impression he was making. When he had finished—both the equation and his meal—he fumbled around for a tip. The waitress handed it back to him and, in a tone mixing pity and kindness, reckoned "You need it more than I do."

Sources

A. Greta Foff Paules, *Dishing It Out* (Philadelphia: Temple University Press, 1991), p. 37.

B. Jim Leary heard Tom Ritzinger tell this story "on himself" at Rice Lake, 1962. Letter from Leary to me, Jan. 28, 1995.

"Talking Back."

Background

Greta Paules includes "Blew Your Tip" in discussing conflict between waitresses and customers, often centered on a tip's size, or the act of being "stiffed." The word *stiff* has served variously to name a rough person, tramp, or workingman. By extension, a stiff corpse became a race horse held back from victory, as well as a deadbeat customer, moocher, or cheapskate. Some waitresses have also added phallic meaning to their descriptions of nontipping stiffs.

Journalists, economists, sociologists, and labor historians have long commented on tipping practices. Here, I stress only the traditionality of the punch line put-down response by the waitress in Paules's anecdote. In a 1946 article entitled "Tipping," a *Life* editorialist wrote, "New York cab drivers have been known to hand back a dime with the time-honored insult, 'Here, bub, you need it more than I do.'" Sociologist Fred Davis, in 1959, reported "a forever repeated [taxi-driver] story": "After a grueling trip with a Lady Shopper, [the driver] hands the coin back, telling her, 'Lady, keep your lousy dime. You need it more than I do'" (163).

In 1953, Morton Hunt attributed a similar retort to a New York waiter, who counseled his brothers to throw small tips back on the table. Hunt wisely added, "But this . . . is folklore or wishful thinking, for every waiter says he knows someone who has done it, but no waiter I met has actually done it himself" (72). A waitress in England dreamed up a fine closing twist: If she received a 10p coin after much service, she'd give it back, saying, "It's all right, thank you, I've got enough change for my bus fare home" (Mars and Nicold 1984, 75).

In Jim Leary's recollection of Tom Ritzinger's tale, we hear a fine switch in the familiar ending for "More Than I Do." The Wisconsin waitress is not angry at being rejected or stiffed; rather, in rewarding a lost soul, she acts out of an innate sense of decency. We expect good storytellers to modify that which they pass along. Indeed, such alteration confirms our hunch of a tale's longevity and appeal. Folklorist Leary makes the added point that Tom's account functions as a portrait of the absentminded professor/scientist/intellectual absorbed in a problem-solving trance.

Dorothy Sue Cobble, in a comprehensive study of waitresses and trade unionism, treats tipping as an element within the conjunction of occupational culture and economics. She observes: "Although tipping permitted a certain amount of autonomy in service work, it also fostered individual entrepreneurship, competitive behavior, and dampened the ardor for collective effort. . . . This intimate transaction created a more ambiguous kind of worker consciousness than the classic adversarial 'us versus them' attitude" (1991, 43).

Despite considerable scholarly and popular/media attention to waitressing, no one seems to know the age of "More Than I Do." A half-century ago, *Life* labeled it a "time-honored insult." How did the journal establish this tale's chronology? Has anyone noted an "original" variant in print? I suspect that a search for the appearance of *stiff* in food-service lingo will uncover more-than-I-do jokes before *Life*'s usage in 1946.

In recent years, tipping practices have altered somewhat with the placement of penny pails, charity boxes, and glass or plastic decorated tip jars on food-service counters and other business establish-

ments. Sandra Cate sums up emergent tip-jar lore in "Counter Intelligence," a University of California master's thesis (1991). We
await new tellings of "jar tales" by workers who continue to count
tips as necessary income.

20

Donkey's Breakfast

A. Kapok Mattress

And speaking about kapok-filled mattresses, a celebrated story, perhaps apocryphal, is told on the West Coast, about a certain sailor, of South-Slavic extraction, who took a nosedive over the side and was lost at sea. About a day out, the steward, while the sailor was on watch on deck, decided to change the mattresses, and casually took his old one and threw it over the side, as was the habit then, and replaced it with the new one. Amid all the shouting and commotion, the story was finally untangled. It seems that the sailor had his life savings sewed up in the mattress. Through the years as the story is told and retold, the amount of money keeps growing.

B. Straw Mattress

I [Joe Murphy on the Swedish steamship *Welinder*] stowed my gear and then Arne motioned me over to his bunk, his back to the others. "These donkey's breakfasts aren't so hot," he said patting his thin straw-filled mattress, "but at least it's a good place to hide things," and he withdrew five booklets with red covers and the familiar IWW symbol on them. I could see they were all in Swedish. . . .

Except for Arne, the shipmate I came to like best was the genial Sicilian, Giuseppe. . . . One day when we were alone in our quarters, he said: "Looka, Joe. I trust you. I wanna show you something." And he turned over his straw mattress and showed me where he had hidden his money—almost ten years' pay. And then he gave me the address of his parents in Sicily and made me promise I would send them the money—except for a hundred dollars for myself—if anything happened to him. I promised him I would.

Two days later when I came topside for supper I saw a strange sight. It looked like the steward back near the stern throwing some kind of large objects into the water. "What the hell?" I asked Arne who had just come up behind me.

He laughed. "Ve have a good surprise, Yoe," he said. "In Seattle the captain he buy some good mattress for us. Ve no longer have to sleep on straw. The steward he trow avay the old donkeys."

I smiled. "Great," I said. It was about time we had some improvement. Then it hit me. "Jesus! Giuseppe's got his money in there!" I said. . . .

I cast a brief look in the mess room and then plunged down into the engine room. Giuseppe was just entering our quarters. When he finally grasped what I was saying he gave a wild shriek and rushed to his bunk. There they were—the new mattresses. He sank his head on his bunk, sobbing. Then he let out another yell and darted for the nearest ladder leading topside. . . .

There was a furor on the deck as the crew rushed aft to peer at the receding wake. Nothing was visible but water now. I rushed after Giuseppe up to the bridge, there on one open wing, Arne stood confronting the captain. It seemed evident the stone-faced skipper had no intention of turning back. . . .

After a couple of minutes Arne and I took Giuseppe between us and led him slowly below. Arne got a bottle of akvavit he had stashed somewhere and made the Sicilian drink some of it. His bronze skin seemed almost a deathly white now. Presently he lay down in his bunk on the new mattress and turned his face to the bulkhead.

Next day Giuseppe seemed almost back to normal. He said little but seemed ready to resume his work philosophically. But as Arne and I came up on deck for our noon hour meal we were confronted by a startling sight. Back toward the stern by the gangway stood Giuseppe, all decked out in his Sunday best, tie and polished high-top shoes and a funny little hat, and even more strangely, a neat little suitcase in one hand.

Before I could think or move, he moved toward the midship structure, gave a funny kind of salute, then turned toward the side of the ship, stepped out jauntily like some bozo taking the first step of the wedding march, and then he was gone.

Sources

A. J. E. Gladstone, "To Make the Run: A Seafarers Memoir," an unpublished typescript, Santa Cruz, 1990, p. 42.

B. Eugene Nelson, *Break Their Haughty Power* (San Francisco: Ism Press, 1993), pp. 156 and 163.

Background

Joe Gladstone wrote a memoir for grandchildren and a few friends. Active in the Sailors' Union of the Pacific, Joe maintained a lifelong belief in rank-and-file unionism and radical politics. After reading his memoir, I queried him about "Kapok Mattress." He told me that he had heard the tale in 1940 on the *Wilmoto,* a slow-moving Hog Islander, at sea since World War I.

Eugene Nelson's biographical novel treats the life of Wobbly Joe Murphy (1906–87). After reading the manuscript, I asked Nelson about the source for his "Straw Mattress" episode. He had not learned it from Murphy, but rather from a member of the Sailors' Union of the Pacific, Mike Moriarty, at Forestville on the Russian River in California.

In contrasting the two variants, readers note the difference in style between Gladstone's bare-bones anecdote and Nelson's fictional elaboration. "Kapok Mattress" scoffs at the celebrated story by commenting upon exaggeration as it is retold. "Straw Mattress" embellishes a folktale in order to give authentic color to a novel. One technique is not automatically superior to the other. The contrast in these modes selected by Gladstone and Nelson helps readers understand alternate choices in presenting folk narrative.

21

Soapbox Heckler

A. More Brains

My [Barney Mayes] first experience as a soapboxer began with the noonday meetings in front of the candy plant [in Chicago]. I had absorbed some of the tricks from the many soapbox speakers I had heard which now came into good use. Keeping the attention of the audience was imperative, no matter what device you had to resort to. Never permit a heckler to interrupt by quickly discrediting such a threat with ridicule and humor. Always have your claque ready to form and direct the audience's reaction by cheering and booing at the right time.

There were no amplifiers or any other kind of loudspeakers, so you had to learn how to breathe properly when you spoke—not too fast or strainfully loud. I had seen a number of would-be soapboxers lose their breath and voice in a few short minutes after they started to speak. . . .

In the course of [Communist Party] events, I ran across Jack McCarthy, a dark Irishman with a heavy brogue, who was a fresh arrival from the old country. He was the city circulation manager for the *Daily Worker,* and was determined to get the paper into the hands of workers by any means whatsoever, in spite of its boycott by the newsstands.

One day he asked me to accompany him to a noonday meeting at the Western Electric plant in Cicero. Two other comrades joined us and jumped into his runabout truck, which was loaded with copies of the paper. On the way, he explained that the day before some mugs had roughed him up, also scattering his papers.

When we arrived there were hundreds of workers milling around in front of the plant, eating their lunches while they listened to a

"Soapboxing."

number of soapboxers selling everything from contraptions to keep you eternally young to cures for rheumatism and lumbago. McCarthy jumped upon his soapbox and began spieling off his sales pitch, waving the *Daily Worker* in one hand and pounding the air with the other. We stood by with papers under our arms.

No sooner had McCarthy launched into his speech, when a member of the audience that had gathered and who was not dressed as a worker shouted, "Do you know what I would do with that paper, even if you gave it to me?"

McCarthy, smiling, listened and then asked him what he would do.

"I'd wipe my ass with it," he bellowed.

The audience broke out into roaring laughter. But before [the heckler] could lead them away, McCarthy—still smiling—shot back at him, "Well it all goes to show that you have more brains in your ass than in your head."

B. Any Way They Can

Woody Guthrie and his friend Cisco Houston were playing at a union hall one time. And they had brought along some leaflets to pass out to the people there. As Woody was about to start playing, somebody at the back of the hall yells out, "I'll tell you what I'm going to do with this leaflet, I'll use it for toilet paper." About six guys went to grab him, but Woody says, "No, leave him be. Some people need to get this information any way they can."

Sources

A. Barney Mayes, untitled, undated, unpublished autobiographical type-script, Labor Archives and Research Center, San Francisco State University, p. 135.

B. Anecdote in Guthrie, "Tale from Woody," *Talkin' Union* issue 5 (Nov., 1982): 6. Reprinted in Paul Buhle, *Labor's Joke Book* (St. Louis: WD Press, 1985), p. 34.

Background

Barney Mayes (1905–78) exemplifies one radical's trajectory from membership in the Young Communist League in the early 1920s, to editorship in the late 1930s of the San Francisco-published union newspaper, *Voice of the Federation,* (Maritime Federation of the Pacific), to anti-Communism in the 1950s. His "More Brains" Chicago story dates to about 1925. I assume its prior circulation among left partisans, but have found no variant before that of Mayes.

In conversations with me, Russ Scheidler indicated having learned "Any Way They Can" from Harry Stamper, a Coos Bay, Oregon, long-shoreman. In turn, Harry told me that he heard it at a convention of the International Longshoremen's and Warehousemen's Union in a report by Jimmie Hermann, international president. By linking the tale to Woody Guthrie, Hermann, or a previous storyteller, had widened this traditional tale's appeal beyond sectarian circles.

22

Dog's Tail

A. Bones

"Captain" George Gates, the well-known rebel who, during the first revolt in Mexico, confiscated an engine shaft and, though deep in the *bosque* [woods, brush] contrived to metamorphose it into a "Long Tom" [canon] for Madero, tells the following story:

"Once upon a time a man and his dog were lost in a far deep desert. They were without food. The dog was a good and useful animal and had always been a good pal. Consequently, though the man was consumed with a gnawing hunger, he did not want to kill the dog. Finally, he hit upon the scheme of cutting off the dog's tail—a large juicy one—and using it for food.

"Curtailment duly followed this economic discovery, and the tail was cooked and eaten. It was in this manner the man's life was saved. When he had picked the bones quite clean of their rich nutriment, he fed them to the dog, and thus saved its life, and—"

"Well," questioned George's listeners.

"Well, those bones—them's wages!"

B. Fido's Wages

[Wobbly soapboxers told stories about] the man who was out hunting with his dog, and he couldn't find anything to eat. He got very hungry, and after a long time, needing something to eat, the hunter called his dog to him. He took his little hatchet and chopped off the dog's tail. He made a stew or soup out of the tail so he wouldn't die of starvation. Then he gave the bones to the dog, and told the dog, "Them's your wages."

Sources

A. Frank Pease, "Bones," *International Socialist Review* 14 (Mar., 1914):
548.

B. Fred Thompson told story to Joyce Kornbluh and me during a visit
at his home, Chicago, June 22, 1963. Tape deposited at Southern Folklife
Collection, University of North Carolina, Chapel Hill.

Background

The "Dog's Tail" story, under various titles, has moved in and out
of labor repertories throughout this century. I do not know whether Frank Pease heard George Gates relate "Bones" in Mexico during the 1910 revolution or after Gates returned home. Fred Thompson first told me this soapbox classic on November 22, 1959, then
naming it "Fido's Wages." Here, I transcribe his taped version from
1963, noting simplicity in delivery. Fred indicated that he had used
it often in 1933 when the IWW appealed to Depression-weary auto
workers in Detroit and factory hands in Chicago.

In 1963, Don Barrett, a Mississippi student, turned the tale away
from class-oriented economics to comment disparagingly on then-
current national civil-rights programs. Hostile to Washington, Barrett compared "Federal aid to the starving hunter who whacked off
part of his famished dog's tail, ate off the meat, and threw the bone
to the beast. Whereupon the 'whimpering dog,' like recipients of
Federal aid, gratefully 'licked the hunter's hand'" (Long 1963, 116).
This inversion of a radical story illustrates the ease with which a
single narrative jumps ideological fences.

23

Drilling in Venezuela

There is a story they tell about when they first went down to Venezuela drillin' the field down there. They had this rig sitting out there in the jungles down there. Every time they'd make a trip—which is when they bring the pipe out of the hole and put a new bit on the bottom and put it back down in the hole—well, the derrick hand noticed, sittin' over in a tree right outside the derrick there, an ape sittin' there watchin' him, eyeballin' 'em.

Roughnecks are notoriously lazy anyway, ya know, any way they can get out of work, get somebody to do it for 'em, well that's fine. The ape was eyeballin' 'im pretty close; he thought well, you know, if I can get that ape over here and teach him how to work my job that'll be fine. I'll just sit here and draw my pay and have him, you know, do the work.

So he coaxed the ape over there on the derrick board there. He watched for two or three days and finally he motions to the ape, ya know, maybe he could try it. So sure enough, he reached out and he just latch on just like any derrick hand, and after about three or four days he had him trained. He just, every time he'd be ready to make a trip, he'd just go up there and sit down and call the ape over, ya know, and he'd work for him.

You got this ape here, did this job pretty good, ya know, and the driller was watchin' this, and the driller got thinkin'. Well now that ape's doing that derrick man's job, and, so obviously, I don't need that derrick hand. What I can do is, I can just run the derrick hand off and they still payin' for a derrick hand up here. I'll just collect his check and mine too, ya know, and that ape can work without pay up here.

So he called the derrick hand down and said, "All right, spool 'em up," he said, "That's all you're goin'." The guy said, "Why?" He said,

"A 'Swivel-Neck' Rotary Driller."

"Well I don't need you any more, I got the ape up there." So the guy come on back to the United States, ya know. He was up here for about six or eight months and he got a letter. A letter from this damned ape. He says, "You can come on back and take your derrick job 'cause I'm pushin' tool down here."

Source

Collected from Delbert Gilbow by Jim Thaman, Berkeley, Nov. 26, 1970. Text in Folklore Archives, University of California, Berkeley.

Background

At age fifteen (1949), Gilbow followed his father into oilfield work in Texas, and continued in western states and Alaska until 1963. He had heard oil lore at home from childhood, and on many jobs before enrolling at the University of California. Thaman recorded Gilbow for a folklore class, obtaining a fine tale as well as explanations of technical processes needed to decode "Drilling in Venezuela."

On the rig, roughnecks (ordinary hands) distinguish the tool pusher (foreman in charge) from the derrick man or monkey man (who stands on an overhead platform to handle hoisted drill pipe sections). Other roughnecks on the drilling platform deck below handle the actual bit (cutting tool) attached to the descending steel. Literally, the crew joins as many stands of pipe as needed for the depth of the intended hole.

Gilbow's story turns on three characters (derrick hand aloft, driller/tool pusher below, agile ape), and their respective moves: lazy hand teaches ape; pusher substitutes ape for derrick hand; ape replaces tool pusher. Gilbow also treats his listeners to occupational speech, technical and metaphoric, in "make a trip" (changing drill bit), "spool 'em up" (fired), and "I'm pushin' tool down here" (final irony as ape becomes foreman).

Guy Logsdon, Oklahoma folklorist, has heard this tale's elements zipped into occupations other than oil. Such variants often close with the line, "The ape's got my job." Ultimately, Delbert Gilbow speaks for workers who use self-deprecating humor, animal analogies, and wordplay to deflect job danger and economic uncertainty.

24

Pay Equity

Remember when you were a teenager and your very first job was as a baby sitter? You were 13 years old. Taking care of 2 kids—one of them sick—for 50 cents an hour sure wasn't easy. The entire house was in your hands and, to make sure that things were safe and sound, the parents would call you, sometimes every hour, to see if the fever on their youngest child had gone down.

Meanwhile, your brother was mowing the lawn or cleaning out the garage and getting paid *twice* as much as you were. And for what? You had 2 kids on your hands; the worst he could do was run over the azaleas with his lawn mower.

If you remember having had an experience like this then you're lucky. You're beginning to understand what the movement for PAY EQUITY is all about.

Source

Told by Diana Rock at a union reception, College Park, Md., Nov. 1, 1984. Text printed by Saul Schniderman from memory in *Talkin' Union* issue 11 (Dec., 1984): 11.

Background

Saul Schniderman edited and published seventeen issues of *Talkin' Union*, 1981 through 1988, dealing widely with labor music, history, and happenings. A member of the American Federation of State, County, & Municipal Employees, he heard Diana Rock tell "Pay Equity" at an AFSCME gathering. In correspondence with me, Saul credited the story to Eve Johnson of AFSCME's Women's Rights department. In 1980, she had elaborated a baby-sitting anecdote about her own son and daughter into a didactic tale which appealed to union activists.

I gained a sense of the popularity and circulation of Eve Johnson's story upon meeting Lisa Hubbard at a Sacramento conference of the California State Employees Association, Service Employees International Union Local 1000. Hubbard had served on the Washington-based National Committee for Pay Equity, and had worked on economic issues with Judith Heh, secretary-treasurer of the Pennsylvania AFL-CIO, who told the story frequently during the 1980s.

"Pay Equity" illustrates the application of traditional narrative forms to "new" problems faced by women workers. We can date the story to 1980, and name unionists across jurisdictional fences to whom it appeals. In readying this tale collection for print, I am aware that the computer revolution pushes pay inequality beyond gender lines. Workers without access to the "Information Highway," or uneasy with modern technology have become industrial outcasts, also subject to wide pay differentials. Who will note emerging yarns about present-day occupational pariahs?

25

Organized

A. Buggy Whip and Hornets' Nest

Years ago, down South in days before autos, a white gentleman was being driven somewhere by his Negro hostler, Sam. Sam had a noted expertise for doing tricks with his buggy whip. So the gentleman asks him to show his skill—to pick off an ear of corn in the field they were passing. Sam got his whip circling, flicked his wrist, and the ear of corn was at the old gentleman's feet. Next, he was told to do likewise with the ear of a mule they were passing. Once again, the tip of the ear was at the old man's feet.

Then the boss saw a hornets' nest, and said, "See what you can do with that." Sam refused, saying, "An ear of corn am an ear of corn, and a mule's ear am a mule's ear, but a hornets' nest—dat am an ORGANIZATION."

B. Blossom and Fly

An old Negro, on a southern plantation, was an expert with the whip and could show his prowess anytime he was called upon by his employer for the amusement of his guests. One hot afternoon, he was called into the yard, and had shown his great skill by knocking off the blossoms of a flower, and then by striking a fly from the sunny steps. Finally, one of the guests pointed to a hornets' nest. The old darky shook his head. "A blossom am a blossom, and a fly am a fly," he said sagely, "but a hornets' nest am an organization."

C. Stay Organized

> The stagedriver passed over the trail one day
> past meadows and woodlands, he took his way.

His long whip lashed with a deadly aim,
whether standing or moving, was always the same.
A grasshopper fell, as his smoky lash
shot out as sure as the lightning flash.
A butterfly here, and a grasshopper there,
fell prey to his aim, as they winged through the air.
Now a hornets' nest hung on a limb near by,
but the driver passed it carefully by.
"What?" the passengers cried, surprised.
"Well," he answered, "Them hornets is organized!"
The butterfly, the horsefly and the grasshopper, too,
have a lesson and a warning to me and to you.
We'll all flutter and fall, with the hopper and flies,
unless like the hornets, we stay organized!

"Hornets' Nest."

Sources

A. Fred Thompson, letter to Saul Schniderman, Nov. 25, 1982.

B. Sterling Brown anecdote in a mimeographed collection of jokes gathered in the 1920s and 1930s. B. A. Botkin deposited Brown's "Negro Jokes" among the former's papers, University of Nebraska Library, Lincoln.

C. Author unknown; poem submitted by Micky Wells, business agent,

Carpenters Local 201, to *Wichita (Kansas) Plaindealer*, Sept. 17, 1990, p. 17. Subsequently reprinted in other labor newspapers.

Background

African-Americans, in slavery's era, shared an abundant body of lore to assuage pain, lubricate toil with jest, educate children, and hold steady freedom's promise. One tale cycle centered on the doings of an old slave and his master. The former, alternately stupid and wise, generally tricked the latter. The slave, of course, couched in humor messages of individual endurance and racial solidarity.

During the 1920s, J. Mason Brewer, the first black folklorist in Texas, heard "Dey's Auganized," incorporating it in "Junteenth" for *Tone the Bell Easy*. Brewer's tale concerned coachman Ananias and Massa. The former amused his master by wielding a whip to split a horsefly and tear apart a bumblebee. However, Ananias refused the command to cut a hornets' nest off a limb by observing, "dey's auganized" (1932, 23).

We hear a parallel to Brewer's tale in "Blossom and Fly." The latter may have circulated in the South for decades before Sterling Brown included it in his unpublished "Negro Jokes." At some point, a union partisan heard a variant of the Brewer/Brown find, and dropped it into labor's story bag. I base this assertion on early talks with Fred Thompson, who asked me to visit Cleveland soapboxer Frank Cedervall, a master storyteller among Wobblies.

I failed to obtain Cedervall's bullwhip and hornets' nest anecdote. Fortunately, Thompson wrote out its text for Saul Schniderman, adding a contextual detail. At factory gates in the 1930s, Fred, organizing for the IWW, had imitated black speech while telling this tale. In 1982, he asked Saul whether such affected dialect might not prove offensive in the present decades.

Thompson's sensitive question touches the utility, today, of old lore hinging upon peculiarities in dialect, custom, or belief of American minorities. When do we offer a narrative in pristine form; when do we soften or alter its rhetoric or moral? One answer presents itself in the anonymous "Stay Organized." *Plaindealer* editor Lynne Baker identified the Kansas carpenter who submitted the poem, but could not name its ultimate source.

We assume that the author of "Stay Organized" had heard or read some form of the hornets' nest tale, retaining its message but consciously altering the master-slave theme and black-speech pattern. In listening to and reading folktales, we compare old and new forms, note changes over time, and view fresh meanings against a backdrop of personal and community norms.

26

Wormwood Table

A man saw a table in an antique shop and asked about it. The dealer said, "Ah, my friend, you have taste; that is a genuine wormwood table. All those little holes and burrows in the wood might not appeal to everyone, but those vermiculations show that it is genuine. And I can see that you have an eye for the rare and the unusual."

But the price was more than the man could afford. He looked at the table, walking around it and noting the height and width, the shape of the legs, and everything about it. He went home and began to think about the table and how he could get one like it.

"What does he take me for. Does he think that I'd pay that much for a table? I could make one for far less than that."

So he set to work. He bought wood and cut and planed it and he worked at making patterns for the legs, the top, the stretchers underneath the table. He went back often to look at the original. He sanded and sawed and cut and stained the wood. And he painstakingly bored holes and burrows into the wood trying to get them to look like the patterns he had seen in the antique table at the dealer's.

After some months of work, he had his own wormwood table; the money he had spent hadn't been half of what the dealer wanted to charge him. He'd show that dealer that he couldn't be charged like that.

So the man invited the dealer to his house. After dinner he took the dealer to his workshop and showed him the table.

"Where did you get it? It looks just like the one I have for sale."

"Of course it does," said the man. And then he told how he had bought the wood and cut and sawed and planed and sanded, and how he had taken such pains to draw the pattern for each piece just so. And the vermiculations—what a chore.

"But this must have taken you a long time."

"Oh, a couple of months, maybe, working every day. But the materials cost less than half what you wanted for the table. So I have my wormwood table for less than half of your price."

"But that's not the entire price of the table," said the antique dealer. "If you worked for two months making it, you have to count the price of your wages as part of the cost of the table."

"Oh no," said the man. "Do you think I got paid for working on that wormwood table? Nothing doing. I just did it because I wanted to do it."

"Well," said the antique dealer, "It just goes to prove what I've always said: Some men will work cheaper than worms."

Source

Mrs. Robert (Ita) Kanter, letter to Archie Green, Feb. 9, 1985.

Background

Robert L. Kanter, the son of immigrant workers, entered the Detroit tool-and-die-maker trade in the Depression years. Committed to trade unionism and socialism, he joined the United Automobile Workers at its inception. After serving the UAW in many technical capacities for three decades, he "retired" to a teaching position at the University of Connecticut, 1966–76.

I heard Kanter tell "Wormwood Table" during a laborlore session, in 1961, at Wayne State University. It made a strong impression on me; I sought, but failed, to find analogs. After her husband's death, Ita Kanter reconstructed the story from memory, noting that Bob had learned it from his father, Fred, a great raconteur.

In her letter to me, Mrs. Kanter added a warm personal message: "Fred taught his children that a working person had the right to be paid honorable wages for a contribution to the well-being of the world."

27

Mother Carey's Chickens

There are a few stories well known to all sailors, one of which I [Charles W. Brown] hope I shall be indulged in telling, for I have never seen it in print. Imagine that you are being told this yarn under the lee of the forward house, in the midnight watch, all sails and stunsails set, the strong trade winds blowing two points abaft the beam, and the good ship bowling along twelve knots an hour. There is nothing for the watch on deck to do but to await orders. The spray is dashing over the weather rail, and the watch on deck are comfortable in their snug shelter, their pipes lighted, and no time limit on the old salt who spins his yarn with such length and variations as suit his pleasure. He will tell this one in substance about as follows:

Those little black web-footed birds that frequently are seen following in the wake of ocean steamers are called Mother Carey's chickens. It is a common sailors' superstition that they contain the souls of departed seamen.

Many, many years ago an old Western Ocean packet, carrying an unusually rough, tough crew (although they were all bad enough), while crossing the Atlantic struck an iceberg and immediately sank, with all on board. The wicked sailors were promptly and properly consigned to the lower regions. As they became somewhat acquainted with their new surroundings they began to growl, in accordance with their previous custom. They growled hard, vigorously, persistently. They did not like the climate; they alleged that the grub was poor and insufficient; they fought among themselves, and the language that they used shocked even the sin-hardened denizens of Gehenna.

Satan was greatly displeased with his new subjects. He interviewed St. Peter, and flatly refused to take any more sailors in his charge. He said that he had conducted a good hot hell for many years, and had given very little trouble, but he desired to have this last consignment of sailors immediately removed. The good Saint pacified his petitioner, and a more satisfactory temporary disposition was brought about.

Satan was obliged to listen daily to the disparagement of his domain. The sailors said that hell was not as hot as the Red Sea in the summer season; that the temperature of the lower regions was mild compared with the "brick fielders" coming down from the Australian Desert, and that the accompanying hot dust was much worse than anything experienced in the lower regions. Hell was declared to be a much more comfortable place than the yard-arm of a vessel beating up Boston Bay in the winter season, when the sailor perched up there was trying to make a frozen topsail fast, with biting snow and sleet driving in at every gust.

The ordinary yarns that these sailors told made the muck-rakers, fishermen, politicians and other high-grade liars turn green with envy. They rebelled against all the lawfully constituted authorities. They were insolent, abusive and quarrelsome, and made more trouble than had been experienced for several centuries.

His Satanic Majesty again went aloft to make another vigorous complaint, and finally insisted on resigning if he was obliged to continue to keep the sailors in his custody. St. Peter was perplexed, but finally had to submit to the demands of the guardian of the lower regions, who returned joyfully and told the sailors that they could clear out.

A conference was held, and the old salts talked over the hardships that they had endured in their former life. Cape Horn, bucko mates, poor grub, and other unpleasant nautical subjects were fully discussed. Finally, it was unanimously decided not to leave their present warm, comfortable quarters, where they had all night in.

Under these circumstances it became a real problem how to get these unwelcome guests back to the upper world.

At this time it was customary to serve grog on shipboard, and one of the principal complaints made by the sailors was that their liquor supply was cut off. An old boatswain told Satan that he would get these fellows out if he could have a permanent job below, with tobacco and rum included. This being agreed to, the old man went outside the gates and piped his whistle for grog. The eager seamen

promptly responded, and all rushed out to the grateful and familiar sound. Satan, however, did not keep his promise, but with his
usual deceit and perfidy shut the gates, and there have never been
any sailors sent to hell since. As they were not qualified for a better fate, they and their successors have been turned into Mother
Carey's chickens.

Source

Charles W. Brown, *My Ditty Bag* (Boston: Small, Maynard, 1925), pp. 60–
64.

"Stormy Petrel."

Background

In the course of completing *Calf's Head and Union Tale,* folklorist
Tom Walker sent me Charles Brown's "Mother Carey's Chickens."
Enjoying this "old salt's yarn" with its strange name for stormy pe-
trels, I set out to trace its origin. The quest led to voyage accounts
by Philip Carteret and James Cook; scientific observations by Joseph
Banks and Daniel Carl Solander; ornithological studies, old and new,
by Alexander Wilson, John James Audubon, Louis Halle, and Ronald
Lockley; and novels by a diverse lot—Frederick Marryat, Herman
Melville, Charles Kingsley, Kate Douglas Wiggin.

Antiquarians and students of proverbial speech (for example—
Athenaeum, Bassett, Brewer, Weekley, Whiting), as well as the ed-
itors of the *Oxford English Dictionary,* contributed chips to the
Carey mosaic by suggesting that sailors had invoked the Latin prayer
opening "Mater Cara" (mother dear) while facing storms at sea.
Somehow, these crews linked prayer, petrels' flight, and the act of
predicting or defying bad weather. Some writers identified Mother
Carey as a witch or devilish hag calling up storms. Still others associated the bird's white feathers with snowfall. In this range from the
Virgin Mary to a powerful witch, we sense the elasticity within a
story linking seabirds, destructive storms, and sacred doctrines.

Learning that Mother Carey shared quarters with Jolly Roger,
Davy Jones, the Flying Dutchman, and Father Neptune, I put my
etymological search aside and returned to Captain Brown's traditional tale ("well known to all sailors" and "never seen it in print"). I do
not know the extent of his elaboration of a shipboard yarn. He may
have reported a gifted storyteller's full narrative, or spliced fragments together from scattered sources.

"Mother Carey's Chickens" compels attention for its portrait of
yarning at sea: verbal play intervals to break work routines; pleasure
to spice monotony and drudgery. We welcome stories that entertain;
also, we treasure them for insight into the human condition. Brown's
offering reveals diverse themes: work at sea harder than life in Hell;
interchange between St. Peter and Satan; wily boatswain betrays
shipmates for tobacco and rum; souls of departed seamen (petrels)
eternally suspended between Heaven and Hell.

Perhaps the most intriguing element in Brown's story lies in his
twisting of the "Heaven's Gate" motif, where a trickster aiding St.
Peter moves fellow workers to Satan's abode. The boatswain does
invert his mates' journey but cannot get them into Heaven. Who-
ever first consigned a jack tar to eternal purgatory and then linked
his fate to the vernacular name for stormy petrels made a profound
statement regarding the status of seamen over the centuries.

Folklorist Herbert Halpert pointed me to another arena in which
mariners may have tied a story about dead comrades to the stormy
petrel. In his case study "Neither Heaven nor Hell" (1979), Halpert
discussed the widespread tale "The Smith and the Devil" in which
God rejects a blacksmith; smith outwits Devil; God and Devil sus-
pend smith between their realms. In some nautical tellings, the

midway place acquired an unusual name, *Fiddler's Green,* where ghostly sailors enjoyed wine, women, and song.

I have not found a folk narrative, other than that by Charles Brown, tying motifs from "The Smith and the Devil" or the locution *Fiddler's Green* directly to a Mother Carey story yet the relationship is present. Sailors' work always involved the possibility of death at sea. No one could avoid asking about the fate of drowned shipmates. Did they simply vanish? Did they return as petrels or as revenants? Did they warn companions of future danger?

David Taylor at the Library of Congress has pursued maritime folklore for two decades. He, too, found Captain Brown's story intriguing, and added to its life by tracing Mother Carey citations in Britain, New England, Canada, and Newfoundland. Tom Walker, David Taylor, and I shall continue to "salvage" stormy petrel lore as we puzzle over its meanings: Each time a sailor dies at sea, Mother Carey arranges for a baby petrel to be born. She punishes wicked captains by turning them into petrels doomed forever to fly over the ocean deep. Sailors who harm or hunt her flocks will be devoured by sharks. Mother Carey's chickens emulate St. Peter by walking on water.

To close, I pose a set of questions for readers who wish to go beyond Captain Brown's yarn: When do colloquial names for petrels, along with stories believed for centuries to be true, drop out of narrative tradition or transfer into allusion or proverbial saying? As we approach the year 2000, do any mariners on giant tankers or computer-loaded and guided container vessels still voice a special name for stormy petrels, or recognize mystery in their sacred aura? Who now accepts the role of retelling Captain Brown's "Mother Carey's Chickens"?

28

Best Boss in the World

During thaws in the Cold War, Russians would come over to visit our factories. They liked Silicon Valley—new technology, pastel colors, elevator Muzak. One day the Ruskies arrive at our plant, a real entourage: the commissar, two interpreters, State Department guides, KGB heavies, FBI agents, our company CEO.

The boss treats the Russians to a regular lunch in our cafeteria, just to show what good eats we get. The commissar says he likes the formalities, but he'd like to talk to an ordinary American worker— no Potemkin Village stooge, no American spy. The CEO says, "Sure, Ivan, just go over to the food line and pick any one."

Ivan walks over, points to a guy, and says, "You!" The guy, Joe, is really startled by all the brass descending on him, but the Russian and American interpreters huddle and explain the Moscow mission.

The commissar, after a few pleasantries, asks the heavy question, "Joe, are you class conscious?" Joe is floored; he doesn't understand the Russian word. The interpreters go into high gear and come up with something like *klassen bewusst*. Joe's still bewildered; he doesn't know German either.

Ivan thinks it over and starts again. He tells the interpreters to tell Joe in English, "Class consciousness—that means, do you hate your boss?"

Now Joe is really ticked off, "Hell no, I don't hate my boss, I've got the best boss in the world!" The CEO gives the commissar a very superior look, but the Ruskie, incredulous, has just warmed up.

He says "Joe, tell me why you like your boss."

Joe launches into a long spiel, leaving the interpreters trailing in the dust. He gestures out the window to the parking lot. "One night it was raining hard. I had to work overtime and I missed my carpool ride home. I got soaking wet running to the bus stop way out on the highway."

Pausing for emphasis, Joe continues, "Just then, the boss pulls out on the highway, slows his Caddy, and asks, 'Where do you live, Joe?' I say, 'Sunnyvale.' He says, 'That's awfully far. Why don't you come up to Hillsborough with me, and I'll have James spin you home right after dinner.'

"I figure I have nothing to lose, 'O.K.'

"He drives to his posh mansion, and escorts me inside. The valet shows me to the shower and gets rid of my wet work clothes. He hands me a fine silk robe. I come to a really big dining room—only me and a huge mahogany table. The butler brings out sherry. Fine stuff! We get a great dinner—Havana cigars, caviar, private-blend Java, you name it.

"It's still pouring outside so the boss says, 'Joe, why don't you spend the night. No trouble. In the morning, I'll have James drive you in. Don't worry about being late. I'll call the timekeeper to punch you in early.'"

Meanwhile, the interpreters are translating all this palaver back and forth, back and forth. The commissar doesn't get all of it—like the bit about punching in. He's still amazed.

Finally, the Russian's had it, up to here. He breaks in determined to trap Joe, and demands, "Did all this happen—caviar, coffee?"

Joe laughs, "Sure did, I told you I had the best boss in the world."

Ivan, flabbergasted, is about to give up, but he takes one last shot at Joe. The big shot barks out, "On Lenin's tomb, swear that all this really happened!" The interpreters and stoolies line up behind the commissar, and glare at Joe.

Joe knows the jig's up. He faces Ivan, man to man, and sheepishly admits, "No, it didn't happen to me, but it did happen to my sister."

Source

I told this story frequently from 1958 to 1965 at union meetings and labor-education conferences. I had read or heard it about 1955, but, at that time, did not note a source.

Background

While telling the "Best Boss in the World" at Madison, Wisconsin, November 18, 1959, I met Joseph Mira of the American Labor

Education Service. Mira stated that he had heard the story, years ago, in his native Austria, where it centered on a peasant describing a visit to the royal palace in feudal days. Subsequently, at a Detroit gathering, Henry Santiestevan, a United Auto Workers' staff member, reported to me that he had heard a similar yarn about Mexican workers at a factory in the United States. Sadly, I did not record these two significant variants.

Despite knowing this tale for more than three decades, I have failed to trace its movement from Europe to the Americas, or the circumstance of its incorporation into trade-union repertoires. However, I have found one printed text attributed to Tom Ranford, president, Los Angeles Central Labor Council: "The Moral Is Clear: Avoid 'Friendly' Boss" (*Service Union Reporter,* Sept., 1958). Ranford placed his story in a local plant during an organizational drive where a nonunion worker, refusing to join, lauded his own "best boss."

While readying this book for publication, I shared curiosity about "Best Boss in the World" with Joanne Delaplaine of the Labor Heritage Foundation. In turn, she interviewed Henry Santiestevan, now retired from the UAW but active in the Washington, D.C., area. He had first heard the story in 1942 during army training at Camp Roberts, California. Then, Henry disliked the "joke," taking it as a slur on Mexican men and women. Further, it distressed him to hear it told by a Jewish GI, who should have been sensitive to ethnic jests.

Santiestevan's feeling about a particular story stretched from 1942 to 1995. He reminds us to see humor in its many guises, to appreciate how a single story can sting for decades, and to recharge our efforts to trace and place work tales as they move across the identity walls of diverse communities.

29

Dramatic Stuff

A. *Mother Jones and the Thugs*

I've [James Farrance] been told the reason [Mother Jones] became a fighter for union organization was that her husband and her son was killed by coal company yellow dogs, and she became angry at all non-union outfits.

I saw her one time here in Monongah [West Virginia]. We was trying to organize our mines. She came down Pike Street in a buggy and horse. Two company thugs grabbed the horse by the bridle and told her to turn around and get back down the road. She wore a gingham apron, and she reached under it and pulled out a 38 special pistol and told them to turn her horse loose, and they sure did. She continued on to the park, and spoke to a large bunch of miners. She wasn't afraid of the devil.

B. *Mother Jones and the Gunmen*

[Mother Jones] surveyed the scene [Cabin Creek Junction bridge guarded by coal-baron gunmen] with a critical eye and walked straight up to the muzzle of one of the machine guns and patting the muzzle of the gun, said to the gunman behind it, "Listen here, you, you fire one shot here today and there are 800 men in those hills (pointing to the almost inaccessible hills to the east) who will not leave one of your gang alive."

The bluff worked; the gunmen ground their teeth in rage. Mother Jones informed me [Fred Mooney] afterwards that if there was one man in those hills she knew nothing of it. . . . "I pulled the dramatic stuff on them thugs."

"Mother Jones at Carnegie Hall."

Sources

A. James Farrance, letter to Archie Green, June 16, 1958. Details in my *Only a Miner* (Urbana: University of Illinois Press, 1972), p. 260.

B. Fred Mooney, *Struggle in the Coal Fields* (Morgantown: West Virginia University Library, 1967), p. 28. Details in *Only a Miner*, p. 269.

Background

Mother Jones and Joe Hill share honors as labor figures in history around whom legends have clustered. They, together with legendary Paul Bunyan and John Henry, tower over other exemplars of workers' strength and spirit. Mother Jones sparked considerable lore during incessant travels from strike zone to convention hall. She had kissed the Blarney Stone as a child in Ireland. In the United States, she married iron molder Frank Jones in 1861; she lost her husband and four children in the yellow fever epidemic of 1876. For the rest of her life, Mary Harris Jones mothered countless "adopted children" in mine, mill, and sweatshop.

These dual texts by West Virginia coal miners James Farrance and Fred Mooney are mini-tales recalled from memory long after the events described. Each account displays the vernacular voice of an Appalachian native. In a personal letter and a memoir, both narrators claimed eyewitness truth. Farrance saw Mother Jones on Monongah's Pike Street; Mooney saw her at Cabin Creek's bridge.

We gain a clue to Mother Jones's flamboyant style, Irish wit, and superb blend of innocence and guile by standing at her side as she told Mooney about pulling "dramatic stuff" on the gun thugs. Literally, she had the capacity to enlarge her character as well as to place herself in the stream of labor tradition. In life she wrote and lectured constantly; in death she generated a huge body of commentary. (For her rhetoric in letters and speeches, see Edward Steel's studies of her speeches and correspondence.)

30

Pillsbury's Best

It was in 1899, McKinley was President and the country was in a terrible economic depression. Millions were out of work, there was no relief, no unemployment insurance, and hunger, poverty and great wretchedness were abroad in the line. At that very time, the Massachusetts Legislature debated the selection of a wild flower as a symbol to grace the State. Democrats and Republicans made eloquent speeches proposing the trailing arbutus, the cowslip, the wild rose, the buttercup, the daisy.

Jim [Carey] swung his chair around, with his back to the speakers, in utter disgust with this shameless and heartless proceeding. The House always welcomed a speech from him. The members enjoyed his remarks and his unfailing good humor. But Carey had no desire to enter in this senseless debate. Finally, some members goaded him into saying something. "Hasn't Mr. Carey anything to offer? Surely, Mr. Carey can propose an appropriate flower for our great state?" said a member.

Slowly, Jim rose to his feet. "Yes, Mr. Speaker, I have a proposal. In the need of this great hour of hunger and suffering of the working people of our land I suggest a much needed flour. I recommend Pillsbury's Best."

Source

August Claessens, *Didn't We Have Fun!* (New York: Rand School Press, 1953), p. 15.

Background

Gus Claessens, Socialist Party stalwart and veteran public speaker, offered many soapbox and party-forum tales in his delightful gar-

land, *Didn't We Have Fun!* I have not found a precise analog for
"Pillsbury's Best," but do not doubt its traditionality. Claessens did
not claim authorship for stories he had heard in his years of agita-
tional/educational work. He identified this wordplay yarn on one of
America's most durable brand names as a "classic story."

31

Mary Ovington's Story

An Irish friend was talking on trade union matters, and she said: "Do you know, yisterday I dined with a naygur. Little did I ivir think I wud do sich a thing, but it was this way. You know my man is sicretary of his union, and the min are on strike, and who should come to the door at twelve o'clock but a big black naygur. 'Is Brother O'Neill at home?' seys he. 'Brother O'Neill,' thinks I; 'well, if I'm brother to you I'd better have staid in Ireland.' But I axed him in, and in a minute my man comes and he shakes the naygur by the hand, and says he, 'You must stay and ate wid us.' So I puts the dinner on the table and I sat down and ate wid a naygur."

"Well," I said, "how did he seem?"

"To tell you the truth," she said, "he seemed just like anybody else."

Source

Mary White Ovington, "The Negro in the Trades Unions in New York," *Annals of the American Academy of Political and Social Sciences* 27 (May, 1906): 96. Reprinted in Herbert Gutman, Preface to Sterling Spero and Abram Harris, *The Black Worker* (New York: Atheneum, 1968), p. xiii; Gutman, *Work, Culture, and Society in Industrializing America* (New York: Knopf, 1976), p. xiii; and David Roediger, *Towards the Abolition of Whiteness* (London: Verso, 1994), p. 160.

Background

Mary White Ovington used the anecdote as an exemplum, or moral tale. It had been "heard the other day, whose every word I can vouch for," as it illustrated her passionate belief that "caste lines [would] disappear when men are held together by a common inter-

"The Laborer."

est" [in unionism]. She did not doubt that labor solidarity would overcome exploitation and injustice.

In 1968, Herbert Gutman called up Ovington's Irish "dialect tale" to comment upon the corrosion of spirit among black and white workers faced by race division. Gutman returned to the story in 1976 to show the need for social historians to learn about Brother O'Neill, his wife, and their black trade-union friend—part of "the unknown country" of rank-and-file workers invisible to many Americans.

Mary Ovington, a white woman, pioneered in efforts at the turn of the century to improve the lot of urban black workers. In 1994, David Roediger drew additional meaning from her 1906 tale in that she had pursued reform within a setting of male trade unionists solving fraternal problems. He commented on the ethos of early union attention to race as subscribing to the "logic of manly work and protected homes." Today, issues of gender, ethnicity, and work are intertwined to the point that Mrs. O'Neill's granddaughters will have to treat issues of justice on the job and at the hall, as well as at the family dinner table.

Although Professor Gutman gave no precise source for the O'Neill anecdote, he linked it to Claude McKay (1890–1948), Jamaica-born poet and novelist. Mary Ovington (1865–1951), a social worker and civil libertarian, served as cofounder of the National Association for the Advancement of Colored People. She met McKay in 1921–22 in Greenwich Village, when both contributed to the *Liberator,* a militant cultural/political magazine.

I do not know whether Ovington told her story after 1906, nor whether McKay had ever heard or read it. I have not found any precise analogs in print. Despite the dated dialect in "Mary Ovington's Story," it retains power—conflict over race has not vanished. Old tales make moral points; they also pull readers to those who cherish folk narratives. (For additional reading, see Mari Jo Buhle on Ovington, and Wayne Cooper on McKay.)

32

Discretion versus Valor

Pat and Mike were the two employees in a Boston coalyard. Pat was the dominant one and a real agitator. He and Mike groused about their dirty jobs, their low pay, and their new boss. Dissatisfaction grew until Pat finally announced that a showdown was the only way to solve their problems.

Pat told Mike that at the end of that day's work, he, Mike, was to go to the boss's office and demand a nickel an hour raise, or else! Mike was charged up by Pat's urging, his relating how abused they were, and how they would force the boss to give in to their demands.

At quitting time, the fired-up Mike strode to the office and banged on the door. The door opened and the boss glared at Mike, shouting, "What the hell do you want?"

Mike blurted, "Me and Pat want a nickel an hour raise or else!"

"Or else what?" growled the boss. Taken aback and considering his weak backing, and how Pat wasn't even with him, he gulped and stammered, "Or else we'll keep on working for what we're getting," as he slunk away to report his defeat to Pat.

Source

Ron Weakley, letter to Labor Archives and Research Center, San Francisco State University, May 20, 1993.

Background

As a young laborer in the early 1940s, Ron Weakley helped organize Pacific Gas & Electric Company's employees into the Utility Workers Organizing Committee (CIO). Then, the International Brotherhood of Electrical Workers (AFL) also chartered several

PG&E rival locals. Facing divisive conflict within this giant utility's work force, the CIO cadre, in 1951, merged into a systemwide consolidated IBEW Local 1245. Weakley, the big union's driving spirit, served as business manager until his retirement in 1971.

Weakley heard CIO president Phil Murray tell a didactic tale, "Discretion versus Valor," in New York, 1943, when some UWOC militants proposed a wartime nationwide utility strike. Murray also cautioned the young organizers, "Never start a strike you can't win." Pat and Mike stories are legion; I have not encountered Murray's variant in print, and thank old-timer Ron Weakley for sharing it with laborlore readers.

33

Seize Her, Bill

A farmer in the Midwest hired some men. One of them named Bill would not join the IWW when asked to do so. This Bill had a boss-mind and always tried to do two day's work in one. The farmer had some mean cows which he did not want to handle, or trust to the IWW hired hands. Bill was willing to do the job. Every time a cow came along the farmer hollered, "Seize her, Bill."

This often-repeated phrase soon got associated with Bill and it became his nickname. When the work was finished, all the hands were discharged. Soon, the IWW men started to associate any boss-minded worker with "Seize her, Bill" and it became shortened to scissorbill.

Source

John Neuhaus related this tale to me in about 1956; I used it, with commentary, in "American Labor Lore," *Industrial Relations* 4 (Feb., 1965): 61.

Background

Linguists affirm "folk etymology" when speakers conjure fancy notions to explain word origins. In short, *folk* in this sense suggests falsehood, absurdity, or circuitous theory well after a term has gained currency. Members of the Industrial Workers of the World, in the union's early years, used *scissorbill* to ridicule a yokel, yahoo, or unclass-conscious worker—a "slave" who ignored common cause with the proletariat. Joe Hill's song, "Scissor Bill" (first printed in the *Industrial Worker,* Feb. 16, 1913) helped firm the term in labor speech. Hill, aware of then-current disputes on evolution, branded a "scissor bill" as "the missing link that Darwin tried to trace."

"Scissorbill Hog."

Essentially, the IWW meaning for *scissorbill* fell back on a formula of false consciousness favored by many Reds who enjoyed belittling creatures of inferior intelligence or confused values. This label consigned victims to an inferno of sloth and despair. Occasionally, a brave Wobbly protested the pejorative usage and asked how the IWW could organize workers after demeaning them in speech and print.

Peter Tamony, seeking the etymological setting in which Wobblies had added *scissorbill* to their daily vocabularies, indicated that the "put down" arose out of long familiarity by workers with a pig and a bird: the half-wild, long-tusked razorback hog (also scissorbill, landshark, or Carolina racer)—hungry and destructive; the scissorbill bird (also razorbill, skimmer, or shearwater)—skimming over water, shearing the waves. Tamony asserted that Wobblies had extended *scissorbill* from greedy pigs and skimming birds to their human counterparts (1957).

In the mid-1950s, Tamony, Neuhaus, and other friends met informally at my home to explore laborlore matters. While Peter traced *scissorbill* and revealed his findings, John recalled that Jack McDonald (1889–1968), a San Francisco bookstore owner and longtime contributor to the *Western Socialist,* "knew" the pejorative word's origin, dating it back to 1908. McDonald's yarn, relayed by Neuhaus and some Wobblies, clearly had been made up, tongue-in-cheek, to rationalize *scissorbill* after it had entered union speech.

The IWW dates its charter to 1905. On April 29, 1909, the *Industrial Worker* carried a squib, "E. J. Foote is organizing in Portland and reports encouraging prospects from that scissor-bill town." Clearly, Foote had viewed Portland negatively, but what were its faults? In August, 1909, the IWW issued its first little red songbook holding Dick Brazier's "Meet Me in the Jungles, Louie," in which unemployed Louie becomes a hobo on the hog. He shares mulligan stew in the jungle and helps in catching the "scissor Bill's rooster." This suggests either a farmer's bird or a rural town householder with a backyard chicken coop. Is the rooster's owner especially stupid or backwards?

As the then-strange word circulated in IWW ranks, a reader wrote to the *Industrial Worker* to ask for definitions of "scisorbill" and "Palouser." (*Palouse* holds many meanings from the French for a grassy expanse to western grass lands, Nez Percé Indians, Appaloosa pony, rancher's homemade lantern, sunset, and greenhorn.) On July 2, 1910, editor Hartwell Shippey responded:

> A Palouser is always a scissorbill, although a scissorbill is not always a Palouser. According to Hoyle, a Palouser is an animal with the human form who roams the region known as the Palouse country, an agricultural district of the state of Washington. He wears a look of greed, a sickly grin, billy-goat whiskers, and is often found wearing clothes.
>
> The scissorbill is like Tom Paine—the world is his country. He is confined to no limitations of latitude or longitude, but roams where'er the fool killer is not. Is found in great numbers in the land of the "Skee and the home of the Slave," but is not absent from other scab localities. He has been classified variously as yap, mut, leather-head, etc., but as he is always very conspicuous where labor is not organized the term NON-REBELLIOUS SLAVE is perhaps the most correct application.

This tongue-in-cheek definition, together with McDonald's explanatory tale (set back to 1908), reveals that *scissorbill* had become attached to non- or anti-unionists in the IWW's formative years. However, editor Shippey shed no light on how or when this pejorative reached the labor movement. Accepting Tamony's belief in the transfer of a hog or bird's name to workers identifying with bosses, I learned of several possible settings for such verbal shifts—zoology to ideology.

In San Francisco, Merle Croy (a carpenter foreman under whom I worked in 1958 on an addition to St. Elizabeth's Infant Shelter) told a lunchtime story about scissorbills. Merle, an Oklahoma coal miner and UMWA partisan prior to his trek west, recalled response to union safety rules at times of underground danger. At the whistle's warning blast, miners had to drop tools and leave the pit. Sometimes a hungry man lingered behind to finish loading his car. If detected, his mates placed the job-hog on trial in the union local, fining him for scissorbilling.

In Pennsylvania, George Korson reported a parallel scene: "The custom of 'loading the turn of the mine' was traditional in bituminous mining. Planned to equalize the opportunities of all miners, it was often abused. . . . Some worked in the mines on Sunday, holidays, and other idle days without compensation, piling up coal for future loading, but were rewarded with extra turns when work resumed. Men guilty of these practices were characterized . . . 'free clickers,' 'free turn men,' 'scissorbills,' and 'coal hogs'" (1943, 179).

Without precise dates for either the Oklahoma or Pennsylvania reports, we speculate whether miners or Wobblies in other trades first moved *scissorbill* from razorback boar to coal hog/job hog to safety-rule breaker to boss-minded wage slave. This sequence involving swine puts aside the possible verbal transition from scissorbill birds to stupid workers.

Three accounts suggest a flight path. In 1958, *Louisville Courier-Journal* columnist Allan Trout offered a Kentucky interpretation: "Sometimes a chick or turkey poult is hatched out with a crossed beak. Because the ends of a crossed beak do not come together, they cannot eat normally. As a result, they are always hungry and lean. This kind of a beak is called a scissorbill." University of Illinois sociologist Bernard Karsh, in a conversation with me in 1959, stated that *scissorbill* derived from a Tennessee rooster with a crooked or crossed bill who crowed from both sides of his mouth, much like a man indulging in double talk.

Eugene Barnett, a "double-header" member of both the IWW and the United Mine Workers of America, had been imprisoned in Walla Walla for the Armistice Day, 1919, American Legion attack on the IWW hall in Centralia, Washington. During my visit at his home in Spokane, June 5, 1961, he advanced a regional explanation:

Scissorbill comes from a bird on the Coast, there, that has its bills crossed, and he can't catch a fish. He'll set up on a big tall tree, and watch the gulls 'til a gull gets a fish, and then it'll swoop down and take it away from the gull. In other words, it reaps the benefit that the other bird works for, and the human scissorbill—he goes around and plays the Chink [gambles] and drinks the dehorn booze [whiskey that emasculates workers] and waits 'til the other man gets a raise, then he runs him out and takes the job (Barnett 1961).

When I pressed Barnett for a source, he asserted that his story was well known on the Northwest Coast. "All the clamdiggers know what they [scissorbill birds] are." Essentially, Barnett was more concerned with accurate nomenclature for birds than with a definitive etymology for a favorite Wobbly term.

However we respond to the explanations advanced by Trout, Karsh, and Barnett, they help us approach a tenable base for the name progression from a shearwater/skimmer/scissorbill sea bird or a beak-deformed domestic fowl to a worker seen as lean, hungry, defective, hypocritical, or living by thievery. I can imagine sailors and fishermen likening subnormal mates to scissorbill birds. Similarly, such a comparison could have been made by persons tending cross-beaked chickens. In short, we do not yet know the precise rout of *scissorbill* from birds and beasts to the labor movement.

In a current study of our word, historian Patrick Huber suggests a plausible link via farmers or farmhands from bird/pig to unclass-conscious worker. He notes examples in print from 1917 to today equating *scissorbill* with *hick, hoosier, hayseed,* and similar slurs for rural provincials. Further, he points to the practice of farmhands in slack seasons seeking temporary work in logging, mining, oilfield drilling, and construction. Raw bumpkins, often untrained and un-skilled, often undercut union wages or placed regular workers in harm's way. In memories of entering the shipwright's trade, I hear in mind's ear the absolute contempt directed against apple knock-ers and cherry pickers—scissorbills, one and all—who didn't know stem from stern or ass from elbow.

Scissorbill (bird) appeared in whalers' speech in 1839, and (hog) in drovers' speech in 1871. Huber continues to search for nine-teenth-century citations of this term in agrarian settings. In time, he'll trace a single word's convoluted journey: whaler, drover, logger, miner, oilfield roustabout, construction stiff, farmhand, Wobbly. Shall we ever map the precise path?

I am not confident that scholarly research, however technical, can drive colorful yarns of word origin and meaning out of circulation on the job and at the hall. Folk etymology is alive and well. Nevertheless, light of heart, I offer the McDonald-Neuhaus tale "Seize Her, Bill" as another detour on the laborlore journey.

"Scissorbill Bird."

34

Measuring Rod

When Bert Davis took charge of a job building a vault in a bank, he picked [apprentice] Francis to go along with him. The contract called for cutting out a section of the wooden main floor, temporary underpinning, protective railing around the opening, a poured concrete 12-inch slab, and, of course, a lot of other details not material to our story. While the laborers got the dirt out, the forms were made up.

Things were going nicely for Davis until they hit rock at a depth of 13 feet 6 inches. The plans called for excavation down to 14 feet from the floor level. Now Davis was in a pickle. He figured if the architect were told about this he would insist on his 14 feet, rock or no rock.

On the other hand, he might possibly let it go and permit a 6-inch slab. When ignorance is bliss, it's folly to be wise—Davis decided to stay mum and pour a 6-inch slab. Who'd know the difference when the job was finished? Considering the rock, there would be no harm done.

Everything was ready for pouring and Davis and Francis were jackassing the chute into place when in walks the architect. "Ready to pour, carpenter?" He asked. "All ready, sir," said Davis. "Got 14 feet down there?" "Yes sir," lied Davis. I'd like to check it," said the architect. "Got a measuring rod?"

They had a rod, all right, but Davis wasn't going to say so. Maybe he could stall him off. Then up pops Francis. "Yes sir," he said. "We've got a rod, I'll go get it."

As he passed behind, Davis, already sweating blood, lashed back with his foot, but fortunately he missed. That little so-and-so! Now the jig was up for fair.

Francis returned with the rod, a dressed length of 1 x 1 crayon-marked in feet and half-feet all the way up to 16 feet. The architect took it and dropped it in the hole. Reaching down, he checked off the floor level with his thumb and pulled the rod up. "Fourteen feet," he read.

He walked around to the adjoining side and checked. This time he got 14 feet scant. Once more he checked and found 14 feet full.

"Nice work, carpenter," he said. "Go ahead and pour." For a long time after he left, Davis stood gaping pop-eyed into the hole. What the devil happened? He took the rod and checked. Fourteen feet, it read. An hour ago it was 13 feet 6 inches.

He turned to Francis. "When you mentioned the rod, I could have crippled you," he said. "Now something has happened, I don't know what. We're down to 14 feet."

Then Francis explained the miracle. When he heard the architect ask for the rod, an idea shot into his erratic mind. On his way out, he grabbed a saw and cut off the first 6 inches!

Davis looked, and sure enough, the rod was cut off at the first half foot mark. "How much wages are they paying you?" he asked. Francis told him. "You're working too damn cheap," said Davis. "I'm going to put in a word for you next pay day."

So Francis got his first raise. Don't you think he earned it?

Source

John Hart, "All about Francis," *Carpenter* 75 (Sept., 1955): 29–31.

Background

John Hart, New York City Local 366, contributed a monthly feature, THE LOCKER, which ran for years in the *Carpenter.* Along with thousands of other UBCJA members, I read his column regularly for its Duke's mixture of trade tips, homilies, and union cheer. In one story, Hart cautioned readers, "Any thing we say about [Francis] should be warily considered. A carpenters greatest fault is the exaggeration of the truth. Who said that? Well, if you never heard it before, we said it. So you just weed out the exaggeration, and whatever is left is the truth."

Beyond issues of veracity, Hart employed much in-group construction language. Does the sketch "Measuring Rod" (in our vernacular, a *story pole*) seem strange to those who never worked on a below-ground concrete pour, jackassed a chute into place, or sweated out an architect's signal?

All construction hands know of actions involving "war" with architects, inspectors, or contractors. Did trickster Francis actually cut a half-foot off a rod? Only John Hart knew the truth about his most unusual apprentice. Hart left to THE LOCKER's readers the task of scaling the distance between experienced event and traditional anecdote.

35

Mike Casey and the Strikebreakers

In 1901, San Francisco teamsters fought for their union in a big citywide and waterfront strike. Three young Irish-born drivers emerged as popular labor leaders: Michael Casey, John McLaughlin, John O'Connell. During the strike, the employers imported a bunch of tough strikebreakers from the East. These strong-arm men were well paid and didn't work very much. They knew more about cracking skulls than driving wagons.

Back then, San Francisco was a wide-open town with a thriving red-light district. The strikebreakers began to spend evenings in a few Tenderloin sporting houses. These men were really big spenders. Mike Casey, knowing some of the madams, made a little arrangement. Whenever several strikebreakers visited a house, the madam sent a quiet message to Casey. He dispatched four or five loyal teamsters to each house. You might say that the teamsters caught the toughs with their pants down.

The teamsters hustled the strikebreakers to a kind of a bull pen back of the union hall—let them cool down for a while. They asked each tough where he lived. Did he come from St. Louis, Chicago, New York, or some small town in the East? The teamsters promised to send each strikebreaker home by train—no questions asked, just stay away from San Francisco during any strike.

Meanwhile, Casey made another arrangement with a yard crew of Southern Pacific trainmen. The teamsters hauled each night's load of strikebreakers down to the Bayview rail yard, and loaded the catch into a conveniently empty boxcar.

MIKE THE BITE.   'BLOODY' BERNSTEIN.   DUM DUM DAVITT

"Strikebreakers."

Two days later, the strikebreakers woke up to find their boxcar door open. With relief, they stepped out into the bright morning sunshine of the Imperial Valley. By coincidence at that time of the year, Valley growers were shorthanded. They put the stranded men to work in the fields at a dollar a day, sunrise to sunset. It was the first honest labor for these strikebreakers, and not a red-light parlor in sight.

Source

Sam Kagel told this story at a Union Pioneers luncheon San Francisco, Nov. 20, 1987. I wrote out his text a few days after the event.

Background

Sam Kagel, a labor arbitrator/negotiator since the 1930s, attributed this story directly to Mike Casey. Whether or not the teamster leader had embroidered an early yarn about revenge against despised strikebreakers, or swore by the truth of his own experience, I do not know. Zeese Papanikolas, in a poetic history of Louis Tikas and the Ludlow Massacre, offers a related anecdote told by a Colorado coal-wars veteran between 1913 and 1914.

"The Greeks [immigrant miners] had other allies—some as un-likely as the girls in the Walsenburg whorehouses, who would tip them off when a bunch of scabs were enjoying themselves in the rooms. Then the Greeks would go down and clean the scabs out and there would be torn knuckles, bloody heads and a few arrests. This was the way the working girl showed her solidarity with the working man" (1982, 184).

36

No Smoking

A. Smoking in the Dynamite Room

A worker has nothing to do; he goes down to the Dynamite Room for a smoke.

The boss comes along, and exclaims, "Why are you smoking in the Dynamite Room?"

The worker replies, "Why should I pay attention to you? We have a strong union."

Eventually, this smoking blows up the plant.

The worker survives and resumes his defiance. He tells a buddy, "I'm going down to the Dynamite Room for a smoke."

The buddy asks, "Do you still have your job?"

"Sure."

The buddy asks, "How about the boss?"

"Oh, we've got a new boss."

B. Powder Factory

A bunch of lumberjacks were toasting their shins around the bunk-house stove. The old axeman spoke:

There was a powder mill down near my home town in Vermont. One day I went to see a friend in this factory. They had pretty strict rules there against any smoking or lighting of matches. I was smoking my pipe when I went there. I read the printed sign forbidding any smoking on the premises. I paid no attention to it. I thought it would do no harm to smoke a bit if I was careful.

As I walked into the factory I saw heaps of powder on every side. While I was passing some of these powder piles I stumbled and fell down. The burning tobacco from my pipe fell on one of them, and, would you believe it, set fire to the powder and burned up several bushels of it, before I could stomp the fire out. It was a close call to burning up the hull powder factory, I can tell you.

Sources

A. Peter Tamony, heard on a San Francisco radio station, June 20, 1964.

B. William Bartlett to Charles Edward Brown; published by Brown in "Wisconsin Parallels to Indiana Folktales," *Hoosier Folklore Bulletin* 3 (Dec., 1942): 101.

Background

For many years, Tamony and I exchanged word citations, musical references, and ephemeral bits. His massive collection has been preserved at the University of Missouri, Columbia. Upon hearing "Smoking in the Dynamite Room," Peter typed it on a file-slip without naming the radio raconteur, but noting that it had been told in a Bronx Jewish accent. Could it have been Myron Cohen? (See "Scissors Story.") Tamony gave me a copy of the joke on the chance that I had heard or could trace it. I have long assumed the traditionality of this dig at "strong unions" but have not found a text in print.

By contrast, "Powder Factory" has had a long life in tradition. Although it came from a north Wisconsin lumber camp before 1932, its narrator ("the old axeman") had set the story back to native Vermont when he measured powder, gun or blasting (?), by the bushel basket. Very likely, he had reached Wisconsin before the century's turn; his story may have been old when he first heard it in Vermont.

Without citing all our tale's forms, I note a few details from three variants: In a "Liars' Club" yarn, the careless hand who started a small fire carried powder by pail day and night before he "got it all moved to safety." Hearing this, a credulous listener stated: "You'd 've been in a helluva shape if it had ever blown up" (Halpert 1943, 12.) This Indiana whopper approaches "Smoking in the Dynamite Room" in its merging of fire and explosion terror.

Among the tales gathered on the Idaho WPA Writers' Project, and published handsomely by Vardis Fisher, we find a lesson on careless smoking: A threshing crewman told his buddies about past work in a Du Pont mill. "I lost my job that time. For twelve tons of the best powder we had burnt up before we could put that fire out"

(*Idaho* 1937, 399). Finally, "Oregon" Smith (an Indiana character) moved the fire story directly into an on-site bull session, "Me 'n' a bunch of other men were sittin' 'round in a powder room in the old days tellin' tales" (Halpert and Robinson 1942, 165).

Had the radio humorist who told "Smoking in the Dynamite Room" heard any previous powder-mill-fire tales similar to those noted here? No powder workers escape fear of accidental death, yet some continue to joke about smoking bans and their narrow escapes in beating the odds of fatal consequences. Who can trace "Powder Factory" to its source, or relate it to current "strong-union" offspring?

37

Comes the Revolution

A. *Peggy Hopkins Joyce*

A communist soapboxer was haranguing a few onlookers at the edge
of Cadillac Square [in Detroit]. Pointing up to the elegant Brook-
Cadillac Hotel, the agitator asked, "Who is sleeping on the hotel's
top floor? I'll tell you who—Walter P. Chrysler mit (with) [playgirl]
Peggy Hopkins Joyce." Pausing for emphasis, the soapboxer raised
his voice, "And they are there every night, but, comes the revolution, you know who will be there? Comrades, the United Automobile Workers of America will be there every night."

A guy in the audience gives the speaker the raspberry. The soapboxer turns to the heckler, "What you say, comrade?" The skeptic
shoots back, "I don't like Peggy Hopkins Joyce." The Red speaker
blasts the wise guy, "After the revolution, you'll like Peggy Hopkins
Joyce." Returning attention to his audience, the soapboxer points
scornfully to the heckler, "Look, comrades, a Trotskyite."

B. *Go to Harvard*

"Comes the revolution," [a Union Square speaker] says, "and everybody will go to Harvard." His ragged audience applauds. "Comes
the revolution"—the speaker pauses—"and everybody here will
sleep with Peggy Hopkins Joyce," an actress then famous for her
persistent habit of getting married to millionaires. More cheers from
the audience, but there is one man who growls, "I doan *wanna* sleep
with Peggy Hopkins Joyce." "Comes the revolution," the speaker
says, wagging his finger, "you'll sleep with Peggy Hopkins Joyce *and*
like it."

C. *Strawberries and Cream*

There was a stock story [Wobblies] would tell, usually delivered with a heavy Russian accent.

The [Communist] party faithful were gathered and the leader was holding forth. "Come the revolution, comrades," says he, "we will have strawberries and cream."

A voice from the audience: "But, comrade speaker, I don't like strawberries and cream."

Whereupon the speaker fixes the interrupter with a gimlet stare.

"Come the revolution, comrade, you will have strawberries and cream—AND LIKE IT!"

Sources

A. Phillips Garman told this story at my home, San Francisco, June, 1985. I wrote out his text several months after the visit.

B. Malcolm Cowley, *The Dream of the Golden Mountains* (New York: Viking, 1980), p. 154.

C. Gilbert Mers, *Working the Waterfront* (Austin: University of Texas Press, 1988), p. 155.

Background

Garman (1910–86) served as UAW research director in the mid-1930s. We met at the University of Illinois in the 1960s, where he encouraged my laborlore pursuits. In placing a story about Peggy Hopkins Joyce in Detroit, he also noted auto mogul Walter Chrysler's reputation as a playboy. Garman's text, although brimming with sexual humor, also recalled bitter conflict between followers of Joseph Stalin and Leon Trotsky.

Literary critic Cowley set "Go to Harvard" in Greenwich Village at the Great Depression's nadir, when some intellectuals speculated on life after their call-to-duty at revolutionary barricades. Texas Gulf Coast longshoreman Mers used "Strawberries and Cream" to illustrate tension between members of the Communist Party and the Industrial Workers of the World.

Under various titles, this anecdote circulated widely among radicals. August Claessens, socialist pamphleteer and soapboxer, felt it to be too well known to repeat (1953, 157). Malcolm Cowley noted that the tag line, "Comes the revolution and you'll *eat* stromberries wit cream," had been shouted by the audience "in chorus at the Players Club" to punctuate performances (1980, 153). I suspect that most veterans of left sectarian movements in the United States share special memories of this joke cycle.

"Meeting Hall."

38

In the Stacks

An old-maid librarian (with such stereotyped characteristics as a bun, corrective shoes, glasses, and a propensity to Shh) is the branch librarian in a branch of the Los Angeles Public Library. A patron comes rushing out of the book stacks to the reference desk. The patron is very upset and says to the librarian, "There's a man masturbating in the stacks." The patron runs out of the library.

All the library personnel (clerks and book shelvers) who hear this are bewildered as to what to do. Meanwhile, more people are leaving the library because of this offensive man. So, finally, the old-maid librarian, very befuddled herself but being the person in charge, with authority (a front), goes back in the stacks, and actually confronting the man masturbating, loses her cool and stammers, "May I help you?"

Source

Undated text submitted by Lee Davis to folklore class; Folklore Archives, University of California, Berkeley.

Background

Lee Davis first heard "In the Stacks" while a student at the University of Southern California Library School, spring, 1973. Initially, she believed it to be true as it fit her preconception of librarians and patrons. After hearing the same story in a San Diego library, and elsewhere, she recognized it as a folk narrative.

Davis, in commenting on her story, noted varied elements: wordplay or double entendre in the question, "May I help you?"; initiation ritual for student librarians; statement on repressed and deviant sexuality in a particular workplace.

39

Paddy Doyle

[Paddy Doyle or Paddy West] is usually said to have lived in Great Howard Street, Liverpool, where he kept a seaman's boarding-house of singular fame. For here he would make a farmer into an able-bodied seaman in a couple of days! In his backyard he had a ship's wheel rigged up where the candidate would learn to steer, while Paddy's wife would chuck a bucket of cold water over him to "git yer used to the cold nor' westers."

Practice in furling sail was gained on the window sill of the attic, and the final ceremony was the stepping over a piece of string and the circling of a cow's horn standing on the front parlour table. "When the mate axes ye where ye've sailed, tell him ye've crossed the Line, and bin three times around the Horn but don't tell him it wuz a cow horn!"

Then, fitted out in dungarees, with a "nice clean ropeyarn for a belt," and with "wan suit av oilskins 'tween ye an' yer mate . . . I'll tell the mate ter put ye in diff'rent watches." . . . A dead seaman's discharge papers in his pocket, the newly-made A.B. would be introduced to some hard-case packet, and as he trundled aboard with a sea-bag filled with bricks covered with an old jersey and a torn shirt, Farmer Jack, now Sailor John, had little idea of what awaited him out on the broad Atlantic!

These Paddy Wests were supposed to be a shade better than shanghaied drunks, and the equal, at any rate, of pierhead jumps. They'd had a *little* coaching in the craft of a seaman, even if it was darned little!

Source

Stan Hugill, *Shanties from the Seven Seas* (London: Routledge and Kegan Paul, 1966), p. 334.

"Shantying."

Background

Gifted shantyman Stan Hugill came from Britain to San Francisco many times to participate in maritime festivals at the National Park Service's Hyde Street Pier. On January 15, 1985, I heard him sing the shanty "Paddy West," introducing it with remarks on crimps rounding up or shanghaiing hayseeds, bank clerks, and greenhorns for "coaching" in a Liverpool saloon. Hugill added that when steam replaced sails, Paddy's recruits would shovel coal into a barrel to qualify as stokers and firemen.

In his performance—set on a pier converted to an outdoor museum site for ancient ships—Hugill broke narrative barriers by casually moving from shanty to ballad to tale to enactment with gesture and grimace. Additionally, he reminded his audience that the twins "Paddy Doyle"/"Paddy West," in song and story, had been as familiar in San Francisco and Valparaiso as in London and Sydney.

Jokes abound to describe inadequate training for raw workers, as well as to put down proprietors of "quickie" trade schools. Wayland Hand, in treating Irish immigrant miners in Butte, Montana, reported: Straight from the "auld sod," and never having seen a copper mine, the job seekers would be escorted to the basement of the Florence Hotel, or "Big Ship." There, they were taught to operate a "slugger" (piston drill). This machine "wised up" green hands, giving them confidence to "climb the Hill" for employment (1946, 177).

Shantyman Hugill and folklorist Hand brought sham training practices to the surface. While penning these lines, I scan political reports demanding work-fare as a substitute for welfare, real jobs instead of handouts. Will neophytes, for decades ahead, tell stories about walking around plastic cow horns, or boast about mastering computer-programmed "sluggers" in dank "Big Ship" basements?

40

Hudson Touring Car

This glaziers apprentice on completing his apprenticeship was given a journeyman's book, a traveling card, and bid "God Speed and good luck," as was the custom at that time.

This young man hopped a Northwestern Pacific freight and bummed his way to the Twin Cities. He secured a day's work and was encouraged to go to Chicago. In Chicago he presented his card to the [Glass Workers] Business Agent and was invited to attend the union meeting that evening. So he went to the meeting that night, and got a seat up front for better observation and to hear the speakers.

Under new business the B.A. made a motion to nearly deplete the treasury and purchase a Hudson touring car. The motion was seconded. No speakers asked for the floor, so our West-coast educated-labor worker took the floor, and started his speech on depleting the union cash for such a luxury item.

Without further ado, two members grabbed our critic, manhandled him to the door, and threw him down a flight of stairs. He went to the nearest bar to heal his wounds. After the union meeting ended, a few members drifted in. Our West-coast traveler asked: "What kind of a union do you run here"?

The reply: "The car was for the crew that throws the rocks."

Source

T. A. "Tiny" Thronson told me this story in Tacoma, Apr. 13, 1991, at an open-house celebration in Local 23's hall, International Longshoremen's and Warehousemen's Union. Subsequently, he sent me a typed text.

Background

"Tiny" Thronson, born in 1905 in Tacoma, shipped out in his teen years on a tramp steamer. He returned to home-port docks in 1928, working and running longshore crews until his retirement in 1971. In recent years, he has served his local's new members in an educational capacity as a tradition bearer and sage. Reflecting on his nickname, Thronson recalled that as a young docker, he stood 6'4" tall and weighed 220 pounds.

I trust that "Hudson Touring Car" makes a perfectly clear connection between the glass workers' trade and rock throwing. In-group humor is intensified with the knowledge that building-trades glaziers rejected Wobbly beliefs in sabotage. Thronson's detail on his West Coast labor-educated worker reveals another subtle story facet: Many Pacific-slope unionists felt their locals to be morally superior to midwestern and eastern unions. Thus, a Tacoma youngster in Chicago had much to learn about rough-and-tumble predatory tactics.

41

Running for the Streetcar

A. *Too Tired*

[Joe Glazer tells a Detroit worker's (United States Rubber) Depression anecdote.]

I want to tell you how it was when I got out of work.

I was workin' but they pushed you; you had to work, work, work. I used to get out of the plant, and I had to take the streetcar right across from the plant. I'd sit down on the sidewalk. Streetcar would come by.

[JG] "What happened?"

I was too tired to get on it. I had to wait two, three streetcars.

[JG] "What do you mean?"

I was just too damn tired to get up, because if you complained about working too hard, there was always six-thousand guys outside ready to take your job.

B. *Day's End*

This happened before the [San Francisco] '34 strike. At the end of each day, the guys would walk from the docks to the front of the Ferry Building, where the Market Street and Muni both circled back. One evening a Matson longshoreman got to the turnaround and noticed that his car was just taking off. He sprinted and with a flying leap just made the car.

The next morning when he walked down to the Matson dock, the boss met him at the gate and fired him flat out. The boss had seen him sprinting at the circle. The boss snarled, "Any son-of-a-bitch who can still run for a streetcar hasn't put in a real day's work for me."

Sources

A. Included by Joe Glazer in a Robert L. Kanter Memorial Lecture at Storrs, Conn., Apr. 10, 1984. Transcript distributed by Labor Education Center, University of Connecticut.

B. I heard this story on the San Francisco waterfront in 1941, but no longer recall who told it.

Background

These two anecdotes, part of a cycle of end-of-the-day streetcar accounts, seemingly contradict each other. The fatigued Detroit rubber worker could not budge from the sidewalk; the San Francisco longshoreman could still sprint to catch a trolley car. Had he held back a bit of energy from the Matson Company? Yet, both tales unite in commenting on grueling work.

Beyond content, we hear differences in tone in each narration. The factory hand bitterly relayed the truth of a remembered experience. The waterfront worker talked with tongue in cheek, highlighting his boss's absolute power. Joe Glazer used "Too Tired" seriously to illustrate depression conditions. The longshoreman who told me "Day's End" employed humor to ridicule his slave drivers.

In commenting upon "Day's End," I am conscious of its wide circulation in the 1940s; everyone on the waterfront seemed to know it in some form. I associate "Day's End" with veterans of the 1934 Pacific Coast maritime strike. Although this event generated massive commentary and subsequent fiction and film, no one drawn to its drama has published a collection of "Big Strike" folklore.

I know of no logical explanation for our uneven study of labor tradition. Some '34 strike historians have emphasized cruel exploitation, righteous militancy, and rank-and-file unionism. Others have stressed tension between pragmatic, syndicalist, and socialist leaders in competing for position within the involved unions. Still others have been entranced by the strike's revolutionary potential and have sought to name betrayers—New Dealers, shipowners, craft unionists.

It is my conviction that much expressive lore can be found to complement all perspectives advanced by scholars in treating the "Big Strike." For example, "Day's End" reminds us that in a major maritime strike led by sophisticated unionists, simple humor persisted in helping workers survive everyday toil. To joke about running after a streetcar and being fired gave storytellers and auditors a shared view of the physical cost in handling cargo and power relationships on the docks before 1934. The anecdote, narrated after the strike, gained added meaning: We've won; We'll set the pace; We're free to chase trolleys if we so desire!

42

Form of a Fist

A. Close That Hand

[Delegate Pat O'Neil from Arkansas addressed the first convention of the Industrial Workers of the World in Chicago, June 27–July 8, 1905. He entered the debate on the Manifesto by commenting on craft unionists scabbing against each other during strikes.]

Suppose a man had his hand just in that position with each finger sticking out by itself (illustrating), would it be of much benefit to him? Possibly he could keep the flies off if he tried, but that is all. Well, now, here, take the hand of labor today. Today, we have got the blacksmith finger, here, we have got the carpenter finger, here, we have got the miner's finger, and over here we have got the railroad finger; and all that that hand of labor has ever done has been to keep the flies off of the face of the capitalist, while he enjoyed your product.

Now, then, instead of having this hand distorted and paralyzed in its trade autonomy, I want it so that I can bring those fingers up and close them into a grip and make the hand a weapon of offense and of defense; and that, Mr. Chairman, is my reason for issuing the Manifesto. I want it so that every one of those fingers can rely upon the finger next to it and the finger furthest from it. As it stands today, the capitalist shears come along and clip that out and then this and the others, through the opportunity that you give capital. I want that opportunity of capital removed. In other words, I want the teeth of the animal removed, and the only way I can see how to pull them is to close that hand.

B. Five Fingers

[Daniel De Leon lectured in Milwaukee shortly after the founding convention of the IWW. While speaking on "The Preamble of the

IWW," and explaining vital differences between craft and industrial unionism, he noted delegate Pat O'Neil's gesture without naming him.]

Illustrating the point with the five fingers of his right hand far apart, [O'Neil] showed that to be the posture of the craft or autonomous unions—disconnected from one another for all practical work, and good only to act as a fan, a fan that had hitherto done nothing but scare the flies away from the face of the capitalist class; and, proceeding thereupon to illustrate the further point by drawing his five fingers tightly into a compact fist, he showed that to be the posture of Industrial Unionism—a battering ram, that would leave the face of the capitalist class looking materially different from the way it looked when it was merely fanned. The impotence wherewith the right of the working class has hitherto been smitten, is now to be transformed into a might without which that right is but mockery.

C. Fingers on My Hand

[A. Philip Randolph commented on racial policy at the American Federation of Labor fifty-sixth annual convention, Tampa, Florida, November 16–27, 1936.]

The American labor movement will never be effective so long as there is not an effective labor movement in the South, and there will never be an effective movement in the South as long as the Negro workers are not accepted by the unions upon a basis of equality. As a matter of fact, the white and black workers of the South cannot be organized separately as the fingers on my hand. They must be organized altogether, as the fingers on my hand when they are doubled up in the form of a fist, in order that they may be able to strike at the proper moment. If they are organized separately they will not understand each other, and if they do not understand each other they will fight each other, and if they fight each other they will hate each other and the employing class will profit from that condition.

Sources

A. Pat O'Neil, portion of remarks at IWW convention, *Proceedings,* 1905, p. 133.

B. Daniel De Leon speech at Milwaukee, July 10, 1905. Address originally titled "The Preamble of the I. W. W."; reprinted as "Socialist Recon-

ЕКОНОМИЧЕСКОТО ОБЯСНЕНИЕ на РАБОТАТА

BULGARIAN—AN ECONOMIC INTERPRETATION OF THE JOB

Цѣна 25 цента

Издание на

ИНДУСТРИАЛНИТѢ РАБОТНИЦИ НА СВѢТА

1001 W. MADISON ST., CHICAGO, ILL.

"Job Talk."

struction of Society" in numerous pamphlets and in his *Socialist Landmarks* (New York: New York Labor News, 1952); extract above, p. 227.

    C. A. Philip Randolph at AFL convention, 1936; extract from *Proceedings,* p. 660.

Background

Although the raised clenched fist has been used widely in labor and radical movements across national boundaries, the origin of this gesture remains obscure. I cite O'Neil, De Leon, and Randolph to reveal differences in rhetorical style, as well as to show distinct uses of an emblematic act within parallel settings—craft separation versus industrial unity; solidarity of workers across lines of race.

    Pat O'Neil exemplifies countless rank-and-file workers known only through the circumstance of a stenographic convention report. Attending the IWW gathering "empty handed and alone" without credentials from any union, he impressed fellow delegates with his downhome speech (razorback hog, train in ditch, calf leaving its mother). In short, he spoke from canebrake and ship's deck announcing that he was seventy-five years old, had helped organize the Sailors Union of China in Hong Kong in 1848, and, most recently, had mined coal at Spadra, Arkansas.

    De Leon and the Socialist Labor Party have generated an immense body of literature. Similarly, Randolph and the Brotherhood of Sleeping Car Porters have full histories. Here, I focus only on one detail in De Leon's talk. He had left Chicago enthusiastic over the achievements of the then-new IWW. Observing delegate O'Neil closing his fingers to form a fist, thus illustrating the "posture of Industrial Unionism," De Leon used this gesture to make visible his deep belief in proletarian emancipation through revolutionary unionism.

    We assume that Randolph, with close knowledge of socialist traditions, had seen comrades clench fists to mark solidarity, to salute each other, and to silently signify their politics. His remarks on the AFL's convention floor in Tampa were particularly dramatic in light of the struggle by black unionists during New Deal years for a voice in labor's house. In mind's eye, I see A. Philip Randolph greeting Pat O'Neil for his humor and his faith.

43

Scissors Story

This seemingly fantastic tale takes you into the heart of one of the factories in the garment industry, where, as you know, many thousands of girls are employed daily. One of these little girls found it necessary to leave the machine for just a moment to go to the ladies room. Upon her return to the machine, she found her scissors missing. She turned to the girls about her:

"Jennie, maybe you got by me my scissors? You ain't got, hah?" "Sadie, you took from me the scissors, maybe, hah?" "Rose, you got by me the scissors? You just borrowed, maybe, a-hah? Of course, the sisters by me in the union, they wouldn't take the scissors. Who in the world could-a took by me such a little thing like scissors? What could it mean to anybody, a treasure, a possession, something? It's my scissors, what they need—must a-be that dirty dog, the boss, he stole by me the scissors."

She wasted no time, burst into the showroom, it was crowded with customers. She walked right up to the boss, she says: "Give me back my scissors!"

He says: "Wha'?"

She says: "Look, how he don't know from anything. Give back my scissors!"

He said: "What you hollering from scissors? Who knows from scissors?"

She said: "Come on! Don't start with me no riddles. I know you got the scissors."

He said: "I don't know from no scissors. What kind?"

She said: "Look how he wants to know what kind-a scissors. What I shall do? A diagram I shall draw you? Blueprints you need? What is a scissors? You never saw a scissors? You don't know from what is a scissors? It's my scissors! Now kick in with the scissors!"

"Sweatshop."

He says: "Ged oudda here! Don't make me no trouble in the showroom. I got here customers, I got important people."

She says: "Drop dead with the important people together. If not for me and my scissors you wouldn't have customers. Now give back the scissors."

He says: "Ged oudda here! I don't know from no scissors. What you making a whole ting, here? You ruin me my business."

She says: "Never mind! You don't know what's happening in the factory, hah? You de boss? Isn't?"

"So."

"So, since when a boss doesn't know what's in the factory happening? I suppose you don't know I went in the ladies room?"

He says:" I don't give a darn where you went, so long as you didn't went by the machine."

She said: "Never mind with the wisecracks! Kick in with my scissors."

He says: "Now get ouda here! I got from you plenty, already. I took dis *chaleria* [curse of cholera] from you. Now, ged oudda here, and go back to the machine before I knock you out the brains."

She said: "Don't touch me, don't curse on me. I'll report you to the union."

He says: "Drop dead with your lousy union together."

She says: "Now I got a case!"

The next morning there was an executive board meeting. The little girl is ushered in.

The executive chairman addressing her, says: "Mine dear sister, tell the brothers what happened. Word for word, leave out noting!"

She says: "Mr. Chairman and mine brudders, I couldn't help it. It's nature. I have to leave the machine for a second, you shall excuse me, to go in the ladies room. When I come back to the machine, was missing by me the scissors, and I know that that dirty dog, the boss, he stole by me my scissors, and I demand, for the first time in twenty years, protection from mine brudders in my union."

She sits down, and the executive chairman says: "Mine dear brothers, what is your pleasure with regards to this situation?"

One delegate gets up, he says: "Mr. Chairman, mine brothers, and my bereaved sister, I happen to know that this particular case has got merit. Because, mit twenty years ago when I first come in this country, I was a cutter working in a shop and, this particular boss, he was also a cutter working with me by the same table. The fact that he become a boss, he should drop dead, but I also had to leave the table for a second to go in the ladies room. You see, it was a co-ed shop. I was away a little longer, 'twas a heavier scissors. And when I come back to the table, that dirty dog, he stole by me mine scissors. So if he had already such-a habits with twenty years ago, then it's no question about, that he took by that girl that scissors."

Another delegate says: "In view, in view, from what we heard it, looks to me already a clear case, CAPITAL AGAINST LABOR, and I demand we shall go deeper."

Third delegate says: "What do you mean, 'go deeper?' That's only one solution what regarding it. Teach that dirty dog, pull him down the shop! We'll call a strike 'til he gives back the scissors. Teach him! That's the only way to teach."

Number four gets up, and says: "Whadda ya mean, teach him? We could teach all them dogs. We could use extra scissors. We'll pull out the whole darn industry—a general strike."

Three weeks they're out. Not a wheel turns. Suddenly, one morning, three weeks to the day, in comes the little girl.

She says: "Mr. Chairman, and mine brudders. My sisters and me, we suffered already for three weeks. We didn't enjoyed a good meal in Lindy's all this time. Please, you'll have to excuse me, I couldn't help it. I overlooked it. I found the scissors in the ladies room."

Source

Myron Cohen, 78-rpm disc, Banner 2098. Recorded in New York ca. 1950. Text transcribed by Archie Green. "The Scissor Story" and other material reissued ca. 1965 on an LP album, *Myron Cohen* (Audio Fidelity 701). The 78 and the LP differ in that the latter holds a dubbed-in laugh-track.

Background

Myron Cohen (1902–86), a silk salesman in Manhattan's garment district, had heard traditional tales in Yiddish during childhood. Entering the "rag trade," he developed a joke line to entertain prospective buyers. Lore clung to him like lint in a dress shop. Breaking into show business, he found the nightclub stage and television studio more congenial than lugging his sample case in the "jungle." Achieving success as an entertainer, and with a loyal audience of fans, Cohen published a bag full of jokes in *Laughing Out Loud* (1958) and *More Laughing Out Loud* (1960).

To explain his shift from salesman to stand-up comic, Cohen repeated two intertwined anecdotes: Cohen's boss, tired of humor on company time, called him on the carpet, "Myron, you're a wonderful storyteller, you should get paid for telling jokes, but not by me." In another account of his move to show biz at Leon & Eddie's, Cohen told his boss, A. E. Wullschleger: "I'm gonna quit." (W) "Why?" (C) "They're gonna pay me $2500.00 a week." (W) "What, for the junk you tell?" (W, shaking his head sadly) "Remember, Myron, you can always have your old job back."

Needless to say, Cohen never had to return to "real work." His low-key delivery, coupled with a superb command of Jewish and other "greenhorn" dialects, endeared him to national audiences. Cohen's "Scissor Story" captured the humor of gifted needle-trades raconteurs, as it also helped unionists (International Ladies Garment Workers Union, Amalgamated Clothing Workers) laugh at their most sacred practice, the strike.

44

At the Door

There was a little girl who went to the door and a harvest hand, a Wobbly, was at the door asking for some work to do in order to get something to eat. She said, "Mamma, there's a bum at the door," and Mamma answered, "That isn't a bum; that's a harvest worker." A month later, the harvest was over and the same Wobbly was at the door rapping for some work and the little girl says, "Mamma, there's a harvest worker at the door," and Mamma replies, "That's no harvest worker; that's a bum."

Source

Joe Murphy, interview at Occidental, Calif., Sept. 23, 1978, for film *The Wobblies*. Text in Stewart Bird, Dan Georgakas, and Deborah Shaffer, *Solidarity Forever* (Chicago: Lake View Press, 1985), p. 45.

Background

In reportage and remembrance, IWW members have presented a grim portrait of the exploitation of transient labor in the Midwest wheat belt between 1915 and 1925. Sadly, some farmers, lawmen, and railroaders joined hand with criminals (then called "hi-jacks") to degrade workers who helped put bread on tables. When Joe Murphy, in *Solidarity Forever*, described acts of violence against harvesters, as well as Wobbly retaliation, he also noted other aspects of migrant life by recalling "At the Door."

"We told stories like that to amuse ourselves. You see, the IWW had a sense of humor, which the other radical organizations never did." Murphy was on target in asserting that Wobs exceeded other radicals at scoring laughter, although he overstated the case in his "never did" assessment. Paul Buhle displayed the breadth of occupational and radical humor in *Labor's Joke Book,* while historian David Roediger commented perceptively on left approaches to such material and modes in my *Wobblies, Pile Butts, and Other Heroes* (1993b, 131).

In seeking details for "At the Door" and possible sources, I queried Joe's widow, Doris Murphy. From her earliest meeting with Murphy in 1942, at a San Francisco bohemian bar, she recalls his reciting doggerel poems and singing IWW songs. In a letter to me, Doris suggested that Joe frequently told an ironic story, "At the Door," as "a vivid illustration of the hypocracy in which the employing class (even dirt farmers one harvest ahead of a bank foreclosure) treated workers fairly well if they could be useful to them, and humiliated them if they could not be. 'Just a month's difference' Joe would say 'between a bum and a harvest worker.'"

We are left to speculate on when and where Murphy first heard "At the Door." Although I have not found a variant, I do not believe that it belonged only to the IWW. I assume that other parallel texts will be found in settings beyond its farm-door threshold.

45

You Can't Buy Me

A. Randolph's Blank Check

What you heard was true. They [Pullman Company] went to him [A. Philip Randolph] twice and offered him some money. I don't know how much money they offered him, but he told them that the Brotherhood [of Sleeping Car Porters] wasn't for sale. And the third time they sent an instructor out of New York over to his office with a check. Blank. And told him to put his figures on him. And Mr. Randolph took the check and had it photostated, and he sent the check back, and he kept the photostat and framed it and put it in his office. Anyway, he had that check—it's true, he had that check. It's true, he had that check. He wouldn't sign it or accept it. It's framed, it's right in Mr. Randolph's office.

B. All the Gold in the World

You have heard the saying that a man couldn't be bought with all the gold in the world. Well, Victor [Berger] couldn't be bought with all the gold plus all the honor and flattery in the world. During the free-silver campaign of 1896 he had written in his *Daily Forward* a powerful argument against the fallacy of bimetallism. The argument was so devastating to the Bryan forces that the Republican National-al Committee, with millions to spend, had offered to purchase a large edition of the *Forward* for national distribution at his own price.

Victor refused. He was no more interested in the success of McKinley than in that of Bryan. And that . . . at a time when his treasurer, Louis Bayer, told me, Victor was so hard pressed for money that he paid the printers in nickels and dimes whenever they became too unruly. I myself saw the letter in which Hearst offered Berger fifteen thousand a year to write a weekly editorial for the Hearst chain. He turned that offer down, at a time when I know he came a darn sight nearer *owing* than owning fifteen hundred.

Sources

A. Fred Fair, interview with Jack Santino, Mar. 30, 1983. Text in *Miles of Smiles, Years of Struggle: Stories of Black Pullman Porters* (Urbana: University of Illinois Press, 1989), p. 62.

B. Account in Oscar Ameringer, *If You Don't Weaken* (New York: Holt, 1940), p. 296.

Background

In preparation for the Smithsonian Institution's Festival of American Folklife on the National Mall in 1978, Jack Santino interviewed retired Pullman porters. He staged a panel of porters recounting their experiences and, subsequently, extended fieldwork to produce a documentary film (1982) and a book (1989). The latter includes nine variants of the tale centering on Randolph's incorruptibility. In its many forms, this exemplum both honors the leader of the Brotherhood of Sleeping Car Porters and rank-and-file members who made integrity and dignity central to their identity.

Despite the wide circulation of "Randolph's Blank Check" and deep belief in its truth, no one ever saw the bribery paper. Apparently, the story dates to New Deal years when porters obtained an initial Pullman contract, overcoming decades of resistance to unionism among its black workers (Anderson 1972, 224).

The earliest printed reference to the blank-check tale appears in a 1937 article by G. J. Fleming: "Randolph did not run to cover. . . . There have been months on end when he has had to go without salary and during which he has had in his hands signed checks which he was invited to fill out for whatever amount of money he wished, the condition being that he turn his back on the Brotherhood of Sleeping Car Porters, but he drew his belt in a notch and returned the check or tore it up. He wouldn't sell his people down the river" (1937, 333).

Fleming's metaphor, sold down the river, dates to slavery days. Hence, it resonated powerfully among readers of *The Crisis*, published by the National Association for the Advancement of Colored People.

"Union Pride."

Essentially, "Randolph's Blank Check" served as a bridge narrative merging interests of trade unionists and civil-rights advocates.

The hero strong enough to reject worldly favors has long remained a theme in folk accounts of social and political movements. Oscar Ameringer, a socialist editor and raconteur, cited two instances of Victor Berger, Socialist Party leader, rejecting offers to "sell-out"—one from McKinley's presidential campaign staff, one from press mogul William Randolph Hearst. Although Ameringer, Berger, and Randolph shared belief in reform socialism, I do not suggest that only men of their political persuasion became magnets for anecdotes about personal honesty. Sailors' leader Andrew Furuseth—cut of a far different cloth than his Debsian socialist tormentors—allegedly refused a bribe of $10,000 in gold coins (See "Furuseth's Credo.")

The can't-buy-me theme emerged during the 1934 Pacific Coast maritime strike when Harry Bridges rose to power as an insurgent leader in the International Longshoremen's Association. At the strike's end, his associates circulated a tale involving the rejection by Bridges of a shipowners' bribe of "fifty thousand bucks—maybe more." No one seems to know when this account appeared, or the degree to which its initial audience accepted it as gospel truth.

In September, 1935, Tom Mooney testified at a habeas corpus hearing—but one attempt in his long effort to secure freedom. (I shall not detail his case from a Preparedness Day Parade bombing in San Francisco in 1916 to his release from San Quentin in 1939. See books by Richard Frost and Curt Gentry.) At the hearing, Mooney explained why the "big corporations" had put him in jail: "Just as they hate Harry Bridges today, they hated me then. Just as they would like to frame Bridges today, they framed me then" (Gentry 1967, 392).

Mooney was in jail throughout the Big Strike; we do not know who among his labor and political allies told him stories about Bridges. However, Estolv Ward used one such dramatic narrative to open *Harry Bridges on Trial*. (This 1940 paperback treated the government's initial effort to deport Bridges to Australia.) Three decades later, biographer Charles Larrowe summarized the tale: Facing a prolonged waterfront struggle, a shipowner suggested that Bridges would scuttle the strike for the right price. An ex-prizefighter made the offer; the unionist refused.

Larrowe, conscious that critics had questioned the bribe incident, added an ambiguous note bandied about by waterfront commentators: "You can say what you like about Bridges being a Communist or a fellow-traveler, . . . but you have to give the guy this much. He's absolutely incorruptible" (1972, 57). Are we to believe that Bridges was personally honest despite his Red beliefs, that Communists were corrupt, or that Bridges trod a path between idealized purity and daily experience?

Larrowe, sensing that he had found a "made-up" legend tying ideology to personality, attempted to verify the Bridges tale by noting that Randolph Sevier, a Matson shipping executive, had affirmed his company's action in providing the bribe money. Am I being too cynical in suggesting that Sevier may have enjoyed pulling Professor Larrowe into a folkloric bog?

Currently, labor historian Robert Cherny, San Francisco State University, is writing a biography of Bridges. Although the latter never alluded to the bribery story in interviews with Cherny, the historian may find details to elaborate its dissemination. He and I have shared notes on this perhaps-apocryphal story. We remain curious to find the threads that stitch unlikely figures (A. Philip Randolph, Victor Berger, Andrew Furuseth, Harry Bridges) into the "You Can't Buy Me" fabric.

46

Smartest Dog

A. Four Dogs

Four union workers were discussing how smart their dogs were. The first was a United Auto Workers member who said his dog could do math calculations. His dog was named T-Square, and he told him to go to the blackboard and draw a square, a circle, and a triangle; which the dog did with no sweat.

The United Steel Workers member said he thought his dog was better. His dog named Slide-Rule was told to fetch a dozen cookies, and bring them back and divide them into four piles of three; which Slide-Rule did with no problems. The Teamsters member said that was good but he felt his dog was better. His dog named Measure was told to go get a quart of milk and pour 7 ounces into a 10-ounce glass. The dog did this with no problems.

All three agreed this was very good and all the dogs were smart. They all turned to the United Mine Workers member and said, "What can your dog do?" The Mine Worker called his dog, who was named Coffee Break, and said, "Show these fellows what you can do." Coffee Break went over and ate the cookies, drank the milk, screwed the other three dogs, claimed he injured his back, filed for Workmen's Compensation, and left for home on sick leave.

B. Three Dogs

Three workers in the factory were discussing their dogs. The first worker said he had the smartest dog in the world. The other workers didn't believe such a boast and challenged him to prove it. The worker called his dog in:

"Chrysler, show the guys what you know."

The dog walked in on two legs, took a notebook out of his pocket and signed his name.

The second worker called his dog in:

"Ford, show the guys what you know."

The dog walked in, took out a cane, did a soft shoe and then read out of a book he had.

The third worker called his dog in:

"Cadillac [GM], show the guys what you know."

The dog walked into the plant and faked a back injury, got six months full sick pay, and went home and screwed some dogs.

They all agreed Cadillac was the smartest dog.

Source

A. Photocopied sheet obtained in 1977 by Louis Horacek in Moundsville, W.Va., from a UMWA member, a mine-safety inspector.

B. Collected by Richard Sandler, ca. 1980, in Detroit for "You Can Sell Your Body but Not Your Mind" (Ph.D. dissertation, University of Pennsylvania, Philadelphia, 1982).

Background

With the ready availability of office copy-machines in recent decades, thousands of humorous jokes and cartoons have circulated anonymously. I do not know when or where "Four Dogs" originated, and whether this UMWA story had traveled by word-of-mouth before someone typed it out and fed it to a photocopier.

Richard Sandler's "Three Dogs" represents a stripped-down variant of the West Virginia miner's tale. The former, told during an auto assembly-line break, identifies the "big three" auto manufacturers as competing dogs. In February, 1988, the *Industrial Worker* printed "A Unionist's Dog," a variant attributed to Ivan Grozni, in which three management-classified workers (engineer, accountant, chemist) pitted their dogs against Straight Time, a union member's dog, and lost.

47

Scientific Management

A. Efficiency

A Negro, recently from Georgia, came North with the exodusters. In Waycross, he had always been bent on pleasing his boss. He was hired at one of Ford's plants. His job was to thrust a strip of metal into a punching machine with his right hand. Thrust, withdraw, thrust, withdraw for eight hours a day with one hour for lunch and ten minutes out for the can. His foreman noticed that he was dissatisfied. "What's the matter, Booker?" he asked. Booker said, "I was jes' thinkin' that my left hand ain't doin' nothing. Maybe I could punch with my left hand."

So they fixed a contraption so that his left hand could thrust a second strip a little bit above the first. Booker was still dissatisfied. His feet were idle. So Ford got his engineers together and they fixed up a treadle for his right foot to work. Booker pointed to his left foot, just standing there. So they fixed a treadle for that foot. Then Booker was happy pedaling with both feet, punching with both hands.

A week later, Booker was moping again. He thought if they put a metal collar around his neck and attached it to the machinery he could get more work done by bobbing his head back and forth. Henry Ford and his son worked on such an invention, got it patented and put it on Booker's neck. Booker beamed.

Nevertheless, two weeks later, he was nearly crying. The foreman asked him what was the matter. Booker told him that he thought he wasn't doing enough work. The foreman was amazed. After all, he was a benevolent friend of labor. "You got both hands punching, both feet pedaling and your head bobbing. Why ain't you satisfied?" Booker brightened up. "I done figured it out. You see, Mr. Bossman, I believe dat if you stuck a broom up my ass, I could sweep de floor."

B. Mass Production

A certain Jewish mechanic, Abie Cohen, burdened with a large and dependent family, had looked for work for several months. Finally, becoming desperate, he applied at Ford and to his amazement was accepted.

Abie reported for work to his foreman, a Mr. Kuntz, pure Aryan. Kuntz looked his new hand over contemptuously.

"For God's sake, look what they're sending over now," he said, and to himself: "I'll get rid of this Jew bastard in a helluva hurry." "O. K., Cohen," he resumed. "Come this way."

He took Abie over to a corner.

"You see that switch over your head? Keep pulling that up and down every second with your right hand."

"O.K., boss! Like you're saying, so I'm doing."

Two hours later, Kuntz returned.

"How you doing, Abie?" Hoping he was worn out and ready to say quits.

"Fine, boss."

"Well, we got orders to speed up production. You see that switch over your left hand? Well, pull that one, too, every second as well as the right one."

Cohen, thinking of his large and inadequately fed family: "Just like you're saying, boss, so I'm doing."

Two hours later, Kuntz returned.

"How you doing, Abie?" Seeing that the new hand was by this time sweating profusely.

"Fine!"

"Well, we got orders to speed up production even more. New orders for cars coming in, and none in stock. You see that pedal by your right foot? Just press that down every second with your right foot."

"O.K., boss, just like you're saying, I'm doing."

Two hours later, Kuntz returned. Abie had stripped to his undershirt, and was sweating a great deal more freely.

"Well, how you doing, Abie?"

"Fine, just fine, boss!"

"Well, we're way behind. Got orders to speed up production. You see that pedal there by your left foot? Well, just press that every second, too."

"O.K., boss, just like you're saying, so I'm doing."

Kuntz started to walk away when Abie called after him.

"Oh, boss!"

"Yeh?"

"Say, maybe you could stick a broom up my behind and I could also could be sweeping off the floor."

C. TS Man

The autoworker is working on his machine and the Time-Study man comes down and studies him for a while. The TS man calls the foreman over and says:

"Joe is working fine, but notice how he doesn't use his left arm. Now, we have this little job over here that could be done with his left hand and this wrench."

The foreman thereupon assigns Joe to tighten a bolt with his left hand while he is operating the machine. A few months later, the TS man comes back, studies Joe for a while, calls the foreman over, and points out how Joe's right foot isn't doing anything and how, by extending a pedal to Joe's position, he could be operating the press next door.

The foreman assigns the job to Joe, who is not now only working the machine, but twisting the bolt with his left hand and bouncing on his right foot to operate the press. Later, the TS man comes by and looks at Joe for a while and gets the foreman to set a lever that Joe can operate with his left foot. The next time around, the TS man finds a job Joe can do with his right hand during part of the cycle when his right hand is idle.

Finally, the TS man comes by, sees Joe working with both his hands and feet, stands there and studies him. Joe quits working, calls the foreman over, and says:

"Get this son-of-a-bitch out of here! The next thing you know, while I'm doing all these other jobs, he'll have a broom up my ass so I can sweep up the floor."

D. Fayetteville Stretchout

You know, every now and then they'll have what they call a stretchout, make a man turn out more work, maybe run more [textile] machines. So, they had just put on what they call a stretchout, and they'd kind of added more work on everybody. And said this fellow, he went and applied for a job. So they asked him, said, "Do you think you could sit on this stool and work this foot pedal all day?" He said, "I believe I can. I'll try." So he got along all right with it.

The next day, he come back, they'd attached a lever, you know, to his machine. They said, "Do you think that you could work this pedal with your foot and pull this lever with your hand?" He said, "Well, I can try." So he got along all right with that.

A day or two later, they come back, and they'd attached another foot pedal. Said, "Do you think that you can work both of these pedals with your feet and pull this lever?" "Well, yeah, been getting along pretty good so far," says, "I'll try."

A day or two later, they come back, they'd attached another lever, you know. Says, "Do you think," says again, "You've been getting along pretty good with that," says, "You'll make more money if you can pull both of these levers and mash both of these pedals." So he said, "Well, I'll try." So he was getting along pretty good with it.

And the superintendent went to the supply room to get a broom for the janitor, you know, and he come back with this broom, and stopped by to see how the fellow was getting along. And he saw that broom in his hand. He just switched off his work and said, "I'm quitting right now!"

Superintendent says, "What in the world?" Says, "what are you quitting for?" Says, "You're getting along just fine."

He says, "Yeah, but," says, "when I started off here, you started me off pushing one pedal." Says, "and then you come and attached a lever to it." And said, "I got on all right with that." Said, "Then you come and attached another pedal," said, "I got along all right with that. And then you attached another lever." And says, "I've been sitting here a-pulling both of these levers and working both of these pedals," and says, "I'm doing all right with that. But if you think you're going to stick that broom handle up my rectum so I'll be a-sweeping the floor everytime I go to get a drink of water," says, "I'm quitting right now!"

Sources

A. Sterling Brown, untitled tale in a mimeographed undated joke collection. B. A. Botkin included it, as "Efficiency," in *A Treasury of American Anecdotes* (New York: Random House, 1957), p. 48. Brown's sheets

"Machine Man."

of 108 "Negro Jokes" can be found in Botkin's papers, University of Nebraska Library, Lincoln.

B. Dr. Morris Finkel interview with Jack Conroy, Chicago, May 11,
1939. Submitted by Conroy for WPA "Industrial Folk Lore" files, Library
of Congress.

C. William Friedland, letter to Archie Green, May 16, 1994.

D. Malcolm Shaw interview with Doug DeNatale, Spring Lake, N.C.,
June 20, 1978. Transcribed by DeNatale for "Bynum: The Coming of Mill
Village Life to a North Carolina County" (Ph.D. dissertation, University
of Pennsylvania, 1985), p. 423.

Background

Poet and cultural critic Sterling Brown carried superworker/exo-
duster Booker from Waycross, Georgia, to a northern Ford factory,
presumably in Dearborn or Detroit. Did Booker move north before
or after Dust Bowl refugees drove west? At the time of Hitler's
power in Europe, Jack Conroy heard Chicago surgeon Morris Finkel
relate Abie Cohen's adventures at Ford as a contest between a Jewish worker and Kuntz, a "pure Aryan" foreman. Bill Friedland, who
had worked at Hudson Motors and Ford's Highland Plant through
the 1940s, noted the "TS Man's" ubiquity in that decade. Then,
everyone knew the story; many gave it a personal twist. Malcolm
Shaw, who told "Fayetteville Stretchout" to collector Doug DeNatale, had worked in Piedmont cotton mills for a lifetime.

Our four narratives reveal a tale's coexistence in Anglo- and African-American tradition as well as in the auto and textile industries. However, the variants carry no internal dates, thus leaving readers and listeners free to speculate on the age of each. Along with questions of chronology, we ask whether "Scientific Management," in any form, moved from the Carolinas to Michigan, or reversed occupational migration patterns by travel from North to South.

Folk narratives twist through and under thorny hedges. During the New Deal years, the WPA Writers' Project brought together collectors and interpreters who placed their findings in large democratic frames. A ballad or tale might be harnessed to a populist wagon; a blues or a shanty might ring out a worker's courage or cunning; an assembly-line jest might become a parable on capitalist exploitation.

Sterling Brown and Ben Botkin "met" about 1930 through friendly correspondence on "The Blues as Folk Poetry," included in the latter's *Folk-Say, a Regional Miscellany*. After 1936, they shared duties in Washington in the national office of the WPA Writers' Project. I believe that Brown, then seeking a publisher for his joke collection, gave Botkin a copy. Without a firm date for the compilation, we can only speculate on its beginning and fate.

In the late 1930s in Chicago, Nelson Algren, Jack Conroy, and other relief-based writers experimented with turning "folk stuff" and "folk say" into proletarian fiction. Algren conducted "fieldwork" at racetracks and night courts; Conroy, at blue-collar bars and rooming houses. When Conroy heard "Mass Production," reflecting the wound of anti-Semitism in industry, he compared it to a previous tale that he had elaborated into "True-Blue Highpockets from Forks of the Crick."

Stephen Wade, a friend of Conroy, alerted me to a question about the authorship of "Highpockets." Douglas Wixson asserted that Conroy had shared the embellished "Highpockets" with his friend Algren, who turned it in at the Illinois WPA Project under his own name. The new tale aimed a satiric blast at the meeting of a tractable worker and a "time-study man, that mother-robbing creeper who watches you from behind dolly trucks and stock boxes." (For Conroy/Algren, see Wixson 1994, 439.)

"Highpockets" remained unpublished for four decades until Ann Banks rescued it in *First Person America*. The WPA typed sheets upon which she drew credited the sketch to Algren rather than Conroy. We do not know when or where Conroy first heard a joke about an overzealous autoworker, nor the precise circumstance of giving the finished tale to Algren.

I also lack leads on Sterling Brown's prime source for his Ford anecdote, but note that he attributed it to "traditional, freely rendered." He had taught at Virginia Seminary in the mid-1920s, where, in his words, he soaked up the wisdom and strength of his people "like a sponge" (1979, 17). Possibly, someone had found or commented upon a tale similar to "Efficiency" prior to Brown's compiling "Negro Jokes."

Another trail fork remains open. In 1946, Dorothy Shay, "The Park Avenue Hillbillie," recorded "Efficiency," a musical retelling of Brown's joke. She and Hessie Smith secured the song's copyright on March 27. Columbia Records released it within a 78-rpm set (C-119), and, subsequently, on two LPs: *Dorothy Shay Sings* (CL 6003) and *Coming 'Round the Mountain* (Harmony HL 7017). Whether or not Shay ever disclosed the relationship of her song to a traditional tale, I do not know.

In all available variants of "Scientific Management," we follow the adventures of a worker, nominally eager to please, who found a way to get back at various authority figures—foreman, superintendent, engineer, time-study man, efficiency expert. In short, a blue-collar hero turns the tables on white-collar "superiors." Our storytellers have no need to spell out their belief that such creatures are less than manly, unable to do "real" work. True men did not hide behind their slide rules, stopwatches, or college degrees.

On automobile assembly lines, at textile mills, and in countless nondescript plants, factory workers lived in a world of muscle, noise, grime, speedups, stretchouts, and physical danger. At times, job tension culminated in personal violence at home, shop-floor grievances, or bitter strikes. A thread of vernacular humor ran through all such actions, giving tellers and hearers who dealt with efficiency experts the vicarious means to mock bosses and their "scientific" hatchet men.

Stories about the encounter between working stiffs and time-study men have appealed to folklore collectors, writers, and singers. I can date Conroy's "Mass Production" to 1939, and guess that Sterling Brown heard "Efficiency" before WPA days. How long does a tale live in memory? When I visited Bill Friedland (February 14, 1993) at home in Santa Cruz, he reminisced about years "on the line" in Detroit. Subsequently, he wrote out his "TS Man" for me.

Where do additional variants lurk? Can we loop back to the earliest telling of "Efficiency" by an African-American exoduster? In what industries beyond autos and textiles did a parallel story take root? Has it been extended to modern robotized factories?

Do present-day workers who hear the tale's broom ending perceive it as a displaced wish to "shove it" to the time-study man about as far as his slide rule would go? Who makes explicit the hidden suggestion that sodomy might be accepted by a white-collar sissy, but rejected by a rugged factory hand? How many workers in their response move from sexual to social interpretation? Who grasps the linkage of this story's gung ho engineers to Frederic Taylor's formal pronouncements on Scientific Management? These questions roll endlessly. Answers lurk on the horizon.

48

Unhappy Secretary

There was this new young secretary on the job who always looked kind of unhappy. One day she got married. After awhile, one of the older secretaries, noticing that the younger woman still looked unhappy, took her to lunch. She said to the younger woman, "You don't seem to be very happy. Is there anything wrong?"

The younger woman replied that this was her third marriage and she was still a virgin.

The older woman asked, "How can that be?"

And the younger woman replied, "The first time that I was married it was to an old man who was kind and who had a lot of money."

The older woman said, "Oh, what happened?"

The younger woman said, "He died of a heart attack just after the wedding ceremony. I was real sad, but he left me a fortune; so I was OK. Later, I decided that since I had all of the money I would ever need, I would marry a young hunk whether he had money or not. Well, I met this man, and he was really good looking and had a great body, and so I married him. But he turned out to be gay."

The older woman said, "Oh, that's too bad."

The younger woman then said, "So I divorced him. I decided to get practical, and so I married the man I'm with now who's a systems analyst."

The older woman said, "Well that sounds good. So why aren't you happy now?"

And the younger women said, "All he ever does is sit on the edge of the bed and tell me how good it's going to be."

Source

Cathy Lynn Preston, "Folklorists Do It Orally," *Lore and Language* (forthcoming).

Background

Within an article on "Do It" bawdy slogans on T-shirts and bumper stickers, Professor Preston highlights wordplay on male identity expressed by linking sports, occupation, and sexual prowess: Plumbers Do It Deeper, Carpenters Do It Tongue-in-Groove, Stagehands Do It on Cue. Such texts in countless variations appear on clothing, automobiles, photocopied handouts, fax sheets, bulletin boards, latrine walls, and computer printouts.

"Do It" humor also makes its way into formulas aimed at the limited amatory power of intellectuals and white-collar professionals: Lawyers Do It Briefly, Hackers Do It with Bugs, Doctors Do It with Patience. At times, jesters expand slogans both of strength and weakness into anecdotes. Rosemary Joyce, in "Wall Street Wags," cites a joke (parallel to that reported by Preston) about a thrice-married virgin—elderly gentleman couldn't do it; homosexual wouldn't do it; stockbroker told her how great it was going to be (1982, 299).

In "Unhappy Secretary," the joke grows into a full narrative revealing solidarity between old and young office workers, as well as the latter's put down of a contemporary systems analyst caught up by abstraction to the point of impotence. Cathy Preston first heard this in the late 1970s, and notes that it has circulated since then, told by men and women. As an in-group white-collar tale, it has been directed against computer programers, scientists, and engineers who promise more than they deliver, or, symbolically, can only make love to their machines.

I find a rough correlation between the nonperforming third husband in Preston's tale and the time-study men lampooned in the several auto and textile stories clustered under "Scientific Management." Is not the systems analyst but a wimpy offspring of Frederic Taylor's efficiency expert? Here, I commend Professor Preston's provocative article to readers who have been puzzled by contrasts in physical and intellectual work, and have asked whether computer machines really do it to their human wizards.

49

Concrete Burial

A. Hand of Him

He was a cement worker. A good cement worker. He gave his best in the production of the things that make the world a good place to live in.

Not long ago he was employed on a bridge across the Mississippi River at Keokuk, Iowa. He helped build the great cement pillars upon which the bridge was to rest. And while he worked he fell into the mold built for the cast of one of the pillars.

The cement poured in. He was buried. The cement hardened. The mold was taken down. Out from the side of the pillar a human hand protruded. It was his. He gave his life to humanity.

The pillar is his monument. Fate sometimes does strange things; sometimes strikes at the very root of things and burns the truth into the minds of men.

B. Ghost of Suicide Bridge

'Most every one in the Highland Park section has heard the story which credits the spirit of a departed Mexican worker with luring almost two hundred persons to suicide on the famous Colorado Street bridge across the Arroyo Seco [Pasadena, California]. . . .

The story goes that when the concrete was being poured into the forms in the building of the huge pillars or piles which support the bridge, one of the Mexicans engaged in the work lost his balance and fell into the form of slimy concrete. For some reason his absence was not noticed for some time and the form had hardened in the meantime. The story has it that the body was never removed.

So in later years the ghost of that Mexican is said to have haunted the great span, luring those who were low in spirit to their untimely deaths!

C. Bath Bridge

"Your great-grandfather painted this bridge," my mother would always begin as my older sister and I [Angela Waldron] would give each other that here-we-go-again look, but we would nevertheless inch forward from the back seat in anticipation. With a captive audience she would continue, "Your great-grandfather helped to paint this bridge, and one day, as the bridge was nearing completion, an accident occurred. It seems a black man was in charge of the cement-pouring crew. Well, he slipped and fell into the wet cement. His co-workers, horrified, watched in vain as he was slowly cemented in and then died. Later, they put up a plaque to commemorate his death at work."

My mother would then point out the location where he had died and where he is said to remain today, entombed. My sister and I would look at each other and shiver in horror as she explained in detail how he fell and was slowly sealed in the cement in front of the crew. We would always ask why he was not saved and she would always reply that it was impossible because it happened too quickly. Elaine and I would look at each other and exclaim, in all our youthful innocence, "Can you imagine how he must have felt!"

Needless to say, the story, told by my mother with a sense of pride, always instilled in us not only a sense of awe but also an element of the horrific reality of death. Afterwards, we were always quiet and subdued until we had reached our destination [Brunswick, Maine].

D. Night Pour

I [Frenchy Gales] worked on a night pour at one of the anchorages [Golden Gate Bridge].

There were guys down in the cement. You'd walk on it to level it off. They took a count and we were short one guy. Everybody started stabbing around in the cement. We couldn't find the guy. We had to notify his family. The timekeeper asked me if I'd come with him.

It was 1:30 in the morning. We went to his home. Knocked on

the door. The guy answered in his pajamas. The timekeeper nearly fainted. The guy said, "I got tired. I went home and went to bed." That was the end of him on the bridge.

Sources

A. Chester M. Wright, extract from column, "Where the Human Stream Flows," *Los Angeles Citizen*, Apr. 4, 1913, p. 1.

B. "Collectors and Collections: Some California Legends," *California Folklore Quarterly* 4 (1945): 97. Items from 1942, in UCLA files of Southern California Writers' Project, WPA.

C. Angela Waldron, unpublished paper, "Encased in Concrete: A Contemporary American Legend," 1993, in Northeast Archives of Folklore and Oral History, University of Maine, Orono.

D. Frenchy Gale anecdote in John van der Zee, *The Gate* (New York: Simon and Schuster, 1986), p. 182.

Background

For two millennia, gifted storytellers have relished immurement tales about brick and stone masons ordered to entomb live prisoners within walls. Parallel narratives described the ritual offering of humans or animals by burial under or in temple foundations. Similarly, a set of ancient tales treated the sacrifice of living persons within bridge footings to appease gods angered by impediments to the river's flow to the sea.

Wayland Hand noted that human sacrifice to propitiate gods and immuring as punishment for civic crime represent discrete matters. However, Hand saw both acts as contributing to modern legends about construction workers accidentally trapped in cement on massive projects such as the Colorado River's Boulder Dam (1954, 133). Seemingly, building tradesmen have kept alive and blended a variety of ancient entombment motifs.

In 1968, Linda Dégh analyzed eighteen haunted bridge tales gathered by Indiana University students. Selecting a group title, "The Negro in the Concrete," she opened with a Highway 36 story, west of Indianapolis, where a saw protruding from the bridge's center support marked a worker's tragic misfortune. As this plot moved into teenage tradition, it often centered on dares to visit the bridge or adventures in confronting the revenant's eerie screams or moans.

In some Indiana variants the victims were not unlucky workers,

"The Bridge Pier."

but rather slaves and prisoners dumped into bridge chambers to save burial costs (62). Thus, we hear not only ghostly sounds of dead laborers but also the echo of a punishment theme within a series of modern accident narratives. Professor Dégh's tales, collected in the 1960s, can be viewed as twigs on a single branch which combine elements from "Hand of Him" and "Ghost of Suicide Bridge." How long did the former circulate before Chester Wright, in 1913, placed it in a newspaper column for unionists?

The use of iron-rod reinforcing bars in concrete pours to form dams, tarmacs, foundations, and structural building components dates to the 1880s. Hence, tales about concrete burials are "modern." Pietro Di Donato's novel, *Christ in Concrete* (1939), memorializes the death of his immigrant bricklayer father in a building collapse. This book continues to evoke the subliminal fear with which construction hands live.

Frenchy Gale, on San Francisco's Golden Gate span, inverted the morbid burial story by turning anxiety to grisly humor—a worker stupid enough to slip away unnoticed from a dangerous job. Alfred Pierre Gales (1901–92) survived the San Francisco earthquake in 1906, and worked as a laborer and ironworker on the Golden Gate Bridge. A superb raconteur, he appeared in Charles Kuralt's "On the Road" CBS television feature on the bridge's fiftieth anniversary.

Here, I reprint a narrative by Gales describing a nonfatal accident on "his" bridge:

The cement would back up over the top like water from a busted main. I got buried that way once. Oh Jesus, yeah. . . . I was down at the bottom getting ready for a pour—on my hands and knees cleaning up all the debris that the carpenters had dropped on that reinforcing iron, what we called the rattrap. I had a five gallon bucket and was throwing in all these pieces of wood and crap. Right about then, somebody wasn't paying attention and the chute flooded with cement. It backed up over the top and spilled out from about 20 feet in the air right on top of me. They used that huge 2½ rock in that cement, and everywhere the rocks hit me I got cut. I wasn't knocked out because I had a hard hat on but everywhere I was cut I got cement goo under my skin. My back was one big water blister (Cassady 1979, 50).

Frenchy Gale's detailed report of a personal accident, however pain-
ful, can be contrasted with his "Night Pour," a story subject to sardonic embellishment, and, possibly, reinforced by similar whoppers
about dumbells sneaking home. His two accounts, as well as those
above from Pasadena and Keokuk, illuminate wide differences in
tale-dissemination modes.

In Angela Waldron's recollection of an entombment legend heard
in childhood, we move away from the everyday work experience of
her great-grandfather, a bridge-painter, to the response of young-
sters to death. Angela and her sister Elaine heard their mother's
story literally as they approached the Bath Bridge en route to Brunswick to visit great-grandmother. Thus, actual site, family annals, storytelling act, and imminence of death fused into a powerful and
convoluted lesson—the bridge as physical tomb; the tale as child's
bridge from family circle to the external world of perils in work.

My comments on "Concrete Burial" have touched the response
by construction workers to tales of death on the job. I am conscious,
of course, that traditional stories hold multiple meanings. Alan
Dundes has made the point in recent studies of "The Walled-Up
Wife"/"The Building of Skadar," a ballad known from India to the
Balkans. In this narrative, men erect a castle, bridge, or monastery
by day. Each night, supernatural forces level the stonework. To appease the spirits and complete their task, masons entomb a wife or
sister. Dundes offers a feminist reading of this theme keyed to men
asserting power over women, and marriage as a state in which wives
are immured.

Listeners and readers may favor singular explanations for favorite stories or, alternately, fan out in many directions. Construction
men I have known interpret variants of "Concrete Burial" mainly as
a reminder of constant danger on the job. Angela Waldron's "Bath
Bridge," linked to variants from Indiana, Iowa, and California, brings
to the surface a victim's race. Her account, alongside those by
Frenchy Gale—one actual; the other, perhaps, embroidered—helps
us call up varied perspectives in assimilating ancient tales of masonry
immurement: a type of civic punishment; a sacrificial ritual for sacred ends; a metaphor for deep tension in gender relationships. We
are free also to peer ahead anticipating new twists in entombment
narratives as building technology alters daily with science-fiction
tools and laboratory-generated materials.

50

Got That Job

A. Millpond

There was the old story about the sawmill hand, walking along the road, who came to a millpond where the boom man had fallen into the water and was drowning. He yelled for help and the man on the bank said: "Where do you work?" "In that mill, there," came the answer. The man on the bank dashed away to the mill and told the straw boss, "How about a job?" "There isn't any job." "Go on, I just saw your boom man drowning." "Oh, the guy who pushed him in got that job."

B. Out the Window

They told a joke one time. This old two-story part [of textile mill]; the office was down at the lower end. And said this man—they [mill workers] all sometimes when they'd catch up would set up there in the window up there. There's a brick walk two stories down below there. Said this man come there; went down to the office and asked for a job.

[Boss] says, "We don't need no help," says, "Everybody was born and raised here," says, "They don't never change jobs unless someone dies," and says, "You don't stand much of a chance."

He thanked them, and come up on the sidewalk there, got on up there, and a fellow fell out the window, and got killed on the sidewalk.

This fellow run back up there. Says, "Look here," says, "A man just fell out the window up there and got killed." Says, "What about his job?" [Boss] said, "Man pushed him out gets his job."

Sources

A. Harvey O'Connor, *Revolution in Seattle* (New York: Monthly Review Press, 1964), p. 255.

B. John Wesley Snipes interview with Doug DeNatale, at Bynum, N.C., Aug. 22, 1979. Transcribed by DeNatale for Ph.D. dissertation, "Bynum: The Coming of Mill Village Life to a North Carolina County" (University of Pennsylvania, 1985), p. 422.

Background

"Got That Job"'s two variants spread across the continent reveal this ironic tale's ideological utility and traditionality. O'Connor knew partisans in Seattle's politically charged labor movement, from "revolutionary" days in 1919 through New Deal/Popular Front years. DeNatale, during his Bynum study, met several gifted Tar Heel yarners, mainly populist rather than socialist in sympathy. The contrast in rhetoric between "Millpond" and "Out the Window" reveals the range of stylistic expression utilized by workers in the United States.

In 1936, Carl Sandburg offered *The People, Yes,* a book of poetry grown from proverbial talk and folktale soil. A few of his lines parallel "Millpond" and "Out the Window," telling the story of the drowning worker who doesn't want to lose his job at the Malleable Iron and Casting Works. I see Sandburg's fragment, whose conclusion I quote below, as an isle in a Carolina-to-Puget-Sound archipelago raised upon jests about joblessness:

> You're ten minutes late. The man who
> pushed the fellow off the bridge
> is already on the job.

51

Third Nut

A Mexican in a large automobile factory was giving the final tightening to the nuts on automobile-engine cylinder heads. There are a dozen or more nuts around this part. The engines passed the Mexican rapidly on a conveyor. His instructions were to test all the nuts and if he found *one* or *two* loose to tighten them, but if three or more were loose he was not expected to have time to tighten that many. In such cases he marked the engine with chalk and it was later set aside from the conveyor and given special attention. The superintendent found that the number of engines so set aside reached an annoying total in the day's work. He made several unsuccessful attempts to locate the trouble. Finally, by carefully watching all the men on the conveyor line, he discovered that the Mexican was unscrewing a *third* tight nut whenever he found two already loose. It was easier to loosen *one* nut than to tighten *two*.

Source

Stanley B. Mathewson, *Restriction of Output among Unorganized Workers* (New York: Viking, 1931), p. 125.

Background

Mathewson gathered several near-apocryphal tales to illustrate his book's theme—workers devised ways to slow factory production whether or not they had joined unions. While managers found it difficult to cope with passive shop-floor resistance, some members of the IWW seized upon sabotage as a class-struggle weapon, raising stories of job action to rhetorical heights.

"Third Nut" holds special interest in its ambiguous reference to

"On the Line."

a Mexican worker. Although I have failed to trace the origin of
Mathewson's tale, folklorist Michael Heisley (in a letter to me) noted
parallel tactics among California farm workers: "El Plan de Tortuga."
During harvest season in the 1970s, fieldhands—seeking gain in
conditions or contractual advance—might slow down to a turtle's
pace.

A question remains about "Third Nut" in early circulation: Did
its initial narrators imply that a lazy or stupid immigrant new to the
assembly line could not follow instructions, or, more likely, that a
particularly canny character had come north from Mexico carrying
anarcho-syndicalist values? During the 1920s, Mexican authorities
hunted down followers of the rebel brothers Ricardo and Flores
Magon. Some rank-and-file Magonistas, believers in "Tierra y Lib-
ertad," sought refuge in the United States where they served as

radical catalysts in fields and factories. Could the unnamed hero of "Third Nut" have been a Magonista? Do we cast this assembly-line hand as saint or sinner? (For Mexican workers in Detroit, see Vargas 1993.)

52

Aunt Betya's Funeral

During the funeral ceremony, one of the aged comrades stood tear-fully at the head of Aunt Betya's casket, and began to deliver her eulogy praising the deceased's dedication to the cause of the world proletariat. In a voice thicker than *solyanka* [beef and barley soup], he intoned:

"I remember Comrade Betya at mimeograph tirelessly preparing leaflets all night, going at dawn to distribute at factory gate. (Voice breaking with emotion), I remember Betya selflessly making tea and *zakuskie* [sweets] for comrades, sweeping hall, never complaining, always cheerful. So exemplary and worthy of emulation was her conduct, I am tempted (voice gradually assuming the ominous res-onance of the commissar) to overlook many left-sectarian distortions of Leninism of which she was guilty, and idiotic promulgation of Bukharinite deviations in pernicious formulations of right-opportun-ist Lovestone. . . ."

Source

Lou Gottlieb, anecdote in "The Bloomington Conference," a report to *Folk News*, World Folk Music Association Newsletter, Washington, D.C., Sum-mer, 1991.

Background

In May, 1991, Indiana University hosted a conference on the folk-song revival and left politics. In a tongue-in-cheek report on the event, Lou Gottlieb recalled Gene Raskin's "Aunt Betya's Funeral." Enjoying the story for its toe-the-party-line tone and barbs at left-sectarian idiocy, I visited Lou in Occidental, California (May 27, 1994) to ask for the tale's history and to hear him narrate it.

In the early 1960s, Gene Raskin—architect, musician, play-wright—had composed a number of songs, including "Those Were the Days" for the popular trio, The Limeliters (Lou Gottlieb, Glenn Yarbrough, Alex Hassilev). Lou and Gene then shared reminiscences tinted with Yiddish humor touching high culture and radical cause. Lou absorbed Gene's story about Aunt Betya, altering it over the years.

Fortunately, we can reconstruct something of the interaction between two gifted raconteurs in that Raskin reported on his aunt's funeral in "The Kerensky Papers," a sketch within *Citronella*. I summarize: Uncle Aaron Gregorovich, a humble photoengraver, and his wife Aunt Betya, staunch members of the "Sozial-Demokrat Movement," shared the fate of countless Jewish emigrants and refugees from czarist Russia. Aaron enjoyed much prestige, for rumor whispered that he guarded certain documents vital to the restoration of the Kerensky government—a forlorn hope in the face of Soviet power.

Upon Betya's death in 1958, Pavel Pavlevitch stood at her modest coffin in Manhattan's Riverside Chapel and intoned: "Yes, we are here to say goodby to our dear comrade Betya Feodoronna, or just Betya, as we called her in the Movement, in the early, intimate days of the Movement. Ah, those days in Patterson-New-Jersey (it was spoken as one word) when we organized the first American branch of the Movement in 1921, our dear comrade Betya used to make stencils for our mimeograph machine and give us hot tea when we had a late meeting" (193).

In Raskin's full account, an aged comrade, tall and gaunt, followed Pavlevitch to the lectern, denouncing the former's error in that the Providence-Rhode-Island SD branch had preceded the Patterson-New-Jersey SD branch. Not only did the second speaker challenge Pavel on matters of chronology and geography but he moved on to denigrate Betya and widower Aaron by doubting the very existence of the Kerensky Papers. Essentially, the Providence partisan cared less for rituals mourning Betya than for the need to correct historical distortion.

The gaunt comrade continued the attack, contrasting his truth seeking "in the name of the working people of the world" against Pavel's heretical claims. Cries of "Shame! Da! Provocateur! Bolshevik tool" rang in the chapel to silence the traitorous critic. I shall not reveal the tempest's ending, but note that it serves as an example of much humor geared to yawning gulfs among radical trade unionists.

Gene Raskin, from childhood, knew the landscape of immigrant/ escapee radicalism infused with cultural spirit; in the 1940s, he viewed this scene anew, as he and his wife Francesca performed at labor meetings and demonstrations. As well, the duo recorded the first LP album issued by the International Ladies Garment Workers Union.

Lou Gottlieb, holding membership since 1939 in Local 47, American Federation of Musicians, has also observed internecine labor warfare. After visiting Lou, a friend from the 1950s, and corresponding with Gene Raskin, who generously sent me *Citronella,* I undertook to compare their respective stories about Aunt Betya. Three decades had elapsed between Lou's initial hearing of the anecdote and his 1991 recollection. Nor had he read Gene's book to refresh his memory.

Thus, as I pulled the two accounts together and presented them to Gottlieb, he expressed amazement at his adaptations and condensations, as well as how little he had remembered of Raskin's early story. Both narrators helped readers/listeners identify with Betya as against her polemical detractor. Despite Lou's changes, he and Gene converged in morally isolating the zealot unable to respect a peer's final rites of passage. Perhaps, from a proletarian abode, Betya smiles at her gaunt critic knowing that a fanciful tale about her funeral will continue to instruct and amuse working people.

53

Judge Gary's Blast Furnace

In 1950 the steel industry was acting badly, and C. E. Wilson, who was then the president of the General Motors Corporation, called me [Walter Reuther] up and he said, "I would like to talk to you and Philip Murray," who was then the president of the Steelworkers. We got together. C. E. Wilson said "I am getting bad reports from Pittsburgh in the steel industry. It looks like we are going to have a strike."

Now he was worried about the steel being cut off so that GM couldn't make cars.

So Philip Murray and I talked to him. He said, "Can I do anything?" We said, "Yes. You better go down to Pittsburgh and get your friends in the steel industry together, buy them a drink and do some missionary work."

He said, "Do you think it will help?" We said, "It is worth trying."

So he went to Pittsburgh, and he wined and dined the top executives of the steel industry, and he tried to tell them they ought to meet their responsibilities at the bargaining table. He came back a day later and called me up and said, "Come over, I want to give you a report."

I said, "What happened?" He said, "I have never been abused and vilified as I was at the end of that dinner after they ate my food."

And I said, "What happened?" He said, "They said, 'Wilson, if you hadn't been appeasing the labor bosses, if you hadn't worked out a contract with the Auto Workers, we wouldn't have this trouble with Phil Murray and the Steelworkers. What we need in America are fewer people like you who appease the labor bosses, and more people like old Judge Gary who fought the labor bosses [and] who destroyed the unions.'"

"Blast Furnace #1."

And I said to Wilson, "What did you say?" He said, "I said, 'Gentlemen, I have learned on good authority that Judge Gary, despite the fact that he was the President of the United States Steel Corporation for many years, never saw a blast furnace until after he died, and that is the way with the fellows running that industry today.'"

Source

Walter Reuther, extract from transcribed remarks on "Resolution in Support of the Steelworkers" at third constitutional convention, AFL-CIO, San Francisco, Sept. 18, 1959, *Proceedings*, p. 113.

Background

Living in San Francisco, I had occasion to attend union conferences and conventions, including the AFL-CIO gathering in 1959. Walter Reuther evoked great laughter among the delegates with his account of Charlie Wilson and Judge Gary. I happened to be sitting next to several newspapermen, when one cynic commented on Walter's punch line, "It was a good story when Ben Stolberg told it twenty years ago."

This offhand remark led me to *The Story of the CIO*, where, indeed, veteran labor reporter Stolberg had written: "In 1919 conditions in the industry were comparable to those in England at the beginning of the Industrial Revolution. Under the benevolent piety of the late Judge Gary, who never saw a blast furnace until after his death, the steel industry still enjoyed the twelve-hour day, the seven-day week, and the twenty-four-hour shift every two weeks" (1938, 67).

Elbert Henry Gary (1846–1927) a lawyer turned capitalist, represents the triumph of legal-political skill over practical experience. Hated and feared by working people, Judge Gary also became the butt of jokes from fellow industrialists who had started at the open hearth, and who boasted about "dirt under their fingernails." I do not know when the blast-furnace-in-Hell yarn first circulated, or how it reached Stolberg or Reuther.

William Serrin noted an arrangement at Gary's elaborate funeral at Wheaton, Illinois, which seems to have been designed to counter any after-death encounter in Hades (1992, 160). Judge Gary's extra-heavy coffin, made of high-quality steel, had to be carried by ten rugged Northwestern University football players, including Red Grange's brother. Should we believe that this special coffin kept Gary from final blast-furnace judgment?

54

Slow Pay

A. Funny Smell

The culprit was my [Walter Simmons] great uncle, Everett Newman, and it took place in Northeast Harbor, Maine.

As I recall, the story was that he was hired to do some work for some summer people. He took the job because he needed the work despite the fact that they were notoriously slow paying their bills. The work involved new wood paneling (likely tongue and groove in those days) in a living room with a fireplace.

At the end of the job, he presented his bill—and was put off with some excuse or another, and the promise that he would be paid the next day. He wasn't paid the next day or the one after that either.

On the third day, they called to tell him that there was a funny smell in the living room, and asked if he would come over to see what he could do. When he got there, he told them that he could take care of the smell just as soon as they paid him for the work he had already completed.

Once they paid him, he went into the living room, reached up inside the fireplace, and removed the dead cod that he had left on top the damper.

B. Mason's Trick

There is another variation involving a mason here in Lincolnville. Same circumstances [as above] but involving the construction of a new chimney. After the mortar hardened, the owner lit a fire but couldn't get the chimney to draw, and the house filled with smoke. Called to correct the problem, the mason (once paid) climbed to the top of the chimney and dropped a brick down the flue. The brick shattered the glass pane that he had installed midway. Nice trick, because, initially, there was no apparent blockage [when the home owner had peered up the flue to check on the chimney's failure to draw].

Sources

A. Walter Simmons, letter to David Taylor, May 13, 1994.
B. Same.

Background

Construction hands tell stories of being tricked or pressed into public-works jobs ("Baltimore City Jail"), their own schemes against bosses and building inspectors ("Measuring Rod"), or their ploys to get free drinks ("Detroit River Telephone Cable"). To our set of trickster tales, Walter Simmons, proprietor of the Duck Trap Press, Lincolnville, Maine, brings two choice yarns by tradesmen of tricks designed to pry wages loose from slow-paying home owners. Simmons has combined a long career as a boatbuilder with a series of books on his craft from lofting to launching. In *Pigeons and Gudgeons,* a compendium of technical and colloquial boatbuilding terms, he illustrates the ease with which some workers step from shop floor into the arcade of scholarship and publication.

Simmons offered "Funny Smell" and "Mason's Trick" as his own straight reportage—just the facts. We find hidden in each laconic account the distance yet interdependence between summer people (or affluent vacationers) and local blue-collar handymen. No one can deny that home-repair mechanics in Maine dreamed and talked about getting even with tightwad home owners and by-the-day employers. We test the traditionality of such stories by finding relatives from the Atlantic to the Pacific.

Jan Brunvand, the indefatigable collector of urban legends, heard a fine glass-sheet-in-the-flue and choking-clouds-of-smoke tale from a builder in Youngstown, Ohio, who called a radio talk show on which the folklorist had appeared. The builder prefaced his report with a bit of blue-collar philosophy, "The most common bricklaying work is putting up chimneys, and the hardest part of the job is collecting full payment" (1989, 260).

Searching for similar stories, I pause to comment on modern

forms of dissemination for old tales. David Taylor at the American Folklife Center, Library of Congress, and I have exchanged reports on our respective explorations in occupational lore. On May 13, 1994, by telephone, he passed along to me the codfish joke, recalling it from a past visit with Simmons at his Maine woodworking shop. When I asked about the source for "Funny Smell," Taylor called Simmons, who sent it, along with "Mason's Trick," to Washington, D.C., by fax. David then relayed the pair of stories to me in San Francisco by regular mail.

55

F-E's Stenographer

"R-O" was a labor spy and his life, for present consumption, begins with his death. His parents didn't christen him with those cryptic, slightly sinister, hyphenated initials. They were the gift of the Corporations Auxiliary Company, the gigantic industrial detective agency which secretly employed him for the last twenty-odd years of his life. His real name was Jack Peters, or something of the sort, and he lived and followed his profession in Wheeling, West Virginia.

At the time of his death, he was a member in good standing of the Amalgamated Iron, Steel and Tin Workers, the business agent of the Wheeling Machinists local and the president of the Central Labor Union of that city. During the famous and heroic steel strike of 1919, Bill Foster entrusted him with the direction of affairs in the Wheeling district which had been his battleground through thirty years of labor history.

In those stormy days, five years ago, ["R-O"] was always the most impatient of the conservatives, the most eager for radical reform. He was the loudest, too, at denouncing the injustice of press and police, and the most loyal for a delicate or a confidential mission. When he died his unions mourned him and buried him with all suitable pomp. It wasn't easy for the mourners to believe that, during the progress of the strike in which he cut so dashing a figure, he had telephoned hourly reports to the strikers' most malevolent enemies. It seemed outrageous to be told that he was the actual author of many of the Steel Corporation's voluminous blacklists.

The truth about ["R-O"] came so picturesquely to light that it supplies a subsidiary story. In Wheeling, the branch office of this Corporations Auxiliary Company was presided over by one Anderson, known to his spies as "F-E," which initials are interpreted to signify "Field Executive." Anderson would sit at his desk, interview his agents and send his reports off to the Pittsburgh office whence, presumably, they were relayed on to the employers who are willing to pay money for such service. Most unfortunately for the Corporations Auxiliary Company, Wheeling Branch, Anderson's stenographer fell ill.

Now the office of the local Labor Detective is always a target for local labor curiosity and resentment. Anderson's stenographer being, for the time, out of the running, Anderson called in a young lady who worked for a public stenographer in the same building. The young lady was either sister or fiancée to an energetic (and curious) Wheeling labor leader. She reported upon the kind of dictation which was being given her in the detective's office.

The thing, then, was to obtain texts of those daily reports and to identify the confusion of initials numbers by which Anderson referred to his crusaders. This proved difficult. Anderson's habit was to dictate his day's summary of information received and progress made, to sit close by while the shorthand was transcribed, then to destroy the shorthand pages, to mail the original of the typewritten drafts and to lock up the carbon in the safe. The girl herself hit upon the device which defeated his precautions, exposed industrial espionage in Wheeling and turned mourning for Jack Peters' death into regret for his life.

First she made certain that Anderson could not read shorthand. Then she came every morning with a duplicate note-book concealed in her blouse, the approximate number of pages filled with shorthand characters. Exchange of note-books presented no serious problem. Anderson destroyed the counterfeit: labor studied the genuine articles.

Source

Sidney Howard, *The Labor Spy* (New York: [New] Republic Publishing Company, 1924), pp. 2–5.

Background

From February 16 to March 30, 1921, the *New Republic* published a set of stinging exposés of then-rampant industrial espionage in the United States. The year before, Richard Cabot, Harvard professor of

"Mine Guards, Spies, and Gunmen."

social ethics, had provided funds for research by investigators Sidney Howard and Robert Dunn. The magazine also circulated *The Labor Spy,* a pamphlet reprint of the findings. Subsequently, Howard expanded the articles into a paperback book which appealed widely to union activists and liberal allies. A full decade elapsed before the Senate Committee on Education and Labor (the La Follette Committee) brought public attention to bear upon the violations of workers' rights previously revealed by a few dedicated muckrakers.

Sidney Howard (1891–1931) sought a playwright's career while still a student at the University of California. Among his teachers, economist Carleton Parker had influenced him with then-challenging reports on casual labor in agriculture and industry. Howard's wartime experience as an ambulance driver in the Balkans and a pilot in France prepared him both for crusading journalism and realistic drama touching subjects as diverse as rum-running and the conquest of yellow fever.

I have not traced the biographies of agents "R-O" or "Field Executive" Anderson. However, I have touched their unsavory environment in studying the word *fink* (see *Wobblies, Pile Butts, and Other Heroes*). In excerpting "F-E's Stenographer" from *The Labor Spy,* I assume that Sidney Howard had talked to unionists in West Virginia who knew firsthand the havoc wreaked by company detectives and provocateurs. Wheeling labor loyalists also relished a "subsidiary story" about a public stenographer who outwitted the corporate janissary. I share Howard's pleasure in relaying and perhaps embroidering an anecdote of a sister's bravery, and wonder where similar tales can be found?

56

Saloon Doors

A. *Erickson's Saloon*

A favorite story around Erickson's [Portland, Oregon], which had five entrances from three streets, concerned a character called Halfpint Halverson, a troublesome Swede logger who liked to argue about the comparative abilities of different nationalities. On one such occasion, when Halfpint disregarded Jumbo's warning, the bouncer plucked Halverson by the collar and pants and threw him bodily out the Second Avenue entrance.

Halverson presently wandered in through one of the three Burnside Street doors. Out he went again in a heap. This continued until he had been ejected through four different doors. Working his way around to the Third Avenue side, Halverson made his entry through the fifth and last door. Just inside stood the mountainous Jumbo. Halverson stopped short: "Yesus!" he said, "vas yu bouncer en every goddam saloon en Portland?"

B. *Corner Saloon*

J. W. Kelly, the Rolling Mill Man, who invented the joke about the corner saloon with three doors on two streets, had gone on the Celestial Circuit, where he doubtless convulses the angels to this day. Kelly, according to his own story, went into a saloon and drank until the bartender refused him liquor—a prim pre-Volstead custom.

Kelly walked out, went around the corner, saw the other door and reentered, thinking he had found another saloon. Again he was refused. Out went Kelly, only to reenter by the third door. But the bartender ordered him out.

"Good God, man," yelled the astonished Kelly, "do you tend all the bars in the city?"

Sources

A. Stewart Holbrook, anecdote in "The Longest Bar" in *The Far Corner* (New York: Macmillan, 1952), p. 84. Appeared as "Ericson's: Elbow Bending for Giants," *Esquire,* Apr., 1954. Reprinted in Brian Booth, ed., *Wildmen, Wobblies & Whistle Punks: Stewart Holbrook's Lowbrow Northwest* (Corvallis: Oregon State University Press, 1992), p. 221.

B. Edward Marks, *They All Sang* (New York: Viking, 1935), p. 131.

Background

Stewart Holbrook, in a stream of books and articles, helped popularize the exploits of loggers and fellow workers in extractive industries. He veered from ethnographic reporting to fiction, always with an entertaining pen. August Erickson, a native of Helsinki, Finland, presided for more than forty years at a magnificent saloon two blocks from the Portland waterfront. When flooded out in 1894, he chartered a big houseboat, moored it on skid road, and continued to dispense cheer to working stiffs who arrived by fir logs, rafts, and towboats.

Saloons served working people ambiguously—offering welcome surcease from toil as well as health-destroying habits. Each watering hole, also, became a setting for turning job experience into tall tale. Logger Halverson may have actually wandered in and out of Erickson's doors. More likely, a creative soul recycled an old Bowery joke, dating to the 1880s, and attributed, accurately or not, to John W. Kelly, the Rolling Mill Man. I have treated Kelly's Homestead steel strike song, "A Fight for Home and Honor," in *Wobblies, Pile Butts, and Other Heroes.*

57

Rotary Club

This story is usually set in Mexia [Texas], which is where it should have happened, if it happened at all. The Mexia boom came just as the Ranger boom was ending, and drillers from the Ranger area rushed to Mexia looking for work. There they were disappointed, for they were cable-tool men and did not know how to operate the rotary equipment being used in the new field. This meant that if they found work at all, they had to begin as green hands at a considerable loss of pay and prestige.

One day some cable-tool drillers were walking down the street when one noticed a Rotary Club symbol on a restaurant window. "Look," he exclaimed to the others. "The sons of bitches even have a club!"

Source

Mody Boatright, *Folklore of the Oil Industry* (Dallas: Southern Methodist University Press, 1963), p. 199.

Background

For books and articles exuding sheer pleasure in gathering and spreading oilfield lore, Mody Boatright stands taller than the highest Texas derrick. I had the pleasure of swapping waterfront for oil tales with him during teaching visits at the University of Texas.

Mody's "Rotary Club" rests on knowledge of internal rivalry between "old-fashioned" cable-tool crews and "modern" rotary-machine workers. Over the years drilling changed from hand power to steam boilers to diesel-electric motors used in turning the pipe drill-

"A 'Rope-Choker' Cable Tool Driller."

bit (tool). In the 1920s, some cable toolers, facing new rotary techniques, quit the trade rather than take up the despised innovation.
Boatright's story illustrates a wry joke functioning to relieve tension
generated by technological "advance."

West Virginia drillers called themselves "snakes," in boasting that
Appalachian rock formations were so hard that only a snake could
get through the strata. For a literary story on oilfield rivalry, see
"'Snake' Magee and the Rotary Boiler" by Jim Thompson; manuscript in the files of the Oklahoma Federal Writers' Project (Botkin
1944, 538).

58

Pea-Soup Fog

A. Stop-Watch Skipper

These vessels [Canadian Pacific Railroad], which run on the Vancouver, Victoria and Seattle route, are notorious for keeping to their schedules, in spite of heavy mists and fogs that frequent Puget Sound and the Coast. It is rumored that so well do the masters know the courses that they handle their vessels with a stop-watch. For instance, in a fog, the skipper will give a course, hold it for so many seconds, and then change it for so many minutes or seconds more. They have things worked out pretty fine.

One time one of these glorified ferries ran into a pea-soup fog. She had a new mate on board and he was nervous. After four or five hours of pelting full speed, the master sent the first officer for'ard and stopped the ship. "Jump!" he said. "We're there!" "But I can't see a damned thing!" protested the first officer. "Jump anyway!" roared the skipper. "There's the wharf right alongside!"

So the first officer jumped blindly into the fog overside, and sure enough he hit the wharf. That's navigating! Split second stuff! The skipper put his stop watch away and took a drink. They say he didn't even look to see what happened to the mate. He knew!

B. In the Early Morning Dew

At the tender age of 17 years, I [Al Smiley] had taken a job as a Quartermaster, on the old *Skagit Queen* with Captain McDonald, Senior. On this particular trip, we were headed from Seattle and Way-Points to Mt. Vernon, and after leaving Utsaladdy, we headed for the Skagit River, and right into pea-soup fog.

Captain McDonald said, "BOY, go down to the Fore Deck and keep a good look out, and sing out if you see anything."

Being a dutiful "Boy," I took this job seriously (as I should) and after some time, all at once, a Black Patch appeared, and "Boy" shouted, in the best sea-faring-style, "Something dead ahead, Sir."

Captain came back with, "What is it?"

By this time, I could see it was a a flock of ducks, and called back, "It is ducks, Sir."

Back from the Pilot House, came this reply, "Are they swimming or walking?"

Sources

A. Albert Richard Wetjen, letter to B. A. Botkin, 1929, printed in Botkin, *A Treasury of Western Folklore* (New York: Crown, 1951), p. 671.

B. Al Smiley contribution to *Piling Busters Yearbook: Stories of Towboating as Towboat Men* (material gathered between 1951 and 1953, and published for Retired Tugboat Association) (Gig Harbor, Wash.: Peninsula Gateway, 1978), p. 107.

Background

Tall tales of pea-soup fog and magnificent seamanship have entertained mariners and landlubbers in many local and world ports. Such stories recall the days before radar, gyroscopic compass, loran, or computer-directed navigational gear. Then, skippers and lookouts depended on bells, whistles, and generous use of their "seventh sense."

Our two stories from Puget Sound, although decades apart, complement each other. Quartermaster Smiley, resorting to the first-person voice, seemingly avoided the view that folktale equates with falsehood. By contrast, Captain Wetjen, employing the device "it is rumored," cast his tale in traditional form. However, both narrators, despite obvious truth-stretching, reinforced the inland boatman's immense pride in skill at the water's edge.

59

Worked to Death

This fella was suspicious of his wife fooling around and he worked at Ford's. Most of them did hard work, most worked in the foundry, and when they'd come home they were beat because of the heat and hard work.

This fella, he was suspicious of his wife. One day he kisses her goodbye, takes his lunch pail and leaves. Fifteen, twenty minutes later he comes back, tip-toeing into the house, and he sees some son-of-a-bitch there in bed with his wife.

He's ready to slit his throat, but he pulls the cover back, sees he had a Ford badge, and he says:

"Ah, shit, he can't do nothing."

[Aside by narrator, the Ford man's so worked to death he can't do nothing!]

Source

Collected by Richard Sandler, ca. 1980, in Detroit from a Ford worker for "You Can Sell Your Body but Not Your Mind" (Ph.D. dissertation, University of Pennsylvania, Philadelphia, 1982).

Background

Considerable factory humor centers on sex, family life, and mainstream morality. Richard Sandler heard "Worked to Death" as a joke on exhausting labor demanded at the Ford foundry. It also comments on the fear of impotence induced by backbreaking labor—in this instance projected away from a cuckolded foundry hand to a worthless intruder.

In the *Journal of American Folklore* (1993a), I have treated a related tale cycle hinging upon bosses imposing themselves on workers' wives. These sneaking-home narratives range widely from rationalizing cuckoldry to fighting harassment by organizing unions. I believe that "Worked to Death" can also be found in varied settings with diverse messages implied by each storyteller.

60

Saviors

A. Saving the Blacks

When I [David Broder] was sent out on the presidential campaign trail for the first time in 1960, I was introduced to the ritual of "saving the blacks." It was not a civil rights slogan, but a mutual self-protection arrangement among reporters.

When you handed your story to the Western Union man (yes, child, there really were Western Union men in those days), you saved your "blacks" or carbon copies. If one of the brethren were too drunk to write a coherent story of his own, some senior reporter would come through the bus collecting "blacks" from the rest of us. He would borrow a paragraph from this story and another from that and quickly piece together a passable composite under the byline of the besotted journalist.

Thus the paper whose correspondent was out of commission was "protected" from being scooped and the errant soul would get no grief from the home office.

B. Saving the Dupes

In 1923, San Francisco's community churches inaugurated Easter Sunday sunrise services atop Mt. Davidson. Each year the major papers sent reporters and photographers to cover the event. One morning, an *Examiner* photographer could not make the service, calling in with a lame excuse. The resourceful city editor sent for a "dupe," last year's photo. Who would know the difference?

Many irate, keen-eyed readers did complain, for the morning reporter had noted the City's characteristic weather—so thick, one could not see the fog-shrouded top of the mountain's cross. Sadly, last year's picture had been shot on an unusually clear sunny morning.

Sources

A. David Broder, "The Press Is on Shaky Ground," *Washington Post*, Nov. 15, 1987, p. C 7.

B. Lynn Ludlow told me this anecdote, Aug. 31, 1992. I wrote out the text as soon as he left my home.

Background

Following the Gary Hart/Donna Rice debacle in 1986, many reporters wrote reflective and reflexive pieces on political life. Should newspapers extend a protective cocoon to public figures? When should journalists curb voyeuristic impulses and hide dereliction in others?

Raising such issues, Broder recalled "a cozy, comfortable arrangement" in which newsmen protected each other from harm. He identified the custom of saving the blacks as a ritual, elevating his recollection to a self-contained story in which memory joins event to create a moral tale: Reporters who banded together in solidarity on campaign buses, as well as professionally in the Newspaper Guild, might well delay casting "first stones."

Seeking to trace Broder's story, I queried Lynn Ludlow, *San Francisco Examiner* op-ed editor. He knew a related practice as "Saving the Dupes," suggesting a wider range of "saviors" than carbons. Also, Ludlow allowed that his tale might be apocryphal, but confirmed that seniors told it as a form of job-training to warn young reporters against resorting to "dupes."

Storytelling pleasure occurs when a listener adds a corroborative detail. I had read "Saving the Blacks" in 1987 and heard "Saving the Dupes" in 1992. On June 3, 1994, in Seattle, I told both to a group of Pacific Coast labor-press editors. Roger Yockey, Local 1105, United Food and Commercial Workers, had worked in 1962 on the *Milwaukee Sentinel.* In those precomputer days, his fellow reporters called carbon copies of their stories "dupes."

Ted Schuchat, retired Baltimore newsman, in a letter to me, added a lexical twist to these accounts: He had heard *blacksheet* as a call-for-help verb rather than a carbon-copy noun. Ted illustrated: "I didn't make the story, will you blacksheet me on this one?" We sense such language's utility and longevity in Ben Bradlee's comment on the *Washington Post* during its sleepy era. Then, the paper's Pentagon correspondent had skimmed other reporters' carbons for his stories; his "nickname was 'Black Sheet' (as in carbon paper)" (279). Newsmen across the continent—Broder, Ludlow, Yockey, Schuchat, Bradlee—confirm that even the least-mysterious tale holds promise for future study—strange words, odd symbols, fresh meanings.

61

Vacation Time

A. Request Denied

Back in the old days, Sam Gompers hired a few staff assistants, usually men who had advanced in office in their respective international unions. Some of them would get a top union job, a sinecure, and stop working. Some of them could never be reelected in their own unions after their initial victories. (Now, we call them regional reps of the AFL-CIO.)

One day, a rep came in to see Mr. Gompers, and said, "I've worked for you faithfully for twenty-two years, and now I'd like to take a vacation."

Gompers looked at the supplicant and shot back, "Request denied. You've been on vacation for the last twenty-two years."

B. Chair-Warmer

One of the many manifestations of the conservative AFL bureaucracy is the so called chair-warmer type of organizer. Such organizers draw big wages and do nothing constructive. About the only time they can be galvanized into action is when it is a case of fighting back some progressive movement struggling to improve the unions, on which occasions they display an amazing vigor and activity.

Chair-warmer organizers have long been targets of attack by progressives and revolutionaries in the labor movement. But I [W. Z. Foster] never knew a criticism more effective than one made offhand by Samuel Gompers, himself the king of labor chair-warmers, to a typical AFL conservative, do-nothing organizer in Pittsburgh.

Gompers happened to be in Pittsburgh, and in the course of his conferences, the organizer, an old veteran, requested that he be

"Samuel Gompers."

granted a month's vacation. Gompers, with a drink or two under his belt, listened to the request and then inquired:

"Now, let's see, Tom, how long have you been on our payroll?"

"It'll be twenty-five years next November," replied the organizer.

"Well," said Gompers with a sly grin, "don't you think that's vacation enough?"

Sources

A. John F. "Jack" Henning, secretary-treasurer, California Labor Federation, told me this joke in his San Francisco office, Dec. 19, 1984.

B. William Z. Foster, *Pages from a Worker's Life* (New York: International Press, 1939), p. 275.

Background

Jack Henning's "Request Denied" and Bill Foster's "Chair-Warmer" come from within and without the labor movement, yet both comment with humor on officials often called "pie cards" or "pork choppers." Henning had heard the joke decades ago from a labor leader who knew Sam Gompers as president of the American Federation of Labor. I assume that Foster also heard a variant in the 1920s or 1930s, elaborating upon it from a "progressive" perspective.

Foster's narration holds a bit of irony. As a longtime leader in the Communist Party of the United States, he, too, warmed a few bureaucratic chairs, managing to survive long periods of drought in his party. Did his own dissident rivals view Foster's tenure as a perpetual vacation?

62

O'Shaughnessy Guards the Gate

Terence Sean O'Shaughnessy was doin' guard duty at the main gate
of the [steel] Works. Comin' and goin', he knew every man jack who
passed through those gates on the day shift. Only the good St.
Patrick himself could get by O'Shaughnessy, the men used to say,
and even then, he'd have to prove to Terry that he *did* drive the
snakes out of Ireland.

Well, anyway, one rainy day, who drives up to the gate demanding to enter but the wives of three Front Office Boys.

"Ye'd oughta know better me pretties," chides Terry in his best
blarneyin' tone. "It's bad cess to us when ladies are among us here.
Old Betsy [furnace] is a jealous mistress. She'll not pour nicely. So,
go ye now home, lassies, to your imroid'ry and cookery. Else your
men will go hungry—and *worse,* this very day!"

Then Terence Sean O'Shaughnessy did a strange thing. He spat
three times, once toward the Monongahela; once toward the Alle-
gheny; once toward the Ohio. Then, mumbling some spell, he crossed
himself and returned to his two-by-four shack out of the rain.

Source

Jacob Evanson, "Folk Songs of an Industrial City," in George Korson, ed.,
Pennsylvania Songs and Legends (Philadelphia: University of Pennsylvania Press, 1949), p. 428.

Background

Among long-held superstitious beliefs, steel millhands, coal and
hard-rock miners, and mariners have asserted bad luck when women
enter their workplaces. When pressed to explain such fear, men

suggested that they had to protect women against the dangers of their work sites. This explanation may well have rationalized other anxieties. Interestingly, O'Shaughnessy's furnace carried a feminine name, Old Betsy.

Jacob Evanson, a Pittsburgh music teacher, pioneered in collecting steel-mill lore. He attributed "O'Shaughnessy Guards the Gate" to Mary Means as told to her by an old-time steelworker. I have not learned the date or circumstance of Mary Means's tale. It holds interest beyond occupational tradition in O'Shaughnessy's attempt to ward off danger by invoking a three-spit ritual topped by the sign of the cross.

63

You're Fired

A. Mr. Sorensen

Mr. Sorensen is often cited as the epitome of the hard-boiled Rouge [Ford Motor Company plant] attitude and he undoubtedly belongs to the two-fisted type of plant superintendent. One of the many stories relates that Mr. Sorensen, strolling through the plant, saw a man sitting on a box, working with a length of wire. Sitting is not encouraged at the Rouge where jobs are strictly of the stand-up variety. So up to the workman went Mr. Sorensen and kicked the box out from under him. Getting to his feet, the workman hit Mr. Sorensen in the jaw. Getting to *his* feet, Mr. Sorensen said: "You're fired."

"The hell I am," said the workman. "I work for the Bell Telephone Company."

B. Ford Executive

The toughness of the Ford management was legendary in the industry. One story about the plight of the Ford workers, used widely by union speakers in organizing talks, went as follows:

A certain Ford executive with a reputation as a toughie was strutting through the plant when he noticed a worker seated on a nail keg, splicing some wires. Sitting down on the job was strictly against the plant rules in that building. Without warning, the executive kicked the keg from under the worker, spilling him on his rump. The worker bounced to his feet and smacked the executive into a tailspin.

"You're fired," the executive roared as he scrambled upright.

"The hell I am," the worker said. "I work for the telephone company."

C. Eager-Beaver MacKie

This story dates from about 1935—at that time it was making the rounds of that part of the AT&SF Railway known as the "Coastlines" (that part of the railroad west of Albuquerque and Belen, New Mexico). It concerned the Assistant General Manager for that part of the railroad, a real eager-beaver by the name of F. J. MacKie. MacKie was the type who would tear the head off some $100.00-a-month station agent if he happened to find two brooms in the warehouse. MacKie would always end by ordering the agent to return one of the brooms to stock as surplus.

Anyway, as the story goes, MacKie was on the station platform at Bakersfield, California, watching the passenger trains arrive and depart. As a train pulled in, he saw a guy dressed in what was then the traditional railwayman's uniform of blue-and-white striped overalls with cap to match—sitting on a baggage truck down by the head-end of the train watching the crew of baggage and express handlers work the train.

MacKie assumed that the guy sitting on the truck was another baggage smasher indulging in a little goofing off. So he walked up to him, gave him a real good ream job, and ordered him to get up on the trucks and help the other boys work the train. The guy slowly slid off the truck and said to MacKie: "You SOB, I'm a Western Union lineman and don't work for your goddam railroad."

And with that he let MacKie have a stiff right to the jaw.

D. General Patton

When old General Patton was holding maneuvers out there in the Mojave Desert, he was chicken as heck about regulations, especially uniforms. There were those poor guys out there dying of heat and thirst, and there was old Patton with them big old .45s on telling 'em to button up their collars. Well, he came along one day riding in a jeep and he saw a guy working up a pole, and, so help me, the guy had on a pair of old sloppy fatigues and his shirt was all unbuttoned and he had no hat on.

Old Patton stopped the jeep and hollered up at the guy, and asked him why the blankety-blank he was out of uniform, and cussed him up one side and down the other. And the guy just sat up there in his belt, and took it, and when Patton was all through, the guy says, "You son-of-a-bitch, I work for Bell Telephone."

Sources

    A. "Mr. Ford Doesn't Care," *Fortune* 8 (Dec., 1933): 132.

    B. Clayton Fountain, *Union Guy* (New York: Viking, 1949), p. 142.

    C. John Meskimen, letter to Archie Green, Dec. 17, 1959; published in "American Labor Lore," *Industrial Relations* 4 (Feb., 1965): 57.

    D. Niel Snortum, letter to Archie Green, Dec. 30, 1964.

Background

"You're Fired," in its four forms above, taps a deep vein of revenge fantasy—a telephone worker or electrical lineman decks a tough "outside" boss after the latter mistakes the former's identity and job skills. Adding his story to my repertoire and embellishing it, I learned something of its continental distribution and popularity.

Clayton Fountain's *Union Guy* offered an autobiographical perspective on UAW adventures. Circumstance brought him to San Francisco in the mid-1950s, where, down on his luck, he drove a taxicab for an uncertain living. Meeting him, I reported great pleasure in reading his book; I quizzed him on his I-don't-work-for-Ford anecdote. Clayton told me that he had not seen an actual encounter between executive and worker, but had heard the story in Michigan UAW organizational spiels in the late 1930s.

In November, 1959, attending a workers' education conference at the University of Wisconsin, Madison, I personalized Fountain's tale by setting it in a San Francisco Bethlehem Steel shipyard. That evening John Meskimen, a former railroad "nut buster" and International Association of Machinists member, related an exciting nail-keg analog. In subsequent correspondence, he wrote out "Eager-Beaver MacKie"; with his permission, I included it in a 1965 article, "American Labor Lore."

In March, 1961, after I spoke at a Wayne State University session on laborlore, Niel Snortum added a variant on General Patton and an aggrieved Bell Telephone lineman. Niel had heard it in the early 1950s, from his brother-in-law, Chalmer Culbertson, a high-tension lineman for the Pasadena (California) Light & Power Company.

With three related tales at hand, I continued my search. During a brief visit to Urbana, Illinois, about 1968, Eli Kovacich, UAW

"Six Auto Workers."

Local 900, Wayne, Michigan, indicated that Joe Pete, an old Serbian millwright and natural-born mimic, had told an especially dramatic "scuttlebutt story" set back in 1941: Peter Martin, a Ford vice president, approached a construction stiff sitting on his ass near the assembly line. In an ungentlemanly manner, Martin demanded to see the outsider's badge. The loafer, not taking any lip, decked the Ford boss. Who can expand or parallel Joe Pete's account?

No tale investigation follows as clear a line as that laid out here. Chance plays a major role in any quest. I met Clayton Fountain at an elegant house party with relaxed time to converse, and Eli Kovacich, on the fly, with but a few minutes to jot his name on the back of a sheet of printing-trades letterhead. John Meskimen and Niel Snortum shared their stories with me directly at public meetings, and subsequently in letters.

I used my Bethlehem cable-splicer variant alongside those of Fountain and Meskimen in "American Labor Lore," and continued to tell all three accounts. In time, a student alerted me to a *Fortune* report (1933) of Charles Sorensen's two-fisted plant-floor bullying. "Mr. Ford Doesn't Care"—the earliest known printing of our mistaken-identity story—did not carry an author's name. I have long wondered about the name of the anonymous journalist, laboring for the magisterial *Fortune,* who first noted a key labor tale. He or she had a fine ear for occupational tradition, stating presciently that "the spirit of the Ford plant is not a normal spirit and it is to be expected that anecdotes breed in it—breed and grow into legend and myth" (1933, 126).

64

Furuseth's Credo

[Federal Judge William Denman, muckraking journalist George West, San Francisco editor Fremont Older, and sculptor Jo Davidson recall related anecdotes about Andrew Furuseth (1854–1938), emancipator of American seamen.]

A. *Carved in Stone*

My [Denman's] first contact with Andy was in 1901, when, as a young lawyer, green then in knowledge of the history of seamen, I was asked to debate with him on the use of the injunction.

To my conventional argument that the orders of courts should be obeyed, he responded with a vivid description of the wrongful use of the injunction in labor disputes. His address concluded with the words now carved on the monument to him on the San Francisco waterfront.

"What would I do if they served an injunction on me to stop the organization of our men? I would put it in my pocket and the judge would put me in jail, and there my bunk would be no narrower and my grub no poorer nor I there more lonely than in the forecastle."

B. *Inyunction in My Pocket*

My [Denman again] first contact with him [Furuseth], in 1904 or 1905 was in a hall near South Park, San Francisco. There in a discussion of the use of "inyunction," as he pronounced it, in labor disputes, in response to a question, "What would you do if our anti-labor injunction were served on you?" He replied, "I would put the inyunction in my pocket and go to yail and in yail my bunk would be no narrower, my food no worse, nor I more lonely than in the forecastle."

C. Fremont Older's Story

I [West] suppose most of the *Survey*'s readers know the classic Furuseth story—how, after a San Francisco court had enjoined him from the normal and necessary activities of a successful strike, and after he had told his friend Fremont Older that he would not obey, and Older had mentioned jail to him, he said: "Very well! They couldn't give me plainer food than I've always eaten; they couldn't put me in a narrower room than I've always had. And they couldn't make me any lonelier than I've always been."

D. Philosophy of Life

Many years ago there was a strike on the water front and Furuseth was, of course, the leader of it. He was arrested at the instance of the shipowners and charged with violating an injunction issued by the federal court. While his case was pending he called at my [Older's] office.

"Are they going to put you in jail, Andrew?" I asked.

Then he poured out to me the philosophy of his life:

"I don't know and I don't care. They can't put me into a smaller room than I have always lived in. They can't feed me any plainer food than I have always eaten." Then with tears gathering in his fine old eyes:

"They can't make me any lonelier than I have always been."

E. Let 'Em Come

One day, when he [Furuseth] was sitting in a bar along the waterfront, someone came in and told him that the dicks were after him, and he had better vamoose. He had been making so-called "seditious" speeches. "No" he said, "they cannot put me in a room any smaller than I have always lived in. They cannot give me food any simpler than I have always had, and they cannot make me any more lonely than I have always been. Let 'em come."

Sources

A. William Denman message read by Silas Axtell at Andrew Furuseth Anniversary Celebration, New York, Mar. 12, 1948; in Axtell, *Symposium on Andrew Furuseth* (New Bedford, Mass.: Darwin Press, 1949), p. 223.

"Holystoning."

B. William Denman letter to Silas Axtell, Feb. 3, 1947; in Axtell, p. 16.

C. George P. West, "Andrew Furuseth and the Radicals," *Survey* 47 (Nov. 5, 1921): 207.

D. Fremont Older, "Andrew Furuseth," *San Francisco Call-Bulletin*, July 4, 1930.

E. Jo Davidson, *Between Sittings* (New York: Dial Press, 1951), p. 240.

Background

We honor a handful of American workers who have acquired near-legendary status: Mother Jones, Joe Hill, Gene Debs, John Lewis, Andy Furuseth. Our memories of these figures ebb and flow with shifts in trade-union vitality, and with revisions in judgment by historians and biographers. Partisans know that no union "saints" have approached the stardom of Babe Ruth or Marilyn Monroe in popular imagination. Yet labor unionists live with their own exemplars—those to whom fate has assigned a modest degree of fame.

I shall not attempt to elevate Furuseth's heroism, nor detail his life story. Born in Romedal, Norway, as a young windjammer sailor he faced then-common exploitation by captains at sea and crimps on shore. Arriving in San Francisco in 1880, he made it his home port, taking a turn as a Northwest coast salmon fisherman. In time, he found his true calling as a union leader and lobbyist for seamen.

Soon after a handful of men organized the Coast Seamen's Union in San Francisco in 1885, Furuseth became active in its ranks as well as in its successor, the Sailors' Union of the Pacific. As head of the International Seamen's Union after 1908, he worked closely with AFL president Samuel Gompers and Wisconsin senator Robert La Follette for legislation to free sailors from serfdom's hold. The Seamen's Act, signed by President Wilson in 1915, stands as but one monument to Furuseth's intensity and perseverance.

Those who knew Furuseth deployed a series of allusions to note his nautical gait, craggy strength, and spartan values: Jeffersonian democrat, Old Testament prophet, Viking ship's prow, Abraham Lincoln of the Sea, Saint Andrew the Sailor. Legendary narratives accrued to him like iron slivers to a magnet. For example, at his death, an unnamed reporter for the *San Francisco News* wrote: "An old acquaintance . . . revealed how Furuseth once saw $10,000 in gold put before him as a bribe. Furuseth became indignant and walked out after shouting a brief refusal." Similar tales of honor have been applied over the years to other labor heroes. (In "You Can't Buy Me" I treat such narratives.)

Well before Furuseth's death, a brief account of his indifference to a court's injunction had circulated in oral and published forms. On Labor Day, 1941, in Embarcadero Park fronting San Francisco's Ferry Building, the SUP dedicated a bronze bust with Furuseth's words inscribed in its granite base: "You can put me in jail. But you cannot give me narrower quarters than as a seaman I have always had. You cannot give me coarser food than I have always eaten. You cannot make me lonelier than I have always been."

In comparing this inscription with the five passages cited above, we find rhetorical variation taken for granted in oral expression, but not anticipated in published form. Apparently, no one at the Ferry Building ceremony was aware of or commented on differences between the chosen text and others then in print.

To this day, I have not found the precise source for the words given to the monument's stonecutters by the SUP officers who commissioned the bronze bust and granite base. Nor have I found a letter, speech, or testimony by Furuseth confirming or denying the words attributed to him; I shall welcome such a discovery. Also, I remain mystified by the circumstance of selection for the pedestal text. Who favored one set of anecdotal words above all others?

Judge Denman in dual recollections of first hearing the credo credited a debate in 1901 and a discussion in 1904–5. Did he consider one occurrence more authentic than the other? George West in 1921 asserted that the *Survey*'s liberal and literate readers knew "the classic Furuseth story" told by Fremont Older. Does not West's statement imply that Older had placed his item in print before 1921? The earliest Older report I have found dates to an Independence Day editorial in 1930 which recalls a text different from those previously attributed to Furuseth.

Sculptor Jo Davidson, meeting the Viking in Paris in 1919 and falling under his spell, invited him to sit for a bust. The sitting occurred in New York in 1929. Decades later, Davidson placed his recollection of the credo, romantically, in a waterfront bar with Furuseth bravely shrugging off "dicks" (detectives). Unlike others, Davidson did not mention law courts or injunctions.

In searching for the first appearance and subsequent circulation of "Furuseth's Credo," I have found clear openings and closed barriers. It reached beyond a trade-union audience in 1916, in a sympathetic sketch for the *New Republic,* when Alvin Johnson reported the story of Furuseth smiling during a strike as friends feared that he'd be clapped into jail. The philosophic sailor calmed his companions, "They can't give me narrower quarters. . . ." Johnson's source has eluded me; his account is the earliest I have found in print.

Paul Taylor in the first academic study of the Sailors' Union of the Pacific wrote, "Older tells one of the best known stories" about Furuseth (1923, 177). In 1959, biographer Hyman Weintraub dated this variant to the San Francisco waterfront strike of 1906. At its close, the Hammond Lumber Company attempted to secure a judgment against the SUP leader. According to Weintraub, Older then asked Furuseth about jail and received his Scandinavian-accented reply (77).

Andrew Furuseth died in Washington, D.C., on January 22, 1938. A week later, the SUP paper, *West Coast Sailors,* ran a front-page photo of its Clay Street hall, flag at half mast and windows draped in bunting for the "Grand Old Man of the Seas." Under the caption, "Andrew Furuseth, SUP Book No. 11," the editor, without comment, presented yet another credo statement: "You can put me in jail, but you can not give me worse food than I have received on board ships, nor smaller quarters than I have been used to. Nor can you make me any lonelier than I have always been."

The *West Coast Sailors* reached a few thousand seamen in 1938 with its tribute to the holder of Book No. 11. Across the continent, the *New York Times* ran a long obituary, "Andrew Furuseth, Labor Leader, Dies" (January 23), and on the following day, an editorial, "The Sailors' Lincoln." Both the *Times* obit and editorial farewell included yet another credo variant: "You cannot make me any more lonely than I have always been. You cannot give me food worse than I have always had. My sleeping quarters will be no more cramped than they have been at any time."

Following Furuseth's wishes, seamen on the SS *Schoharie* scattered his ashes in the Atlantic midway between Europe and America. He could well have chosen any sea on the globe, for he had sailed in all seven. Immediately after his death, SUP members, young and old, sent contributions to union headquarters requesting that a life-sized statue of "Old Andy" be placed on the San Francisco waterfront.

The union's paper endorsed this spontaneous effort in a February 11 editorial. Fund-raising continued for month after month, as the planners wisely scaled the intended statue down to a bust on a stone base. Finally, on December 15, 1939, the paper pictured a clay model of Furuseth's head by local sculptor Hal Bayard Runyan, announcing that it would be cast in bronze by the "lost wax process," and that a granite pedestal had been cut but not yet surface-finished or inscribed.

Previously, in 1935, Harry Lundeberg, a fiery Norwegian-born sailor, had succeeded Furuseth at the union's helm. Involved in constant disputes with with a host of antagonists—shipowners, Stalinists, Maritime Commission bureaucrats, AFL "pie cards" frozen in office—Lundeberg had little time to devote to a memorial site. Nevertheless, committed to honoring his union's champion, he negotiated in 1940 with foot-dragging politicians to place a worker's bust in Embarcadero Park. In time, he enlisted the state legislature and Governor Olson to secure a bit of space for the monument. On August 29, 1941, the *West Coast Sailors* announced a dedication ceremony for Labor Day (September 1).

This front-page announcement held an anomaly—a photo of Jo Davidson's bust of Furuseth without attribution to the famed sculptor. Having marched in the 1941 Labor Day parade, and recalling walks to the Ferry Building site, I, along with many San Franciscans, assumed that Davidson had sculpted "our" bronze. (I return to this matter below.)

After 1941, in war and peace, SUP members and fellow workers gathered annually on March 12, Furuseth's birthday, to place floral wreaths at his Embarcadero monument, swap yarns about the old Viking, and renew their sense of mission. Photos taken at these events reproduced in the union's paper show a gallery of old-timers—a few who had sailed in Andy's early days; the rest, his "children." Facing their centennial in 1985, SUP members commissioned *Brotherhood of the Sea,* in which Steven Schwartz sought the origin of Furuseth's epitaph. Searching the literature, the historian fell back on Judge Denman's "convincing account" of 1904–5 (1986, 42).

It is unlikely now that we shall ever trace the full history of "Furuseth's Credo." Did the sage actually use these words in 1901 during a discussion or debate with young lawyer Denman? Did Furuseth utter his remarks to editor Older in 1906? Could someone else have attributed the anecdote to Furuseth? Are answers buried in faded letters and yellowed newsprint?

With construction of San Francisco's hated waterfront freeway in 1957, the Furuseth bust lost its majestic home at the foot of Market Street. Wisely, the SUP designated a new place for the monument: the outdoor entrance to its elegant art deco building on Rincon Hill (opened in 1950). This appropriate site recalled scenes of major labor battles with police and California guardsmen in the 1934 Pacific Coast maritime strike.

Upon Harry Lundeberg's death (January 28, 1957), the SUP commissioned Edwin Hurt to sculpt and cast a bust for him displaying his characteristic sailor's white cloth cap. On January 28, 1958, the union dedicated this bust, on a granite base similar to that of Furuseth's. The two Norsemen, in bronze flanking their hall's entrance, now stand perpetual watch in calm and stormy weather. In truth, their parallel setting in front of a union hall has become a labor landmark honoring workers of all callings.

Today, for those who pause to read, Furuseth's words cut into polished black stone bring vignettes to mind: sailing ships and icy jails; bucko mates and fights for dignity; heroism and continuity in labor struggle. In personal visits to the SUP hall, I reflect on the credo, bringing to it a folklorist's perspective. I ask: When and where did Furuseth first learn a stoic's response to nature's hardships or threatened jail?

As a schoolboy in Romedal, Andrew had absorbed Norse sagas, not as quaint children's tales but rather as the sinew and marrow of Viking identity. Did he hear or read a saga about a hero impervious to the elements? Presently, I lack knowledge of a particular Norse text which stands behind "Furuseth's Credo" but have found a related passage in the annals of Britain. Bede, writing in the eighth century, and looking back at the exploits of Celts and Saxons, told the story of a visionary monk:

Drihthelm . . . developed habits of extreme asceticism, such as going down to the river Tweed at night and standing in the ice-cold water, saying psalms and prayers, sometimes with broken ice floating round him, and then letting his wet clothes dry on him—terrible! Those who would behold it would say: "It is wonderful, Brother Drihthelm, that you are able to endure such violent cold," to which he simply answered: "I have seen greater cold." And when they said "It is strange that you will endure such austerity" he replied: "I have seen greater austerity." (Chadwick 1963, 335; see also Bede 1990, 284–89)

"Furuseth's Credo" joins two discrete themes: denial of hardship's power and the analogy of jail/forecastle. Brother Drihthelm attested to the first long ago. In 1759, the great eighteenth-century dictionary maker Samuel Johnson called attention to the second matter, when he attempted to release his black servant from abhorrent sea duty. Biographer James Boswell used this action to report Johnson's view of maritime life: "No man will be a sailor who has contrivance enough to get himself into a jail; for being in a ship is being in a jail, with the chance of being drowned" (Boswell [1791], vol. 1, 348).

On a tour of the Hebrides in 1773, Johnson repeated this sentiment to a guide who had been "pressed aboard a man-of-war" (vol. 5, 137). In a subsequent conversation at Skye, he elaborated: "The man in a jail has more room, better food, and commonly better company, and is in safety" (vol. 5, 249). In 1776, at home in London, Johnson enlarged on "the wretchedness of sea-life": "A ship is worse than a gaol. There is, in a gaol, better air, better company, better conveniency of every kind; and a ship has the additional disadvantage of being in danger . . . . Men go to sea before they know the unhappiness of that way of life; and when they have come to know it, they cannot escape from it" (vol. 2, 438).

Boswell's *Life of Johnson* has attracted extensive commentary for two centuries. I pause only to note that Sir James Mackintosh, who served as Recorder of Bombay, had attributed (in a journal entry dated January 26, 1811) Endymion Porter's "Consolation to [James] Howell" as Johnson's source in linking ship and jail. Howell, a Royalist in the camp of King Charles during England's civil war, had been jailed at the Fleet, a London prison. Porter, a fellow Cavalier, then tried to cheer his friend with a pun on the dual meanings of *fleet* (Mackintosh 1853, vol. 2, 83).

Already jailed for four years and uncertain of release, Howell wrote to Porter on January 2, 1646. He thanked him for his "comfortable Advice, that having been so long under hatches in this *Fleet,* I should fancy myself to be in a long voyage at Sea." The prisoner continued:

"You go on to prefer my captivity in this *Fleet* to that of a Voyager at Sea, in regard that he is subject to storms and springing of Leaks, to Pirates and Picaroons, with other casualties. You write, I have other Advantages also, to be free from plundering and other Barbarisms, that reign now abroad. 'Tis true, I am secur'd from all these; yet touching the first, I could be content to expose myself to all those chances, so that this were a *floating Fleet,* that I might breathe free Air" (Boswell [1791], vol. 5, 137; Howell [1646], 431).

I do not know whether Johnson indeed had borrowed views of seafaring directly from James Howell or from previous writers. Perhaps Johnson formed such thoughts out of general knowledge of maritime life during the eighteenth century. I find it significant that wordplay on sea duty/prison dates back at least as far as the 1640s, and suspect that further reading will reveal additional branches on the family tree for "Furuseth's Credo" beyond that treated by Johnson, Porter, and Howell.

Like many seafarers, Andrew had read widely, and, alongside labor activists of his era, had mastered rhetoric's power. Possibly, he had encountered Bede or Boswell and had used their influential books to formulate an ascetic's creed comparing jail and forecastle. Yet, I prefer to believe that Furuseth had tapped into a vein of distant tradition—poetic saga, concise aphorism, circuitous tale—when he had talked to Denman, Older, Davidson, or others about his calm fearlessness in facing the state's dungeons.

Norwegian biographer Haakon Lie (in a letter to me) noted Furuseth's familiarity as a schoolboy with Snorri Sturluson's (1179–1241) classic tomes on the Icelandic sagas. Giving a book to a young relative, Andrew inscribed a few words, "These Norsemen were honest and courageous men. Be thou like them." We do not strain credulity to speculate that Furuseth saw himself as a bold Viking navigator steering a course both by the stars and by the poetry of ancient bards.

With luck we may yet unearth a clue to the earliest printing of Furuseth's defining belief. To complement library and literary search, I suggest visits to the SUP hall on San Francisco's Rincon Hill and to the National Portrait Gallery in Washington. The former holds an outdoor monument to Furuseth; the latter, Jo Davidson's bust of Andrew—a bronze whispering mysteries twined with those of the credo itself.

Here, I turn to the bust's strange story. Maritime attorney Silas Axtell, in 1918, had proposed a statue in Furuseth's honor. The "Old Man" rejected the plans angrily, insisting that the SUP needed men, not monuments. However, in 1919, when Davidson met Furuseth at the Paris Peace Conference, the sailor and the sculptor became friends. A decade passed before Andrew agreed to a studio sitting in New York.

On March 29, 1929, Davidson wrote to Furuseth in Washington that the bronze would be ready at the foundry in a week or two. During the sitting, both men had speculated that the finished bust might be placed at Sailors' Union of the Pacific headquarters. The sculptor liked the idea, providing that the members themselves would contribute directly to its cost without assessing the union treasury. Anticipating that placement details would soon become firm, Davidson entrusted the bust to his friend Lincoln Steffens. Sadly, no SUP fund drive took place (Weintraub 1959, 192–93).

By 1930, the depression left seamen penniless, unable or unwilling to recognize the value in Davidson's artistry or the importance of housing one of his works in a union hall. Also, radicals in the SUP scoffed at the bust, and used hard times to gnaw away at Furuseth's character, thus denying him honor while alive. Fortunately, a few of his friends persisted in treasuring the bronze.

By reading letters in Davidson's papers at the Library of Congress, we sense the uneasiness in labor's ranks when confronted by a piece of art. Apparently, after Steffens failed to effect the bust's purchase by the SUP, the sculptor sent it to Fremont Older in San Francisco. Writing to Davidson, the editor indicated that he had talked to SUP officers who reported their failure in resolving the matter. Older continued: "Some of the men say, why put up a man's bust while he is still alive. Meanwhile this great masterpiece, for that is exactly what it is, stands on my desk, a homeless waif. What shall I do?" (June 23, 1930).

Davidson responded to Older: "It seems to me that this bust of Andy should go somewhere, but where—I really have not the slightest idea. I don't care anything about making any money on it—I had my kick in moulding that extraordinary head of his, for it is an amazing face & I would like to think of it somewhere where those for whom he had given his life would see it" (October 9).

Two details add to Davidson's poignant letter. He had been very well paid for bronze heads by millionaire bankers and industrialists; thus he could offer the Furuseth bust to sailors who, despite empty pockets, might appreciate it. Quite unrelated to problems in placement, the bust's availability in 1929 helped bring to the surface Furuseth's aversion to photography.

On March 25, 1929, Victor Olander, International Seamen's Union secretary-treasurer, had sent a fascinating letter to Davidson expressing pleasure that Furuseth had finally agreed to a sitting. Olander elaborated that years before Andy had refused a Boston paper's request to photograph him in that such a picture might suggest the injection of his own personality over that of rank-and-file seamen in their struggles. This may well have been Saint Andrew's wish. However, I sense also the early belief that a photographer might steal a subject's soul.

Furuseth's "fear" of a picture had been noted previously in *La Follette's Magazine,* March, 1915. Upon passage of the Seamen's Act, editor Senator La Follette combined a tribute to the sailor-lobbyist with an announcement that his face would appear in the April issue:

> [Furuseth] is a picturesque fighter, a curious character, a unique American figure. But a picture of "Andy" has never been seen in the papers.
>
> He has never permitted his photograph to be published. In every American Federation convention his lean, crouched figure rises. His eyes glow. His face is screwed with intensity. His shrill voice tells of the seamen's fight for better things. And year after year, Furuseth has been going before Congress trying to get a bill passed abolishing involuntary servitude on board American ships.
>
> Now his fight is won. With the signing of the seamen's bill by President Wilson, Furuseth has triumphed for his cause.
>
> And the face of Andrew Furuseth will appear in *La Follette's Magazine* for April!
>
> This splendid champion of his fellow men has consented to the first publication of his photograph in this magazine.

True to promise, the April issue featured a front-page photo portrait by Edmonston of Andrew Furuseth, as well as another reminder that he had "refused to be photographed until the Seamen's Bill should become a law." In a previous sketch for the magazine (July, 1913), Carl Sandburg (then freelancing for labor/socialist journals) launched the photography-fetish story by noting that, unlike famed publicity seekers, the sailor threatened severe retaliation for photographers who caught him in their sights. Furuseth "has a reputation for having smashed more cameras than J. Pierpont Morgan."

Sandburg also engaged in a bit of Furuseth legend-building by penning memorable lines: "He takes only seaman's pay as 'salary' from his union. When he attended an international seamen's congress in Europe a few years ago, he worked his passage across, rated as an ordinary seaman. He sleeps in a sailor's bunk at the San Francisco headquarters. He has never married, explaining that a sailor is a slave without a home to share with a woman."

Returning to the matter of Andy's face, Sandburg concluded with a bit of intra-union gossip: "Bill" Mahon, president of the Amalgamated Association of Street and Electric Railway Employees, reputedly held a "secret" photo of Furuseth. Learning of this sin, the sailor's chief threatened to lead a squad to ransack Mahon's Detroit home for the picture totem.

Our photography digression ends happily in 1934, when Dorothea Lange "caught" a serene "Old Viking" a few years before his death. In retrospect, we know that pictures of Furuseth remained scarce until photos of the Davidson bronze began to circulate after 1929. Even before the bust could be seen in public, the ISU made available a striking photo of Davidson modeling Furuseth in clay. A number of labor papers then printed the picture with Olander's story of the "camera-shy" sailor (*El Paso Labor Advocate*).

I have found it as difficult to trace the path of the Furuseth bust as that of his credo. Charles Crane, a former American minister to China, may have purchased or borrowed the "original" piece (first casting) from Davidson in 1929. To get the Crane bronze, or a second casting, to the SUP, the sculptor entrusted it to Fremont Older and Lincoln Steffens, both of whom had friends in the labor movement.

No one seems to know how many castings Davidson made from his clay model, if indeed he made more than one. During 1934, a year turbulent with intense ideological/jurisdictional conflict in labor's ranks, Crane or a maritime-union officer may have "loaned" (perhaps for safe keeping) the Furuseth bust to the Department of Labor for lobby placement. More likely, New Deal Secretary of Labor Frances Perkins, who had known Jo Davidson for many years, may have persuaded him to send the bust to Washington before the dedication (February 25, 1935) of the department's new building on Constitution Avenue.

The *Washington Post* and the *Washington Star* both reported on the building's opening, at which Perkins hosted a musical concert featuring a United Mine Workers' (brass and wind) band from West Virginia and a United Textile Workers' string band from South Carolina. Other performers offered Irish ballads, Negro spirituals, and "People's Chorus" favorites. Adding color to the festivities, Perkins borrowed for exhibit 150 paintings from the Public Works of Arts Project—President Roosevelt's initial foray into relief-based art patronage.

Assuming that Frances Perkins also secured the Furuseth bust from Davidson for her building's dedication, I shared my hunch with Nancy Balz, a Montgomery County, Maryland, librarian, who hit "paydirt" at the National Archives. On February 25, 1935, immediately after the Department of Labor ceremony, John J. Leary Jr. of the Federal Housing Administration sent a typed note to Perkins thanking her for an impressive service and most interesting program.

In bold script, Leary added a personal note of praise: "and bringing in the busts of Mother Jones and Furuseth was positively worthy of Belasco." (The David Belasco analogy invoked memory of a master drama producer, 1854–1931.) With Leary's letter unearthed, we continue to hunt for corroborative details on the perhaps-informal transactions between the sculptor and Perkins in securing busts of the maritime and coal-mine exemplars. Davidson's bronze of Mother Jones on a marble-block base, still in Labor Department hands, rests in its current hall-of-fame lobby installation.

In 1944, Secretary Perkins returned the Furuseth bust not to Crane, Steffens, Older, or any of the former ISU officials but directly to Davidson. Why did he request its return? Sensitive to its loss, Perkins wrote to the sculptor (May 25) reminding him that New York mayor Fiorello La Guardia had promised a replica of the original for the Labor Department. Nothing came of this proposal. The circumstances of the bust's arrival in Washington and its departure remain a mystery.

Seemingly, Davidson, or his heirs, kept the "Perkins" Furuseth bust hidden in storage from 1944 until 1985, when the National Portrait Gallery purchased it (or another casting) from a private art dealer; this bronze is now on display in the Gallery's Davidson room. Curator Brandon Fortune, in tracing the background of the NPG piece, has found a bewildering set of references to other (or derivative) castings. Dr. Fortune's paper trail suggests that the sculptor or associates may have cast as many as eight copies:

Charles Crane (1929)

Lincoln Steffens/Fremont Older (1930)

Department of Labor (1935)

Baltimore Museum of Art exhibit, borrowed from ISU (September 5–30, 1938)

Sailors' Union of the Pacific (date ?)

International Seamen's Union or its successor, the Seafarers International Union (date ?)

United Seaman's Service, N.Y. ($500.00 payment received by Davidson, April 21, 1943)

Andrew Furuseth Club, New York (World War II)

American Academy of Arts and Letters exhibit, New York (November 26, 1947–February 1, 1948)

I have found no trace of any castings except the one now displayed in the National Portrait Gallery, and am uncertain about duplications in the list above. Nor do I know whether the "original" Furuseth bust in Ambassador Crane's possession went to the Department of Labor and, ultimately, to the NPG. Perhaps, we can yet locate a lost Davidson bronze of the spartan sailor.

I add these details on the bust's numbers and locations to my account of "Furuseth's Credo" to illustrate that unresolved questions surround artistry in bronze as well as in words. Seemingly, Davidson had not only captured Saint Andrew's craggy features but also the tension in his lined face—an insider's calm generated by pride in craft played against an outsider's wariness after a life of fighting against odds.

In the years from the "Big Strike" (1934) to Furuseth's death in 1938, waves of militancy again engulfed American seamen. Alone in Washington and in declining health, Andrew rejected old and new "enemies": SUP firebrands, Wobbly syndicalists, CIO industrial unionists, New Deal liberals, waterfront Marxists. The 1936 shift from the cautious and corrupt ISU to the newly chartered SIU left him stranded. It is to the eternal credit of his fellow workers in the Sailors' Union of the Pacific that, despite his sad end, they persisted in a drive for a dignified monument on San Francisco's Embarcadero. He had known its worn docks and finger piers since his arrival from Norway.

In the early 1970s, the citizens of Romedal and labor unionists in Oslo decided to memorialize Furuseth on home ground. Failing to secure a copy of the Davidson bust, they commissioned Nils Flakstad, a local artist, to cast a "substitute." Visiting Norway in 1974 and viewing the Romedal bust mounted on granite, Joe Glazer composed "The Ballad of Andrew Furuseth," rewriting the credo in his song. Haakon Lie included this ballad text in his biography of Furuseth (1993, 235).

Jo Davidson had served as an honorary pallbearer at Furuseth's Washington funeral service in the Department of Labor lobby. The event's dignified brochure held photographs of Furuseth and the Davidson bronze, as well as the credo exactly as incised a few years later on the SUP monument. We can assume that Harry Lundeberg or a staff member gave the brochure text to the San Francisco sculptor or the pedestal stonecutter. Conversely, the brochure designer in 1938 may have obtained a previous text from SUP headquarters in San Francisco, or from an ISU official. In short, I do not know who selected the "final" text and judged its authenticity.

Although I do not see the pursuit of a perfect or original text as the prime task in folkloric study, I believe that close attention to a tale's clustered words can aid working people in calling up their past and in charting a future. We gain perspective on life journeys by decoding "Furuseth's Credo." We enlarge understanding of constant interplay at the poles of job freedom and authority in rereading one sailor's words.

A reflection on the linkage of labor tradition to loss of institutional memory can be found in a poignant event during World War II, told by Captain Richard Harrison of the Liberty Ship *Bret Harte.* Passing the sister Liberty *Andrew Furuseth* at sea, Harrison asked the wheelman if he could identify Furuseth. Not only did the sailor confess ignorance but his shipmates also knew nothing of the hero who had toiled to unshackle them (Axtell 1948, 215).

In opening comments on "Furuseth's Credo," I asserted that no trade unionists had risen very high in our pop-culture firmament. Although some partisans revere Joe Hill and Mother Jones as legends, most workers in the United States remain content to elevate sports and screen stars. Furuseth's name no longer calls up great recognition. Nevertheless, in considering his credo and looking at his countenance in bronze, we open again questions about labor's cause: Who best represents America's workers? Why do we lack a hallowed pantheon? Who deserves beatification?

Walter MacArthur—Glasgow sailor and editor of the *Coast Seamen's Journal*—had worked for decades with Furuseth, observing his zeal as well as idiosyncrasies. Like a seaman facing a fanatical "Old Man" aboard ship, the editor struggled to balance respect for authority with independence in the ranks. In a letter to labor historian Ira Cross (March 13, 1935), MacArthur attempted to place his associate's status in perspective:

> In some minds, the idea prevails that Furuseth is entitled to credit for the very existence of the Union. The fact is the other way around.
>
> From the very beginning the Sailors' Union has contained a large proportion of capable men, to whose courage and initiative is due the continuous existence of the Union and the progress made in the practical conditions of their lives. These men did not make speeches in public, but they spoke the only language that was understood by the crimps and runners on the waterfront.
>
> They patrolled the beach and boarded vessels in all sorts of weather and under all sorts of conditions. They took chances of being clubbed on the docks or thrown overboard in the bay. In short, they "took the gaff," and by so doing preserved the life of the Union. (Camp 1948, 333)

Without resort to mystical or apocalyptic tones, MacArthur revealed the role of rank-and-file sailors in making possible the ascent of a hero. Beyond assessing this vital relationship, we can look back in time and marvel at the mutual exchange between Furuseth and the mariners who kept him in office. He articulated their belief in the Sailors' Union of the Pacific; they supported him in his many eccentricities and singular passion. His credo, far more than a personal statement, made sense to countless tars who plowed the waters.

Ultimately, we treasure "Furuseth's Credo" and art by sculptors Davidson, Runyan, and Flakstad because words and bronze combine to keep Furuseth's name fresh. We know that the head in metal above stone can not speak. Yet, it trumpets that seafarers served variously before the mast, on waterfront picket lines, and in legislative lobbies to uncouple the traditional bond of prison/forecastle.

I continue to seek the source of one salt's text. Do its roots rest in a Viking saga, Bede's chronicles, or James Boswell's writings on Samuel Johnson? Regardless of my quest's outcome, I believe that, today, Andrew Furuseth's sparse words on coarse food and narrow quarters remain meaningful for those who read them in history books, hear them narrated, or trace them incised in a labor landmark's granite.

"Andrew Furuseth."

65

Wordplay

A. Woods Talk

One winter day a tramp stopped at an N. Ludington Co. camp and asked for something to eat. Rugged as life was in those camps, a stranger asking for food was never turned away. The camp foreman asked him if he would like to go to work. The newcomer agreed. "All right," said the foreman, "Grab one of those cant hooks leaning against that tall pine and mount that log car."

The tramp proved himself a skilled woodsman. However, it was not long before he became the victim of an accident on top of the logs, which fractured one of his legs. Top-loading, or "sky-hooking," as the men called it, was dangerous work. The company sent him to the M. and M. hospital in Marinette, Wisconsin. One day, during his convalescence, he got into a conversation with a nurse who asked him how he had been injured.

"Well, sister," replied the victim, "It was this way. I dropped in at one of the N. Ludington camps and as I was the first 'gazabo' who came down the 'pike' that morning and the 'push' needed men, he put me to work 'sky-hooking' on top of a load."

"The first thing that the 'ground hop' did was to send me up a 'blue.' I hollered at him to throw a 'Saginaw' into her, but he 'Saint Croixed' her. Then he 'gummed' her and the result was that I got my 'stem' cracked."

The nurse replied, "I don't have the faintest idea what you are talking about." The tramp replied, "Neither do I."

B. I Don't Understand

Once upon a time, so legend has it, an injured logger was brought to a hospital, which may have been in New Westminster, or maybe

Snohomish, or perhaps it was Tillamook. In any case, the head nurse asked him how the accident had happened.

"Nurse" said he, "It was this way: I was setting chokers on the candy side and was just hooking on to a big blue butt when the rigging slinger says to let her go. The hooker yelled Hi! to the punk, the punk jerked the wire, the puncher opened her wide, and . . . well, Nurse, here I am."

This wasn't too clear to the nurse. "But," she said, "I don't understand." The logger sat up in his cot. "Damned if I do, either," he replied, "unless that haywire rigging slinger was crazy!"

C. Posing as a Farm Lad

Then there's the one about the boomer who was tipped off that he would stand a better chance of being hired if he would pose as a farm lad. He got along okay with the trainmaster, who disliked boomers, until he came to the "Reason for leaving previous employment." This he explained in person to the T.M. as follows:

"The old man was always ridin' me. He pulled me outa service for a week when I Wabashed the grain drill, tryin' to back the hayrack in the clear. And he handed me thirty brownies for burnin' a journal off the mowin' machine. I stood for all that; but the day before yesterday he ran the hired man around me when I stood first out for a ridin' plow and, by golly, I pulled the pin."

D. Nautical Teamster

Another tenderfoot, not finding gold as plentiful as he had expected, was forced to accept employment as a driver of a team hauling lumber from the sawmill to the near-by mining camps. This man had been a sailor most of his life before coming to the [Black] Hills, and the team, consisting of two oxen and an old gray mare caused him a great deal of trouble on the "maiden voyage."

According to the story, the sailor with a few salty oaths started the team, and then things began to happen. The gray mare kicked swiftly with both hind legs, and the oxen, trying to escape, changed places on the tongue so that they were facing the amazed driver, and the team started moving slowly toward the edge of the near-by cliff.

"Hey Cap'n," the driver yelled to the sawmill owner, "You'd best come on deck. The la'board ox is on the sta'board side, the sta'board ox is on the la'board side, the mare tangled up in the riggin', and the whole shooting match is divin' for hell stern foremost."

Sources

A. Anecdote in "'Lumberjack' Language" (reprinted or adapted from an early newspaper), *Marinette County (Wisconsin) Historian,* Apr., 1980, p. 3.

B. From "Introduction" by Stewart Holbrook in Walter McCulloch, *Woods Words* (Portland: Oregon Historical Society, 1958), p. i.

C. Freeman Hubbard, *Railroad Avenue* (New York: McGraw-Hill, 1945), p. 199.

D. Hyman Palais, "Black Hill Miners' Folklore," *California Folklore Quarterly* 4 (Oct., 1945): 256.

Background

These four examples of wordplay feature an insider's grasp of job custom and nomenclature. In three case, the narrator signaled fiction with a time-tested form: Holbrook employed the device, "so legend has it"; Hubbard, "then there's the one"; Palais, "according to the story." Hearing such disclaimers, listeners move to the realm of fanciful humor, once upon a time, and shared heritage.

My grouping of these four items is arbitrary. The Wisconsin and Northwest tales of the logger and nurse are clearly related as they touch the same event and hinge on job-talk mystery. The teamster/sailor and farm lad/railroad boomer tales treat hidden identity, job switching, and trade jargon. Folklorist Jim Leary in *Midwestern Folk Humor* (1991, 245) indicates that "Woods Talk," under different titles, has been collected in Wisconsin and printed many times since 1929. Also, he speculates (in a letter to me) that it may have originated in the Northeast, migrated to the Midwest, and, in time, to the Pacific Northwest.

The Marinette hospital nurse didn't understand the tramp logger's description of a job accident. I shall not offer a full explanation other than to note that the art of sky-hooking involved loading logs high on a sleigh or a railroad flatcar. A blue-butt log, far thicker at butt than tip, would not roll evenly. Hence, skilled loaders would Saginaw or Saint Croix (manipulate) blues with cant hooks or peaveys by retarding or advancing one or the other end of the log.

We find evidence of migration for "Posing as a Farm Lad" in an article on railroad speech. Meeting blacklisted men working under a "flag" (assumed name), brakeman Luis Kemnitzer wrote out several of their stories. (See comments on the Chicago Yardmen's Association strike in my introduction, "Tales Heard and Told," and in "Service Letter.") One CYA veteran on the Southern Pacific gave Luis an "old joke": "[It] tells of a brakeman, in his boomer hat and thousand-miler shirt [badges of experience], showing up to the superintendent and trying to convince him that he had never railroaded before. 'But you're thirty years old—what have you been doing all your life?' 'Well this is my first trip off the farm.' 'Why did you quit [farming]?' 'I got sore—I was *first out* for the ridin' plow, and the old man *run* the hired man *around* me'" (Kemnitzer 1973, 377).

At this juncture, I shall not translate the occupational language of lumberjacks, railroaders, or sailors. Rather, I suggest that curious readers seek work-word lists in *American Speech* and other library sources. We take pleasure in demystifying the treasured lore of friends and strangers. Each job tale heard and assimilated enlarges appreciation of our creativity. Wordplay enthusiasts unite—you have nothing to lose but your wits!

66

Bundle of Sticks

A. *Stick Together*

The old man once had five boys and he got a lesson out of it because he got a bundle of sticks and handed them to each one of them and told them to break them sticks. Well, by all them sticks being together, they was hard to break. And he told them, "Just take one out and break it." It was easily broken. "All right" he said, "now as long as you stick together nobody can break you." He had a reference to uniting and organizing in order to be strong. So we get our strength through the whole labor movement by sticking together. Organize together. What hurts one worker will hurt all.

B. *Quarrelsome Boys*

A Man had several sons who were such quarrelsome boys that they could never agree with each other. So he called them together and had a Bundle of Sticks brought.

"Now, Boys" said their father, "take this Bundle and let me see which of you can break it."

One after the other tried his hardest; but the Sticks were so closely bound together that they would not break. Then the Father untied the Bundle and gave one single Stick to each boy, telling him to break it.

"Oh, that was quite Easy, father," said they.

"You see, my boys," said the father, "you are like the Bundle of Sticks. While you keep together and agree, none can hurt you. When you fall apart anyone may do you Harm."

"Old Man and His Sons."

Sources

A. John Garner, interview with Cliff Kuhn at Pratt City, Ala., July 20, 1984. Text transcribed by Brenda McCallum. For the setting, see McCallum's "The Gospel of Black Unionism" in *Songs about Work,* ed. Archie Green (Bloomington: Indiana University Folklore Institute, 1993).

B. Text without attribution in *Industrial Syndicalist* 1, no. 1 (July, 1910): 24. For setting see Geoff Brown's introduction to *The Industrial Syndicalist* (Nottingham: Spokesman Books, 1974).

Background

Our gathering closes with a pair of classic stories spanning the Atlantic Ocean. Derived from *Aesop's Fables,* these twins have appeared under various titles: "The Old Man and His Sons," "A Father and His Sons," "The Boys and the Sticks." The strength-in-unity motif also appears in Mark (3:24–25), in tales attributed to Genghis

Khan, and in histories of the American Revolution. Variants of "Bundle of Sticks" have been offered by Valerius Babrius, Roger L'Estrange, and Jean de La Fontaine.

I do not know when or under what circumstance a trade unionist in Europe or America first adapted this fable for a labor audience. Brenda McCallum and Cliff Kuhn (in letters to me) identified John Garner as a retired coal miner and member of the United Mine Workers of America. Robin Kelley in *Hammer and Hoe* placed him as a black communist in the 1930s. Kuhn, meeting Garner at age ninety-three, reported that he likened leaving sharecropping behind to enter the Alabama labor and radical movements to an "Exodus from Egypt."

In Garner's colloquial text, and the *Industrial Syndicalist's* printed text, we encounter a fable alive in tradition for two millennia. How long will our book's other gathered tales move about and inspire?

"Vineyard Madonna."

References

This list holds references to published material found in libraries as well as ephemeral items and sound recordings deposited in libraries and archives—all noted in preceding pages of my book. For unpublished material cited from correspondents and interviewees, see individual names in Index. For current research in folktale studies see *Journal of American Folklore, Southern Folklore,* and *Western Folklore.*

Aarne, Antti. 1961. *The Types of the Folktale.* 2d rev. ed. Translated and enlarged by Stith Thompson. Helsinki: Suomalainen Tiedeakatemia.

Adamic, Louis. 1931. *Dynamite.* New York: Viking.

Aesop's Fables. See Joseph Jacobs.

Aiken, Riley. 1964. "Fifteen Mexican Folktales." In Boatright et al., *Good Tale and a Bonnie Tune,* 3–56. Reprinted in Aiken, *Mexican Folktales from the Borderland.* Dallas: Southern Methodist University Press, 1980.

Ameringer, Oscar. 1940. *If You Don't Weaken.* New York: Holt.

Anderson, Jervis. 1972. *A. Philip Randolph.* New York: Harcourt.

Andrew Furuseth 1854–1938. [Memorial Service Brochure.] Copy in Jo Davidson papers, Library of Congress, Manuscript Division.

"Andrew Furuseth, Labor Leader, Dies." 1938. *New York Times,* Jan. 23.

Athenaeum. 1864. Review of J. C. Hotten, *The Slang Dictionary. . . .* No. 1931 (Oct. 29): 557.

Audubon, John James. 1962. *The Original Water-Color Paintings by John James Audubon for The Birds of America.* 2 vols. New York: American Heritage Publishing Company.

Audubon, Maria. 1897. *Audubon and His Journals.* 2 vols. New York: Scribner's.

Axtell, Silas. 1948. *A Symposium on Andrew Furuseth.* New Bedford, Mass.: Darwin Press.

Banks, Ann. 1980. *First Person America.* New York: Knopf.

Banks, Joseph. 1962. *The Endeavour Journal of Joseph Banks: 1768–1771.*

Edited by J. C. Beaglehole. 2 vols. Sydney: Public Library of New South Wales.

Barnett, Eugene. 1961. Interview with Archie Green, Spokane. Tape deposited, Southern Folklife Collection, University of North Carolina Library, Chapel Hill.

Bassett, Fletcher. 1885. *Legends and Superstitions of the Sea and of Sailors in All Lands and at All Times.* Chicago: Belford, Clarke.

Baughman, Ernest. 1967. *Type and Motif-Index of the Folktales of England and North America.* The Hague: Mouton.

Bede. 1990. *Ecclesiastical History of the English People.* Translated by Leo Sherley-Price, revised by R. E. Latham, new introduction and notes by D. H. Farmer. Harmondsworth, Eng.: Penguin Books.

Beaglehole, J. C. See Joseph Banks; James Cook.

Bird, Stewart, Dan Georgakas, and Deborah Shaffer. 1985. *Solidarity Forever: An Oral History of the IWW.* Chicago: Lake View Press.

Boatright, Mody. 1963. *Folklore of the Oil Industry.* Dallas: Southern Methodist University Press.

Boatright, Mody, Wilson M. Hudson, and Allen Maxwell, eds. 1964. *A Good Tale and a Bonnie Tune.* Dallas: Southern Methodist University Press.

Booth, Brian, ed. 1992. *Wildmen, Wobblies & Whistle Punks: Stewart Holbrook's Lowbrow Northwest.* Corvallis: Oregon State University Press.

Boswell, James. [1791.] *Boswell's Life of Johnson.* 6 vols. Revised and enlarged by G. B. Hill and L. F. Powell. Oxford: Clarendon Press, 1934–50.

Botkin, B. A. 1930. *Folk-Say, A Regional Miscellany.* Norman: University of Oklahoma Press.

———. 1944. *A Treasury of American Folklore.* New York: Crown.

———. 1951. *A Treasury of Western Folklore.* New York: Crown.

———. 1954. *Sidewalks of America.* Indianapolis: Bobbs-Merrill.

———. 1957. *A Treasury of American Anecdotes.* New York: Random House.

Botkin, B. A., and Alvin Harlow. 1953. *A Treasury of Railroad Folklore.* New York: Crown.

Bradlee, Ben. 1995. *A Good Life.* New York: Simon & Schuster.

Brewer, Ebenezer. [1870.] *Brewer's Dictionary of Phrase and Fable.* Centenary edition, rev. Ivor Evans. New York: Harper, 1969.

Brewer, J. Mason. 1932. "Juneteenth." In Dobie, *Tone the Bell Easy,* 9–54.

Broder, David. 1987. "The Press Is on Shaky Ground." *Washington Post,* Nov. 15.

Brown, Charles E. 1942. "Wisconsin Parallels to Indiana Folktales." *Hoosier Folklore Bulletin* 1 (Dec.): 100–101.

Brown, Charles W. 1925. *My Ditty Bag*. Boston: Small, Maynard.

Brown, Geoff. 1974. *The Industrial Syndicalist*. Nottingham: Spokesman Books.

Brown, Sterling. ca. 1932. ["Negro Jokes."] Undated, untitled, mimeographed collection in Botkin papers, University of Nebraska Library, Lincoln.

————. 1979. "A Son's Return: 'Oh, Didn't He Ramble.'" In Harper and Stepto, *Chant of Saints*, 3–22.

Brunvand, Jan. 1989. *Curses! Broiled Again!* New York: Norton.

Buhle, Mari Jo. 1990. "Ovington, Mary White." In Buhle et al., *Encyclopedia of the American Left*, 547–48.

Buhle, Mari Jo, Paul Buhle, and Dan Georgakas, eds. 1990. *Encyclopedia of the American Left*. New York: Garland.

Buhle, Paul. 1985. *Labor's Joke Book*. St. Louis: WD Press.

Burke, William Allen. 1943. *Copper Camp*. New York: Hastings House.

Camp, William. 1948. *San Francisco: Port of Gold*. Garden City: Doubleday.

Campbell, Patrick. 1992. *A Molly Maguire Story*. Jersey City: Templecrone Press.

Carpenter, The. 1893. ["Non-Union Sheep's Head."] 13 (Nov.): 5. Reprinted as "Lesson in Unionism." 1993. 113 (Nov.–Dec.): 38.

Carteret, Philip. 1965. *Carteret's Voyage Round the World, 1766–1769*. 2 vols. Edited by Helen Wallis for the Hakluyt Society. Cambridge: Cambridge University Press.

————. See John Hawkesworth.

Cassady, Stephen. 1979. *Spanning the Gate*. Mill Valley, Calif.: Squarebooks.

Cate, Sandra. 1991. "Counter Intelligence: The Popular History and Contemporary Practice of Tipping in the United States." M.A. thesis, University of California, Berkeley.

Chadwick, Nora. 1963. "The Celtic Background in Early Anglo-Saxon England." In Chadwick, *Celt and Saxon*. Cambridge: Cambridge University Press.

Christopher, Carl. 1992. "The Mollies." *Hazleton (Pennsylvania) Standard-Speaker,* July 17.

Claessens, August. 1953. *Didn't We Have Fun!* New York: Rand School.

Cobble, Dorothy Sue, 1991. *Dishing It Out: Waitresses and Their Unions in the Twentieth Century*. Urbana: University of Illinois Press.

Coffin, Tristram P., ed. 1968. *Our Living Traditions*. New York: Basic Books.

Cohen, Myron. ca. 1950. "The Scissor Story." Banner 2098 (78-rpm disc). Reissued on LP ca. 1965, *Myron Cohen* (Audio Fidelity 701).

———. 1958. *Laughing Out Loud.* New York. Citadel.

———. 1960. *More Laughing Out Loud.* New York. Citadel.

"Collectors and Collections: Some California Legends." 1945. *California Folklore Quarterly* 4:96–98.

Conroy, Jack. See Ann Banks; Douglas Wixson.

Cook, James. [1768–80] 1955. *The Journals of Captain James Cook on His Voyages of Discovery.* 4 vols. and portfolio. Edited by J. C. Beaglethorpe for the Hakluyt Society. Cambridge: Cambridge University Press.

Coolidge, Dane. 1937. *Texas Cowboys.* New York: Dutton.

Cooper, Wayne. 1987. *Claude McKay.* Baton Rouge: Louisiana State University Press.

Cowley, Malcolm. 1980. *The Dream of the Golden Mountains.* New York: Viking.

Craddock, Billy. 1978. *One More Tramp Guide.* Hookstown, Penn.: The Bee.

Davidson, Jo. 1929–50. Papers and ephemera. Library of Congress, Manuscript Division.

———. 1951. *Between Sittings.* New York: Dial Press.

Davis, Fred. 1959. "The Cabdriver and His Fare." *American Journal of Sociology* 65:158–65.

Dégh, Linda. 1968. "The Negro in the Concrete." *Indiana Folklore* 1:61–67.

De Leon, Daniel. 1952. *Socialist Landmarks.* New York: New York Labor News Company.

DeNatale, Doug. 1985. "Bynum: The Coming of Mill Village Life to a North Carolina County." Ph.D diss., University of Pennsylvania, Philadelphia.

Denman, William. See Silas Axtell.

Di Donato, Pietro. 1939. *Christ in Concrete.* New York: Bobbs-Merrill.

Dobie, J. Frank, ed. 1932. *Tone the Bell Easy.* Austin: Texas Folklore Society.

Dundes, Alan. 1989. "The Building of Skadar." In Dundes, *Folklore Matters.* Knoxville: University of Tennessee Press.

———. 1995. "How Indic Parallels to the Ballad of the 'Walled-Up Wife' Reveal the Pitfalls of Parochial Nationalistic Folkloristics." *Journal of American Folklore* 108:38–43.

Eckstorm, Fanny. [1924] 1972. *The Penobscot Man.* Reprint with introduction by Edward Ives. Somersworth: New Hampshire Publishing Company.

Eckstorm, Fanny, and Mary Smyth. 1927. *Minstelsy of Maine.* New York: Houghton Mifflin.

El Paso Labor Advocate. 1929. "Seamen's President Long Camera Shy." Apr. 26.

Evanson, Jacob. 1949. "Folk Songs of an Industrial City." In Korson, *Pennsylvania Songs and Legends,* 423–66.

Feintuch, Burt, ed. 1988. *The Conservation of Culture.* Lexington: University Press of Kentucky.

Fife, Austin. 1942. "Popular Legends of the Mormons." *California Folklore Quarterly* 1:105–25.

Fisher, Vardis. See *Idaho.*

Fleming, G. James. 1937. "Pullman Porters Win Pot of Gold." *Crisis,* 10 (Nov.): 332.

Foote, E. J. 1909. "Items of Interest." *Industrial Worker,* Apr. 29.

Foster, William Z. 1939. *Pages from a Worker's Life.* New York: International.

Fountain, Clayton. 1949. *Union Guy.* New York: Viking.

Frost, Richard. 1968. *The Mooney Case.* Stanford: Stanford University Press.

Gentry, Curt. 1967. *Frame-up.* New York: Norton.

Georgakas, Dan. See Stewart Bird.

Gillespie, Angus. 1980. *Folklorist of the Coal Fields.* University Park: Pennsylvania State University Press.

Gladstone, J. E. 1990. "To Make the Run: A Seafarers Memoir." Typescript, University of California Library, Santa Cruz.

Glazer, Joe. 1984. *Transcript of Robert L. Kanter Memorial Lecture.* University of Connecticut, Labor Education Center.

Gould, Ed. 1975. *Logging: British Columbia Logging History.* Vancouver, B.C.: Hancock House.

Gottlieb, Lou. 1991. "The Bloomington Conference." *Folk News,* Summer. World Folk Music Association Newsletter, Washington, D.C.

Greco, Tony. 1995. "A Lockup to Look At." *Hazleton (Pennsylvania) Standard-Speaker,* Mar. 20.

Green, Archie. 1960a. "John Neuhaus: Wobbly Folklorist." *Journal of American Folklore* 73:189–217.

———. 1960b. "Dutchman: An on-the-Job Etymology." *American Speech* 35:270–74.

———. 1965. "American Labor Lore: Its Meanings and Uses." *Industrial Relations* 4 (Feb.): 51–68.

———. 1968. "The Workers in the Dawn." In Coffin, *Our Living Traditions,* 251–62.

———. 1972. *Only a Miner.* Urbana: University of Illinois Press.

———. 1993a. "Boss, Workman, Wife: Sneaking-Home Tales." *Journal of American Folklore* 106:156–70.

———. 1993b. *Wobblies, Pile Butts, and Other Heroes: Laborlore Explorations.* Urbana: University of Illinois Press.

———, ed. 1993c. *Songs about Work.* Bloomington: Folklore Institute, Indiana University.

Grozni, Ivan. 1988. "A Unionist's Dog." *Industrial Worker,* Feb.

Gruenther, Alfred. 1957. Remarks. In *Proceedings,* 2d AFL-CIO convention, 106–13.

Guthrie, Woody. 1982. "Tale from Woody." *Talkin' Union* issue 5 (Nov.): 6.

Gutman, Herbert. 1968. New preface to Spero and Harris, *The Black Worker,* vii–xiii.

———. 1976. *Work, Culture, and Society in Industrializing America.* New York: Knopf.

Halle, Louis. 1970. *The Storm Petrel and the Owl of Athena.* Princeton: Princeton University Press.

Halpert, Herbert. 1943. "Liars' Club Tales." *Hoosier Folklore Bulletin* 2 (June): 11–13.

———. 1945. "Tall Tales and Other Yarns from Calgary, Alberta." *California Folklore Quarterly* 4:40–49.

———. 1946. "Aggressive Humor on the East Branch." *New York Folklore Quarterly* 2:85–97.

Halpert, Herbert, and Emma Robinson. 1942. "'Oregon' Smith, an Indiana Folk Hero." *Southern Folklore Quarterly* 6:163–68.

Halpert, Herbert, and Violetta Halpert. 1979. *Neither Heaven nor Hell.* St. John's: Memorial University, Department of Folklore, Reprint No. 5.

Hand, Wayland. 1946. "The Folklore, Customs, and Traditions of the Butte Miner, Concluded." *California Folklore Quarterly* 5:153–78.

———. 1954. "Immuring." *Western Folklore* 13:133–34.

Harlow, Alvin. See B. A. Botkin.

Harper, Michael, and Robert Stepto, eds. 1979. *Chant of Saints.* Urbana: University of Illinois Press.

Hart, John. 1955. "All about Francis." *Carpenter* 75 (Sept.): 29–31.

Hawkesworth, John. 1773. *An Account of the Voyages.* . . . 3 vols. London: Strahan and Cadell.

Hayes, Alfred. 1968. *The End of Me.* New York: Atheneum.

Heyer, Marigrace. 1995. "Restless Spirits." *Lehighton (Pennsylvania) Times News.*

Hill, G. B. See James Boswell.

Holbrook, Stewart. 1952. "The Longest Bar." In *The Far Corner,* 80–85. New York: Macmillan. Reprinted as "Erickson's: Elbow Bending for Giants." In Booth, *Wildmen, Wobblies & Whistle Punks,* 217–22.

Holtzberg-Call, Maggie. 1992. *The Lost World of the Craft Printer.* Urbana: University of Illinois Press.

Howard, Sidney. 1924. *The Labor Spy.* New York: [New] Republic Publishing Company.

Howell, James. [1646], 1890. *The Familiar Letters of James Howell.* Edited by Joseph Jacobs. London: David Nutt.

Hubbard, Freeman. 1945. *Railroad Avenue.* New York: McGraw-Hill.

Huber, Patrick. 1996. "Scissorbill: A U.S. Labor Pejorative Reconsidered." *Comments on Etymology,* forthcoming.

Hugill, Stan. 1966. *Shanties from the Seven Seas.* London: Routledge and Kegan Paul.

Hunt, Morton. 1953. "How You Look to a Waiter." *Nation's Business* 41 (July): 70–73.

Huxtable, Ada Louise. 1973. "Good Buildings Are Hard to Get." *New York Times,* July 8, Section II: 19.

Idaho, a Guide in Word and Picture. 1937. Caldwell: Caxton Printers.

Ives, Edward. 1964. *Larry Gorman: The Man Who Made the Songs.* Bloomington: Indiana University Press.

———. 1971. *Lawrence Doyle: The Farmer Poet of Prince Edward Island.* Orono: University of Maine Press.

———. 1978. *Joe Scott: The Woodsman-Songmaker.* Urbana: University of Illinois Press.

Jacobs, Joseph. 1894, 1965. *The Fables of Aesop.* Reprint. New York: Schocken.

———. See James Howell.

Jansen, William Hugh. 1944. "Lore of the Tankbuilders." *Hoosier Folklore Bulletin* 3 (June): 27–29.

Johnson, Alvin. 1916. "Andrew Furuseth." *New Republic* 9 (Nov. 11): 40–42.

Johnson, Samuel. See Boswell.

Joyce, Rosemary. 1982. "Wall Street Wags." *Western Folklore* 41:292–303.

Kelley, Robin. 1990. *Hammer and Hoe.* Chapel Hill: University of North Carolina Press.

Kemnitzer, Luis. 1973. "Language Learning and Socialization on the Railroad." *Urban Life and Culture* 1:363–78.

Kingsley, Charles. 1863. *The Water Babies.* London: Macmillan.

Kornbluh, Joyce. 1964, 1988. *Rebel Voices.* Ann Arbor: University of Michigan Press. Reprint. Chicago: Charles H. Kerr.

Korson, George. 1938. *Minstrels of the Mine Patch.* Philadelphia: University of Pennsylvania Press.

———. 1943. *Coal Dust on the Fiddle.* Philadelphia: University of Pennslvania Press.

———, ed. 1949. *Pennsylvania Songs and Legends.* Philadelphia: University of Pennsylvania Press.

Kuralt, Charles. 1985. *On the Road with Charles Kuralt.* New York: Putnam's.

[La Follette, Robert.] 1915. "Furuseth's Picture" and "The Face of Andrew Furuseth." *La Follette's Magazine* 7 (Mar.): 2 and (Apr.): 1.

Lange, Dorothea. [1934.] Portrait of Andrew Furuseth. *Survey Graphic* 27 (Mar., 1938): 134.

Larrowe, Charles. 1972. *Harry Bridges.* Westport, Conn.: Lawrence Hill.

Larson, Carl. 1980. "Mark of the Damned." *Allentown (Pennsylvania) Call-Chronicle,* June 15.

Leary, Jim. 1991. *Midwestern Folk Humor.* Little Rock, Ark.: August House.

Leary, John J., Jr. See Frances Perkins.

Lie, Haakon. 1993. *En Sjoamanns Saga—Andrew Furuseth.* Oslo: Tiden.

Lighter, J. E. 1994. *Random House Historical Dictionary of American Slang.* New York: Random House.

Lockley, Ronald. 1983. *Flight of the Storm Petrel.* London: David & Charles.

Long, Margaret. 1963. "A Southern Teen-Ager Speaks His Mind." *New York Times Magazine,* Nov. 10, p. 15.

Love, John. 1920. "The Wreck on the B. of R.T." *Survey* 44 (Apr. 24): 135–36.

"'Lumberjack' Language." 1980. *Marinette County Historian* 4 (Apr.).

Lynch, Frank. 1958. "You'll Get Pie in the Sky When You Die." *Seattle Post-Intelligencer,* Aug. 29.

MacArthur, Walter. See Walter Camp.

Mackintosh, Robert. 1853. *Memoirs of the Life and Times of Sir James Mackintosh.* 2 vols. 2d ed. Boston: Little, Brown.

Marks, Edward. 1935. *They All Sang.* New York: Viking.

Marryat, Frederick. 1836. *Mr. Midshipman Easy.* London: Saunders and Otley.

———. 1840. *Poor Jack.* London: Longman.

Mars, Gerald, and Michael Nicold. 1984. *The World of Waiters.* London: Allen & Unwin.

Mathews, Mitford. 1951. *A Dictionary of Americanisms on Historical Principles.* 2 vols. Chicago: University of Chicago Press.

Mathewson, Stanley. 1931. *Restriction of Output among Unorganized Workers.* New York: Viking.

Maurer, Meyer Emil. 1936. "Ring around a Rosy." *New Leader,* Oct. 24. Reprinted as "Hop Lee Gives the Pelican a Job." *Industrial Worker,* Dec. 5.

Mayes, Barney. ca. 1970. Untitled autobiographical typescript. Labor Archives and Research Center, San Francisco State University.

McCallum, Brenda. 1993. "The Gospel of Black Unionism." In Green, *Songs about Work,* 108–33.

McCarl, Robert. 1978. "Occupational Folklife: A Theoretical Hypothesis." *Western Folklore* 37:145–60. Reprinted in *Working Americans.* Smithsonian Institution Folklife Studies 3.

―――. 1988. "Occupational Folklife in the Public Sector: A Case Study." In Feintuch, *Conservation of Culture*, 132–53.

McCarthy, William. 1994. *Jack in Two Worlds*. Chapel Hill: University of North Carolina Press.

McCulloch, Walter. 1958. *Woods Words*. Portland: Oregon Historical Society.

Melville, Herman. [1851] 1979. *Moby-Dick*. Handset limited ed. San Francisco: Arian Press.

―――. [1856] 1922–24. *The Piazza Tales;* includes "The Encantadas." Vol. 10 of *The Works of Herman Melville*. London: Constable.

―――. 1924. *Billy Budd and Other Prose Pieces*. Vol. 13 of *The Works of Herman Melville*. London: Constable.

Meltzer, Milton. 1978. *Dorothea Lange: A Photographer's Life*. New York: Farrar, Straus and Giroux.

Mencken, Henry. 1942. *Newspaper Days*. New York: Knopf.

Mers, Gilbert. 1988. *Working the Waterfront*. Austin: University of Texas Press.

Mooney, Fred. 1967. *Struggle in the Coal Fields*. Morgantown: West Virginia University Library.

Morris, Richard B. 1976. *The American Worker*. Washington, D.C.: Department of Labor.

"Mr. Ford Doesn't Care." 1933. *Fortune* 8 (Dec.): 63.

Murtaugh, James. 1905. Remarks. In *Proceedings of the First I.W.W. Convention*. New York: New York Labor News Company.

Nelson, Eugene. 1993. *Break Their Haughty Power*. San Francisco: Ism Press.

Norton, Roy. 1910. "A Job as King." *Saturday Evening Post* 173 (Oct. 8): 4–10.

O'Connor, Harvey. 1964, 1981. *Revolution in Seattle*. New York: Monthly Review Press. Reprint. Seattle: Left Bank Books.

Olander, Victor. 1929. Letter to Jo Davidson on Furuseth bust. Mar. 25. In Jo Davidson Papers, Library of Congress, Manuscript Division.

―――. 1930. See *El Paso Labor Advocate*.

Older, Fremont. 1930. "Andrew Furuseth." *San Francisco Call-Bulletin*, July 4.

O'Neil, Pat. 1905. Remarks. In *Proceedings of the First I.W.W. Convention*. New York: New York Labor News Company.

O'Sullivan, Sean. 1966. *Folktales of Ireland*. Chicago: University of Chicago Press.

Ovington, Mary White. 1906. "The Negro in the Trades Unions in New York." *Annals of the American Academy of Political and Social Sciences* 27 (May): 90–96.

Palais, Hyman. 1945. "Black Hill Miners' Folklore." *California Folklore Quarterly* 4:256–60.

Palladino, Grace. 1991. *Dreams of Dignity, Workers of Vision.* Washington, D.C.: International Brotherhood of Electrical Workers.

Papanikolas, Zeese. 1982. *Buried Unsung.* Salt Lake City: University of Utah Press.

Paules, Greta Foff. 1991. *Dishing It Out: Power and Resistance among Waitresses in a New Jersey Restaurant.* Philadelphia: Temple University Press.

Pease, Frank. 1914. "Bones." *International Socialist Review* 14:548.

Peña, Manuel. 1991. "The 'Treacherous-Woman' Folklore of Mexican Male Workers." *Gender & Society* 5:30–46.

Perkins, Frances. 1935. [Leary letter, Feb. 25, on Davidson bust of Furuseth]. Office of the Secretary; General Records of the Department of Labor, Record Group 174. National Archives, College Park, Md.

Perlman, Selig, and Philip Taft. 1935. *History of Labor in the United States.* Vol. 4 of John Commons, *History of Labor in the United States.* New York: Macmillan, 1918–35.

Piling Busters Yearbook: Stories of Towboating by Towboat Men. 1978 [material gathered 1951–53]. Gig Harbor, Wash.: Peninsula Gateway.

Porter, Endymion. See James Howell; Robert Mackintosh.

Powell, L. F. See James Boswell.

Preston, Cathy Lynn. 1995. "Folklorists Do It Orally." *Lore and Language,* forthcoming.

Randolph, A. Philip. 1936. Remarks. In *Proceedings of Fifty-sixth AFL Convention,* 666.

Randolph, Vance. 1957. *The Talking Turtle and Other Ozark Folk Tales.* New York: Columbia University Press.

[Ranford, Tom]. 1958. "The Moral Is Clear: Avoid 'Friendly' Boss." *Service Union Reporter* (Los Angeles), Sept.

Raskin, Gene. 1980. *Citronella.* New York: Bloch.

Reuther, Walter. 1959. Remarks. In *Proceedings of Third AFL-CIO Convention,* 113.

Rickaby, Franz. 1926. *Ballads and Songs of the Shanty-Boy.* Cambridge: Harvard University Press.

Rock, Diana. 1984. "Pay Equity." *Talkin' Union* issue 11 (Nov.): 11.

Roediger, David. 1994. *Towards the Abolition of Whiteness.* London: Verso.
———. See Fred Thompson.

"The Sailors' Lincoln." 1938. *New York Times,* Jan. 24.

Sandburg, Carl. 1913. "The Face of Andy Furuseth." *La Follette's Magazine* 12 (July): 8.
———. 1936. *The People, Yes.* New York, Harcourt, Brace & World.

Sandler, Richard. 1982. "You Can Sell Your Body but Not Your Mind." Ph.D. diss., University of Pennsylvania, Philadelphia.

San Francisco News. 1938. "World Mourns Andy Furuseth, Sailors' Chief." Jan. 24.

Santino, Jack. 1986. "A Servant and a Man, a Hostess or a Woman." *Journal of American Folklore* 99:311–22.

———. 1989. *Miles of Smiles, Years of Struggle.* Urbana: University of Illinois Press.

Scanlon, Rosemary. 1971. "The Handprint." *Pennsylvania Folklore Quarterly* 16:97–107.

Schniderman, Saul. See Diana Rock; *Talkin' Union.*

Schwartz, Stephen. 1986. *Brotherhood of the Sea.* New Brunswick: Transaction Books.

Serrin, William. 1992. *Homestead.* New York: Random House.

Shaffer, Deborah. See Stewart Bird.

Shapland, Frank. 1936. "Casey's Chronicles of the Work World." *Journal of Electrical Workers and Operators* 35 (Jan.): 24, 38.

Shay, Dorothy. 1947. "Efficiency." Columbia 37190 (78-rpm disc). Reissued 1949 on LP album, *Dorothy Shay Sings* (Columbia 6003), and ca. 1960, *Coming 'Round the Mountain* (Harmony 7017).

[Shippey, Hartwell]. 1910. "Editorial: A Letter of Inquiry." *Industrial Worker,* July 2.

Simmons, Walter. 1993. *Pigeons and Gudgeons.* Lincolnville Beach, Maine: Duck Trap Press.

Smiley, Al. 1952. "In the Early Morning Dew." In *Piling Busters Yearbook,* 107.

Solander, Daniel Carl. See Joseph Banks.

Snorri Sturluson. 1951. *The Prose Edda of Snorri Sturluson: Tales from Norse Mythology.* Translated by Jean Young. London: Bowes & Bowes.

Spero, Sterling, and Abram Harris. 1931, 1968. *The Black Worker.* New York: Columbia University Press. Reprint, with new preface by Herbert Gutman. New York: Atheneum.

"Stay Organized." 1990. *Wichita (Kans.) Plaindealer,* Sept. 17, p. 17.

Steel, Edward. 1985. *The Correspondence of Mother Jones.* Pittsburgh: University of Pittsburgh Press.

———. 1988. *The Speeches and Writings of Mother Jones.* Pittsburgh: University of Pittsburgh Press.

Stolberg, Benjamin. 1938. *The Story of the CIO.* New York: Viking.

Talkin' Union. Feb. 1981–Summer 1988.

Tamony, Peter. 1957. "Scissorbill." *Industrial Worker,* Dec. 23.

Taylor, David. 1992. *Documenting Maritime Folklife.* Washington, D.C.: American Folklife Center, Library of Congress.

Taylor, Paul. 1923. *The Sailors' Union of the Pacific.* New York: Ronald Press.

Texter, Cameron. 1984. "Mollies' Infamous Cell Is Not Doomed After All." *Pottsville (Pennsylvania) Republican,* Sept. 6.

Thompson, Fred. 1947. "Cormorants, Revolt! A Old Fable Brought up to Date." *Industrial Worker,* Sept. 20.

———. 1963. Interview with Joyce Kornbluh and Archie Green, Chicago. Tape deposited, Southern Folklife Collection, University of North Carolina Library, Chapel Hill.

———. 1978. Interview. In Bird et al., *Solidarity Forever,* 215–21.

———. 1982. "Soapbox Story." *Talkin' Union* issue 5 (Nov.): 7.

———. 1993. *Fellow Worker.* Edited by David Roediger. Chicago: Charles H. Kerr.

Thompson, Jim. 1944. "'Snake' Magee and the Rotary Boiler." In Botkin, *Treasury of American Folklore,* 538–40.

Thompson, Stith. See Anti Aarne.

Tietjens, Eunice. 1916, 1917. "Cormorants." *International Socialist Review* 17:169. Reprinted in *Profiles from China.* Chicago: Seymour.

"Tipping." 1946. *Life* 21 (July 15): 30.

Trout, Allan. 1958. "Greetings." *Louisville Courier-Journal,* Nov. 3, 1958.

U.S. National Labor Relations Board. 1959. *H. K. Ferguson Company vs Tuscaloosa District Council of Carpenters* (124 NLRB 20).

van der Zee, John. 1986. *The Gate.* New York: Simon and Schuster.

Vargas, Zaragosa. 1993. *Proletarians of the North.* Berkeley: University of California Press.

Waldron, Angela. 1993. "Encased in Concrete: A Contemporary American Legend." Typescript deposited in the Northeast Archives of Folklore and Oral History, University of Maine, Orono.

Walentis, Al. 1980. "Molly Maguire." *Reading (Pennsylvania) Eagle,* Aug. 31.

Walker, Tom. 1995. "Sailor's Progress: Folklore and Political Culture of an American Merchant Seaman." Ph.D. diss., Indiana University, Bloomington.

Wallis, Helen. See Philip Cartaret.

Ward, Estolv. 1940. *Harry Bridges on Trial.* New York: Modern Age Books.

Washington Post. 1935. "New Building Here Dedicated to the Department of Labor." Feb. 26.

Washington Star. 1935. "Reception and Singing Mark Labor Building Dedication" and "Better Technique Is Pledged Labor." Feb. 25 and 26.

Weekley, Ernest. 1932. *Words and Names.* London: John Murray.

Weintraub, Hyman. 1947. "The I.W.W. in California, 1905–1931." M.A. thesis, University of California, Los Angeles.

———. 1959. *Andrew Furuseth: Emancipator of the Seamen.* Berkeley: University of California Press.

West Coast Sailors. 1938–58. Articles and photographs on Andrew Furuseth.

West, George P. 1921. "Andrew Furuseth and the Radicals." *Survey* 47 (Nov. 5): 205–9.

Wetjen, Albert Richard. 1929. Letter. In Botkin, *Treasury of Western Folklore,* 671.

Whiting, Bartlett J. 1977. *Early American Proverbs and Proverbial Phrases.* Cambridge: Belknap Press.

Wickersham, James. 1938. *Old Yukon: Tales—Trails—Trials.* Washington, D.C.: Washington Law Book Company.

Wiggin, Kate Douglas. 1911. *Mother Carey's Chickens.* Boston: Houghton, Mifflin.

Wiggin, Kate Douglas, and Rachel Crothers. 1925. *Mother Carey's Chickens: A Little Comedy of Home in Three Acts.* New York: Samuel French.

Willson, Meredith. 1948. *And There I Stood with My Piccolo.* Garden City: Doubleday.

Wilmington (California) Daily Press. 1933. "Wilmington Celebrates 75th Anniversary." Sept. 2.

Wilshire, Gaylord. ca. 1902. *Hop Lee and the Pelican.* New York: Wilshire Book Company.

Wilson. Alexander. 1808–14. *American Ornithology.* 9 vols. Philadelphia: Bradford and Inskeep.

———. 1840, 1970. *Wilson's American Ornithology with Notes by Jardine.* . . . Boston: Otis, Broaders. Reprint. New York: Arno.

Wixson, Douglas. 1994. *Worker-Writer in America.* Urbana: University of Illinois Press.

WPA Writers' Program. See William Allen Burke.

Wright, Chester. 1914. "Where the Human Stream Flows." *Los Angeles Citizen,* Apr. 4.

"Scrub Woman."

Illustrations

Index

ARCHIE GREEN, who lives in San Francisco, is a long-time member of the United Brotherhood of Carpenters and Joiners of America. In 1982, he retired as professor of English and folklore at the University of Texas, Austin. He has written *Only a Miner* and *Wobblies, Pile Butts, and Other Heroes,* and edited *Songs about Work.* In the decade between 1967 and 1976, he lobbied for the American Folklife Preservation Act. From its inception, he has been active in the John Edwards Memorial Forum, an archival association treating vernacular music.